Reviews
Duane F. Watson, JBL 108 (1989) 748-50

HERMENEUTISCHE UNTERSUCHUNGEN ZUR THEOLOGIE

Herausgegeben von
HANS DIETER BETZ · GERHARD EBELING
MANFRED MEZGER

24

The Tradition that You Received from Us: 2 Thessalonians in the Pauline Tradition

by

Glenn S. Holland

J. C. B. Mohr (Paul Siebeck) Tübingen

CIP-Kurztitelaufnahme der Deutschen Bibliothek

Holland, Glenn S.:
The tradition that you received from us : 2 Thessalonians in the Pauline tradition / by Glenn S. Holland.
– Tübingen : Mohr, 1988.
   (Hermeneutische Untersuchungen zur Theologie ; 24)
   ISBN 3-16-145203-8
   ISSN 0440-7180
NE: GT

© 1988 by J.C.B. Mohr (Paul Siebeck) P.O. Box 2040, D-7400 Tübingen.

This book may not be reproduced, in whole or in part, in any form (beyond that permitted by copyright law) without the publisher's written permission. This applies particularly to reproductions, translations, microfilms and storage and processing in electronic systems.

Typeset by Typobauer Filmsatz GmbH in Scharnhausen; printed by Gulde-Druck in Tübingen; bound by Großbuchbinderei Heinrich Koch in Tübingen.

Printed in Germany.

There are two reasons why things written are not understood: they are obscured either by unknown or by ambiguous signs.

Augustine
De doctrina christiana 2. 10. 15

Preface

This study was originally a dissertation submitted to the faculty of the Divinity School of the University of Chicago in June, 1986. I would like to express my gratitude to Hans Dieter Betz, who served as dissertation advisor and was always generous with his time, his encyclopedic knowledge, and his acute insights. Thanks are also due to the other members of the dissertation committee, Robert M. Grant and Arthur Droge, who provided many helpful suggestions and words of encouragement. Jerald C. Brauer, Jon Levenson, and Frank Reynolds gave impetus to this work in its earlier stages, while Adela Yarbro Collins made several valuable suggestions as it neared completion. To them my thanks, as also to Donald A. Sykes and Rex Mason, David E. Aune, Karl P. Donfried, Donald Dale Walker, and my colleagues at Allegheny College.

I would also like to thank the editors of the series Hermeneutische Untersuchungen zur Theologie, Hans Dieter Betz, Gerhard Ebeling, and Manfred Mezger, as well as the publisher, Georg Siebeck. Thanks also to Martha Morrow-Vojacek, who prepared the final typescript.

Finally, I must express my gratitude to my family. My parents, Glen and Marjorie Holland, have provided unfailing support. My sister, Nancy Jean Holland, has inspired me by her example, and my sons, Nathaniel and Gregory, have lightened the burden of my work through their complete indifference to it. My wife Sandy has been my friend and supporter in this and all my work; to her this study is dedicated with gratitude and love.

December 1986   Glenn Holland

Table of Contents

Preface VII
Introduction 1

I.   Rhetorical Analysis and Exegesis of 2 Thessalonians 6
    1. Epistolary Prescript 1:1-2 34
    2. Exordium 1:3-4 35
    3. Narratio 1:5-12 37
    4. Probatio 2:1-17 43
    5. Exhortatio 3:1-13 50
    6. Peroratio 3:14-16 54
    7. Epistolary Postscript 3:17-18 57

II. A Comparison of Material in 1 and 2 Thessalonians 59
    1. Epistolary Prescript 1:1-2 60
    2. Exordium 1:3-4 61
    3. Narratio 1:5-12 63
    4. Probatio 2:1-17 67
    5. Exhortatio 3:1-13 73
    6. Peroratio 3:14-16 77
    7. Epistolary Postscript 3:17-18 77

III. The Eschatology of 2 Thessalonians 91

IV. 2 Thessalonians in the Pauline Tradition 129

Select Bibliography 159
Index of Passages 163
Index of Authors 173
Index of Subjects 175

Introduction

Our purpose is to find the place of 2 Thessalonians in the Pauline tradition. This is the movement of theological thought represented in the New Testament by the letters written either by Paul or by those who considered themselves his followers. In the case of 2 Thessalonians, the situation is complicated by the similarities between 1 Thessalonians and 2 Thessalonians, similarities which, taken with other considerations, have led some scholars to doubt the Pauline authorship of the second letter. Both Béda Rigaux[1] and Wolfgang Trilling[2] have traced the history of the theory of the pseudepigraphic nature of 2 Thessalonians, and we shall therefore only sketch it in here. The authenticity of the apocalyptic scenario found in 2 Thessalonians 2:1-12 was the first question to be raised, in 1798 by Johann Ernst Christian Schmidt; he believed that its eschatology was inconsistent with that of 1 Thessalonians 4:13-5:11. Friedrich Heinrich Kern, in 1839, brought the authenticity of the whole letter into question on essentially the same grounds. Various scholars believed that the apocalyptic scenario had clear affinities with the book of Revelation, the legend of Nero *revidivus*, and echoes of the threat of gnosticism, which placed it later than the time of Paul. A new chapter in the interpretation of the letter was begun by the work of William Wrede in 1903[3]. Wrede undertook a comparative analysis of 1 and 2 Thessalonians and reached the conclusion that the second letter was dependent upon the first for its literary form and expression, and yet different from it in other respects, and thus had to be a forgery. Wrede effectively determined the basis on which the debate about authenticity is still carried on. The great majority of commentators on the Thessalonian correspondence still defended the authenticity of 2 Thessalonians. In Germany, Ernst von Dobschütz's influential entry in the Meyer commentary series defended the Pauline authorship of the letter

---

[1] Béda Rigaux, *Saint Paul: les épitres aux Thessaloniciens*, Études Bibliques (Paris/Gembloux: Librairie LeCoffre/Éditions J. Duculot, 1956), pp. 124–32.

[2] Wolfgang Trilling, *Untersuchungen zum 2. Thessalonicherbrief*, Erfurter Theologische Studien, vol. 27 (Leipzig: St. Benno, 1972), pp. 11–45.

[3] William Wrede, *Die Echtheit des Zweiten Thessalonicherbriefs*, Texte und Untersuchungen zur Geschichte der altchristlichen Literatur (Leipzig: I. C. Hinrich'sche Buchhandlung, 1903).

(1909), as did the excellent English commentary by George Milligan (1908) and James Everett Frame's contribution to the International Critical Commentary series (1912). The magisterial commentary of Béda Rigaux in 1956 again defended Paul's authorship, but the next year saw the publication of one of the few commentaries promoting deutero-Pauline authorship, that of Charles Masson. Wolfgang Trilling undertook a major reinvestigation of the question of authenticity in his *Untersuchungen zum 2. Thessalonicherbrief* (1972)[4], and wrote a commentary on the letter that provides an exegesis of its problems on the assumption of deutero-Pauline authorship (1980). The question has continued to be debated and any consensus appears to be as unlikely as at any time since Wrede's study in 1903. Any attempt to place the letter within the Pauline tradition, therefore, must take into account the relationship between 1 and 2 Thessalonians which, in turn, will affect other decisions about authorship.

But how is the relationship between 1 and 2 Thessalonians best to be investigated? That a literary relationship of some kind exists is not open to question[5]. As Ernest Best put it briefly, "There is a great similarity between the two; this is not only of words, small phrases and concepts but extends to the total structure of the two letters which is in addition different from what is taken to be the standard Pauline form"[6]. The problem then is, how best to account for this literary relationship? There are four proposed solutions, three assuming Pauline authorship and the fourth assuming another writer. The first is that Paul wrote both 1 and 2 Thessalonians within a very short time, and that in the second letter he unconsciously imitated the ideas and phrasing of the first[7]. The second is that Paul wrote both letters and had a copy of the first before him as he composed the second, so that he consciously reworked some ideas and phrases of the first letter in the second[8]. The third is that Paul wrote both letters, but that 2 Thessalonians was actually addressed to another

---

[4] Trilling, *Untersuchungen*, pp. 11–45.

[5] This was demonstrated clearly by the analysis of Wrede, *Die Echtheit*.

[6] Ernest Best, *A Commentary on the First and Second Epistles to the Thessalonians*, Harper's New Testament Commentaries (New York: Harper and Row, 1972), p. 37.

[7] Gottlieb Lünemann, *Critical and Exegetical Handbook to the Epistles of St. Paul to the Thessalonians*, trans. Paton J. Gloag, Meyer Commentary (Edinburgh: T. and T. Clark, 1884), pp. 169–73; Wilhelm Bornemann, *Die Thessalonicherbriefe*, Meyer Kommentar (Göttingen: Vandenhoeck und Ruprecht, 1894), pp. 324–26; George Milligan, *St. Paul's Epistles to the Thessalonians* (London: Macmillan and Co., 1908), LXXX–LXXXV; Ernst von Dobschütz, *Die Thessalonicher-Briefe*, Meyer Kommentar (Göttingen: Vandenhoeck und Ruprecht, 1909), pp. 31–49; Rigaux, *Saint Paul*, pp. 149–52; Best, *Thessalonians*, pp. 50–58.

[8] This opinion is represented by Theodor Zahn, *Introduction to the New Testament*, trans. M. W. Jacobus, 2d ed. (New York: Charles Scribner's Sons, 1917), pp. 249–50.

congregation or that 1 and 2 Thessalonians were addressed to two different parts of the same congregation[9]. The fourth solution is that 2 Thessalonians is the product of a later author who consciously imitated the language and style of 1 Thessalonians[10].

In any of these theories, however, there are two separate tasks which must be performed to arrive at a satisfactory conclusion about the relationship between the two letters. The first is an exegesis of 2 Thessalonians in its own right, the second a comparison of 2 Thessalonians with 1 Thessalonians, based upon their common material.

The first of these steps, however, already poses a problem: what does it mean to undertake a study of 2 Thessalonians "in its own right?" There is no denying the influence, conscious or unconscious, of the text of 1 Thessalonians upon that of 2 Thessalonians. It might be argued that ignoring the influence in an attempt at an "independent" exegesis would be as dubious an enterprise as undertaking an exegesis of Matthew while ignoring the influence of Mark. Indeed, most of the exegetical work concerned with 2 Thessalonians has assumed the influence of 1 Thessalonians. That is, under the theory of common Pauline authorship, 2 Thessalonians has been interpreted in the light of 1 Thessalonians; it was assumed that it was entirely proper to make the interpretation of the second letter compatible with (and thus dependent on) the interpretation of the first. Such an exegesis of course tended to reinforce the presupposition upon which it was based, and the majority of commentators have supported the Pauline authorship of 2 Thessalonians. On the other hand, the few exegetical studies of 2 Thessalonians not based upon the assumption of Pauline authorship have been primarily concerned with finding points of apparent disagreement between the two letters, thereby confirming the presumption of another author[11]. Such an approach, controlled by an assumption of discontinuity between the two letters, is also not conducive to an objective analysis. Both approaches create a form of circular reasoning,

---

[9] The first solution is offered by Eduard Schweizer, "Der zweite Thessalonicherbrief ein Philipperbrief?", *Theologische Zeitschrift* 1 (1945): 286–89; the second solution is offered by Adolf von Harnack, "Das Problem des zweiten Thessalonicherbriefs", *Sitzungsbericht der Königlich Preussischen Akademie der Wissenschaften*, philosophisch-historische Klasse (Berlin: Georg Reimer, 1910), pp. 560–78; Martin Dibelius, *An die Thessalonicher I, II, an die Philipper*, Handbuch zum Neuen Testament 11, 3rd ed. (Tübingen: J.C.B. Mohr (Paul Siebeck), 1937), pp. 57–58.

[10] Wrede, *Die Echtheit*, pp. 34–36; Charles Masson, *Les deux épitres de Saint Paul aux Thessaloniciens*, Commentaire du Nouveau Testament 11a, (Neuchâtel/Paris: Delachaux et Niestlé, 1957), pp. 9–13; Trilling, *Untersuchungen*, p. 132.

[11] An example is the exegesis of Wolfgang Trilling, *Der zweite Brief an die Thessalonicher*, Evangelisch-katholischer Kommentar zum Neuen Testament 14 (Zürich/Neukirchen: Benziger/Neukirchener, 1980).

and thereby point up the fragility of an exegesis of 2 Thessalonians based upon a particular presumption of its relationship to 1 Thessalonians.

Is it possible, then, to interpret 2 Thessalonians "in its own right?" The very fact of the existence of the letter argues that it is possible. The author, either Paul or some other, felt it necessary to write the letter to convey information not present in 1 Thessalonians. The letter must make sense in and of itself. It appears that the second letter addresses a different situation than the first, perhaps a situation which arose out of a misunderstanding of 1 Thessalonians. In any event, the new situation can be discerned only through a proper exegesis of 2 Thessalonians. The use of phrases or ideas from 1 Thessalonians in 2 Thessalonians does not necessarily influence the meaning of the latter letter; indeed, 2 Thessalonians appears to be a re-presentation of the material of 1 Thessalonians intended to clarify that material as it relates to a new situation. But in either case, the second letter provides an interpretative explanation (indeed, possibly the first interpretative explanation) of 1 Thessalonians[12]. Just as a commentary provides a particular understanding of a given book of the Bible, so 2 Thessalonians, by its use of the material of 1 Thessalonians, provides a particular understanding of that book, whether that of Paul himself or of some other writer. 2 Thessalonians, whoever its author, is one of the earliest extant commentaries on one of Paul's letters.

It should be clear, then, that a proper exegesis of 2 Thessalonians will also clarify its author's understanding of 1 Thessalonians and can form the basis for examining the relationship between the two letters. It is also clear that such an exegesis must be undertaken without any regard for "consistency" or "inconsistency" in relation to 1 Thessalonians or its supposed meaning. It is this work of exegesis which will constitute the first three chapters of this monograph.

The basis for this work of exegesis will be a rhetorical analysis of 2 Thessalonians. Hans Dieter Betz has demonstrated that "Paul's letter to the Galatians can be analyzed according to Greco-Roman rhetoric and epistolography"[13], and others have applied this method with varying degrees of success[14]. The

---

[12] Cf. the remark of Rudolf Bultmann, *Theology of the New Testament*, 2 vols. (New York: Charles Scribner's Sons, 1955), 2:131; although we would not endorse his view of the function of the second letter in regard to the first, we would agree with his general view, "in a certain sense 2 Thessalonians is a commentary on 1 Thessalonians."

[13] Hans Dieter Betz, *Galatians: A Commentary on Paul's Letter to the Churches in Galatia*, Hermeneia (Philadelphia: Fortress Press, 1979), p. 14.

[14] George A. Kennedy, *New Testament Interpretation through Rhetorical Criticism* (Chapel Hill, N.C.: University of North Carolina Press, 1984), offers an analysis of 1 Thessalonians (pp. 142–44); of the second letter he says only "second Thessalonians resembles 1 Thessalonians but is much shorter and omits the narration" (p. 144). Robert Jewett proposed a rhetorical analysis of both letters in "The Thessalonian Church as a Millenarian Movement", a paper presented to the Social Sciences and New Testament Interpretation Consultation at the Annual Meeting of the Society for Biblical Literature, 8–11 December 1984,

fact that 2 Thessalonians can be shown to conform to the rules of rhetorical composition should cause no surprise. Paul was clearly familiar with these rules[15], and any other who wished to imitate his style would of necessity be familiar with them as well. While it is true that the conventions of composition in the ancient world might vitiate some of the similarities between 1 and 2 Thessalonians, they also remove some of the difficulties another author would have faced in imitating Paul's "style".

The first chapter of this study will be devoted first of all to a rhetorical analysis of 2 Thessalonians, and second to an exegesis of the letter based upon that analysis. The second chapter will investigate the relationship between 1 and 2 Thessalonians on the basis of the earlier analysis and exegesis and will also be concerned with the question of authorship. The third chapter will be devoted to the apocalyptic material in the letter, 2 Thessalonians 1:5-10 and 2:1-12. There are several major exegetical problems presented specifically by the apocalyptic scenario of 2:1-12, and these will be investigated at that point. The fourth and last chapter will be devoted to the problem of placing 2 Thessalonians within the larger context of the New Testament literature and more specifically within the Pauline tradition. It is hoped that the conclusions will prove enlightening not just to the study of the legacy of Paul in the early church, but to an entire movement within the church of the late first century.

---

in Chicago. He divided the letter as follows: 1. *Exordium*, 1:1-12; 2. *Propositio*, 2:1-2; 3. *Probatio*, 2:3-3:5; 4. *Exhortatio*, 3:6-15; 5. *Peroratio*, 3:16-18. Both Kennedy and Jewett have overlooked the significance of ἔνδειγμα (1:5) as an indication of the rhetorical division of the letter. Jewett has also interpreted the thanksgiving concluding the *probatio* (2:13-17) as a second proof, because he has misconstrued the meaning of the false proclamation and taken the general subject of the *probatio* (parousia and in-gathering) as its specific subject (compare our analysis in chap. 1). He does not recognize 3:14-15 as part of the "summation" common to the *peroratio*. He also makes 3:17-18 a part of the rhetorical argument, when its inclusion is (1) related to the conventions of letters (as is that of the prescript, 1:1-2), not those of rhetoric, and (2) a device related to pseudepigraphy.

[15] Kennedy, *New Testament Interpretation*, pp. 9–10; Betz, *Galatians*, pp. 14–15.

Chapter I

Rhetorical Analysis and Exegesis of 2 Thessalonians

The particular species of rhetoric found in 2 Thessalonians is deliberative. It is intended to persuade the readers to choose a particular course of action[1], in this case to "stand firm and hold to the traditions that you were taught" (2:15a). The elements of deliberative rhetoric are exhortation and dissuasion, "since the exhorter advises a thing as being better, and the dissuader opposes it as being worse"[2]. In the case of 2 Thessalonians, the author exhorts the readers to obey the Pauline tradition so that there may be "peace" (3:14-16) and dissuades them from heeding the false proclamation that "the Day of the Lord is here" (2:1-2).

An analysis of the rhetorical composition of 2 Thessalonians will illustrate the argument of the letter and will serve as the basis for exegetical comment. It is not our intention to provide a commentary on 2 Thessalonians but rather to understand the intentions of the author, the nature of the doctrine he promulgates, and his own perception of the function of the letter. Because of our concern with the relationship between 2 and 1 Thessalonians, such an analysis also provides an opportunity for schematic arrangement of the material in 1 Thessalonians parallel to similar material in 2 Thessalonians. By arranging the parallel material according to a compositional outline of 2 Thessalonians, the repetition of material from 1 Thessalonians and its use in particular parts of the argument of the second letter will be made clear. It will be seen that the author of 2 Thessalonians used the first letter selectively and referred several times to the same parts when it served his purpose.

Therefore our compositional analysis of 2 Thessalonians will be divided into four colums. The first column will present the analysis in outline, the second, the text of 2 Thessalonians arranged according to the corresponding categories of the analysis. The third column will present the parallel material in 1 Thessalonians, specifically the parallels that appear in proximate position

---

[1] Aristotle, *Ars rhetorica* 1. 1358b; Jonathan A. Goldstein, *The Letters of Demosthenes* (New York: Columbia University Press, 1968), pp. 100–7.
[2] Aristotle, *Ars rhetorica* 1. 1358b.

in that letter as its parallels in 2 Thessalonians; and the fourth column will present thematic parallels in 1 Thessalonians and parallels in other parts of 2 Thessalonians itself[3].

---

[3] Wrede, *Die Echtheit*, pp. 4–12, undertakes a demonstration of the similarities between 1 and 2 Thessalonians by use of parallel columns. Our analysis includes the rhetorical analysis and secondary parallels, but of course incorporates Wrede's parallels as well.

	I.	Epistolary Prescript 1:1-2	
1:1		A. Name of the principal sender	Παῦλος καὶ
		B. Names of the co-senders	Σιλουανὸς καὶ Τιμόθεος
		C. Naming of the addressees	
		1. Definition of their organization	τῇ ἐκκλησίᾳ
		2. Description of its nature	
		a. Ethno-political affiliation	Θεσσαλονικέων
		b. Religious affiliation	ἐν θεῷ πατρὶ ἡμῶν καὶ κυρίῳ Ἰησοῦ Χριστῷ
1:2		D. Salutation	χάρις ὑμῖν καὶ εἰρήνη ἀπὸ θεοῦ πατρὸς [ἡμῶν] καὶ κυρίου Ἰησοῦ Χριστοῦ
	II.	Exordium 1:3-4	
		A. Description of an act of thanksgiving	
1:3		1. Thanksgiving formula	εὐχαριστεῖν
		2. Statement of obligation	ὀφείλομεν
		3. One addressed in thanksgiving	τῷ θεῷ
		4. Appropriate time of thanksgiving	πάντοτε
		5. Object of thanksgiving	περὶ ὑμῶν
		6. Address	ἀδελφοί
		7. Liturgical statement of obligation	καθὼς ἄξιόν ἐστιν
		8. Reason for thanksgiving: virtues displayed	ὅτι
		a. First virtue displayed	
		1) Evidence of increase	ὑπεραυξάνει
		2) Virtue	ἡ πίστις ὑμῶν
		b. Second virtue displayed	
		1) Evidence of increase	καὶ πλεονάζει

1 Thessalonians (primary)*	1 and 2 Thessalonians
Παῦλος καὶ Σιλουανὸς καὶ Τιμόθεος	
τῇ ἐκκλησίᾳ	
Θεσσαλονικέων	
ἐν θεῷ πατρὶ [ἡμῶν] καὶ κυρίῳ Ἰησοῦ Χριστῷ χάρις ὑμῖν καὶ εἰρήνη [ἀπὸ θεοῦ πατρὸς ἡμῶν καὶ κυρίου Ἰησοῦ Χριστοῦ] (1:1)	
εὐχαριστοῦμεν	ἡμεῖς δὲ ὀφείλομεν εὐχαριστεῖν
τῷ θεῷ	τῷ θεῷ
πάντοτε	πάντοτε
περὶ πάντων ὑμῶν (1:2a)	περὶ ὑμῶν
	ἀδελφοὶ (2 Thess. 2:13a)
μνημονεύοντες ὑμῶν τοῦ ἔργου τῆς πίστεως καὶ τοῦ κόπου τῆς ἀγάπης (1:3a) ὑμᾶς δὲ ὁ κύριος πλεονάσαι καὶ περισσεῦσαι	

---

* "Primary" denotes a parallel in the same or proximate location in both 1 and 2 Thessalonians, or the probable primary reference of the author of 2 Thessalonians. Other parallels appear in the fourth column.

		2) Virtue	ἡ ἀγάπη
		3) By whom displayed	ἑνὸς ἑκάστου πάντων ὑμῶν
		4) Towards whom displayed (subject = object)	εἰς ἀλλήλους
	B.	Description of an act of boasting	
1:4		1. (Re-)identification of actor	ὥστε αὐτοὺς ἡμᾶς
		2. Object of action	ἐν ὑμῖν
		3. Action	ἐγκαυχᾶσθαι
		4. Persons addressed	ἐν ταῖς ἐκκλησίαις τοῦ θεοῦ
		5. Content of boast: virtue displayed	ὑπὲρ
		a. First virtue	τῆς ὑπομονῆς ὑμῶν
		b. Second virtue	καὶ πίστεως
		c. First circumstance	ἐν πᾶσιν τοῖς διωγμοῖς ὑμῶν
		d. Second circumstance	καὶ ταῖς θλίψεσιν αἷς ἀνέχεσθε
III.	Narratio: Episode in the Last Judgment 1:5-12		
	A.	Evaluation of the narrative	
1:5		1. Type of narrative	ἔνδειγμα
		2. Topic	τῆς δικαίας κρίσεως τοῦ θεοῦ
		3. Examination of the verdict	
		a. Purpose: action towards Thessalonians	εἰς τὸ καταξιωθῆναι
		b. Direct object	ὑμᾶς
		c. Indirect object	τῆς βασιλείας τοῦ θεοῦ ὑπὲρ ἧς καὶ πάσχετε
		d. Affirmation of the righteousness of the verdict by appeal to the *lex talionis*	
1:6		1) Affirmative conditional	εἴπερ
		2) Principle of retribution	δίκαιον παρὰ θεῷ ἀνταποδοῦναι
		a) Negative result	τοῖς θλίβουσιν ὑμᾶς θλῖψιν
1:7		b) Positive result	καὶ ὑμῖν τοῖς θλιβομένοις ἄνεσιν μεθ' ἡμῶν
		c) Result of solidarity with "Paul"	

τῇ ἀγάπῃ

εἰς ἀλλήλους καὶ εἰς πάντας
(3:12a)

ὥστε

τίς γὰρ ἡμῶν ἐλπὶς ἢ χαρὰ ἢ   μὴ χρείαν ἔχειν ἡμᾶς λαλεῖν τι
στέφανος καυχήσεως (2:19a)   (1 Thess. 1:8c)
ὥστε γενέσθαι ὑμᾶς τύπον πᾶσιν
τοῖς πιστεύουσιν ἐν τῇ   αὐτοὶ γὰρ...ἀπαγγέλλουσιν...πῶς
Μακεδονίᾳ καὶ ἐν τῇ Ἀχαΐᾳ (1:7)   ἐπεστρέψατε πρὸς τὸν θεόν...
καὶ τῆς ὑπομονῆς τῆς ἐλπίδος...   καὶ ἀναμένειν τὸν υἱὸν αὐτοῦ
τοῦ ἔργου τῆς πίστεως   ἐκ τῶν οὐρανῶν (1 Thess. 1:9-
(1:3b, 3a)   10a)

εἰδότες, ἀδελφοὶ...,
τὴν ἐκλογὴν ὑμῶν (1:4)

                                     εἰς τὸ περιπατεῖν ὑμᾶς ἀξίως
ὅτι τὸ εὐαγγέλιον ἡμῶν οὐκ
ἐγενήθη εἰς ὑμᾶς ἐν λόγῳ μόνον...   τοῦ θεοῦ τοῦ καλοῦντος ὑμᾶς
καὶ ὑμεῖς...δεξάμενοι τὸν   εἰς τὴν ἑαυτοῦ βασιλείαν καὶ
λόγον ἐν θλίψει πολλῇ (1:5-6)   δόξαν (1 Thess. 2:12b)

Ἰησοῦν τὸν ῥυόμενον ἡμᾶς ἐκ
τῆς ὀργῆς τῆς ἐρχομένης (1:10c)

	B. The narrative: Episode in the Last Judgment	
	1. Eschatological setting of the "righteous judgment"	ἐν τῇ ἀποκαλύψει τοῦ κυρίου Ἰησοῦ
	2. Description of the ἀποκάλυψις	
	a. Person to appear (Jesus) implied	
	b. Place of appearance	ἀπ' οὐρανοῦ
	c. Accompanying theophanous phenomena (τόποι)	
	1) First phenomenon	μετ' ἀγγέλων δυνάμεως αὐτοῦ
1:8	2) Second phenomenon	ἐν πυρὶ φλογός
	d. First purpose: action towards the wicked	διδόντος ἐκδίκησιν
	1) Objects of action	
	a) First characterization	τοῖς μὴ εἰδόσιν θεὸν
	b) Parallel second characterization	καὶ τοῖς μὴ ὑπακούουσιν τῷ εὐαγγελίῳ τοῦ κυρίου ἡμῶν Ἰησοῦ
	2) Result of action	
1:9	a) Application of principle of retribution	οἵτινες δίκην τίσουσιν
	b) Description of the δίκη in eschatological terms	ὄλεθρον αἰώνιον ἀπὸ προσώπου τοῦ κυρίου καὶ ἀπὸ τῆς δόξης τῆς ἰσχύος αὐτοῦ
	e. Second purpose: participation of Thessalonians in eschatological glory because of "Paul's" advocacy	
1:10	1) Eschatological setting	ὅταν ἔλθῃ
	2) First characterization of action	ἐνδοξασθῆναι ἐν τοῖς ἁγίοις αὐτοῦ
	3) Parallel second characterization	καὶ θαυμασθῆναι ἐν πᾶσιν τοῖς πιστεύσασιν
	4) Basis of action	ὅτι ἐπιστεύθη τὸ μαρτύριον ἡμῶν ἐφ' ὑμᾶς
	f. Time reference (end of ring composition, cf. 1:7)	ἐν τῇ ἡμέρᾳ ἐκείνῃ
	C. Report of a prayer of intercession	
1:11	1. Reason for prayer (in reference to the preceding section)	εἰς ὃ
	2. Action	καὶ προσευχόμεθα
	3. Appropriate time of prayer	πάντοτε
	4. Direct object	περὶ ὑμῶν

ἐν τῇ παρουσίᾳ τοῦ κυρίου
ἡμῶν Ἰησοῦ (3:13b)

καὶ ἀναμένειν τὸν υἱὸν αὐτοῦ
ἐκ τῶν οὐρανῶν (1:10a)

μετὰ πάντων τῶν ἁγίων αὐτοῦ
(3:13b)

τῆς ὀργῆς τῆς ἐρχομένης (1:10c)
μὴ ἐν πάθει ἐπιθυμίας
καθάπερ καὶ τὰ ἔθνη
τὰ μὴ εἰδότα τὸν θεόν (4:5)
ὅτι τὸ εὐαγγέλιον ἡμῶν οὐκ
ἐγενήθη εἰς ὑμᾶς ἐν λόγῳ μόνον
ἀλλὰ καὶ...[ἐν] πληροφορίᾳ
πολλῇ (1:5a)

αὐτὸς ὁ κύριος

ἐν κελεύσματι, ἐν φωνῇ
ἀρχαγγέλου καὶ ἐν σάλπιγγι
θεοῦ, καταβήσεται ἀπ' οὐρανοῦ
(1 Thess. 4:16a)
αὐτὸς ὁ κύριος ἐν κελεύσματι,
ἐν φωνῇ ἀρχαγγέλου...

(1 Thess. 4:16a)

...τῆς ὑπομονῆς τῆς ἐλπίδος
τοῦ κυρίου ἡμῶν Ἰησοῦ Χριστοῦ
ἔμπροσθεν τοῦ θεοῦ καὶ πατρὸς
ἡμῶν (1:3b)

καὶ οὕτως πάντοτε σὺν κυρίῳ
ἐσόμεθα (1 Thess. 4:17b)

καὶ ἀναμένειν τὸν υἱὸν αὐτοῦ
ἐκ τῶν οὐρανῶν, ... Ἰησοῦν τὸν
ῥυόμενον ἡμᾶς ἐκ τῆς ὀργῆς
τῆς ἐρχομένης (1:10)

ὥστε γενέσθαι ὑμᾶς τύπον
πᾶσιν τοῖς πιστεύουσιν ἐν τῇ
Μακεδονίᾳ καὶ ἐν τῇ Ἀχαΐᾳ
(1:7; cf. 1:5-9)

...περὶ πάντων ὑμῶν
μνείαν ποιούμενοι ἐπὶ τῶν
προσευχῶν ἡμῶν ἀδιαλείπτως
(1:2)

ἐν τῇ παρουσίᾳ τοῦ κυρίου ἡμῶν
Ἰησοῦ μετὰ πάντων τῶν ἁγίων
αὐτοῦ (1 Thess. 3:13b)

...ὡς ὅτι ἐνέστηκεν
ἡ ἡμέρα τοῦ κυρίου (2 Thess.
2:2c)

		5. Primary intentions of prayer	ἵνα
		a. First intention	
		1) Direct object	ὑμᾶς
		2) Action	ἀξιώσῃ
		3) Indirect object	τῆς κλήσεως
		4) Actor	ὁ θεὸς ἡμῶν
		b. Second intention	
		1) Action	καὶ πληρώσῃ
		2) Direct objects	
		a) First direct object	πᾶσαν εὐδοκίαν ἀγαθωσύνης
		b) Second direct object	καὶ ἔργον πίστεως
		3) Attribution of action to divine power	ἐν δυνάμει
1:12		6. Secondary intentions of prayer	ὅπως
		a. Action	ἐνδοξασθῇ
		b. First direct object	τὸ ὄνομα τοῦ κυρίου ἡμῶν Ἰησοῦ
		c. First means	ἐν ὑμῖν
		d. Second direct object	καὶ ὑμεῖς
		e. Second means	ἐν αὐτῷ
		f. Attribution of action to divine grace	κατὰ τὴν χάριν τοῦ θεοῦ ἡμῶν καὶ κυρίου Ἰησοῦ Χριστοῦ
	IV.	Probatio 2:1-17	
		A. Topic of probatio in the form of a doctrinal exhortation	
2:1		1. Exhortatory formula	ἐρωτῶμεν δὲ ὑμᾶς
		2. Address	ἀδελφοί
		3. Topic of exhortation	ὑπὲρ
		a. First topic	τῆς παρουσίας τοῦ κυρίου ἡμῶν Ἰησοῦ Χριστοῦ
		b. Second topic	καὶ ἡμῶν ἐπισυναγωγῆς ἐπ' αὐτόν
2:2		4. Purpose of exhortation	εἰς τὸ
		a. Actions to be avoided	
		1) First undesirable action	μὴ ταχέως σαλευθῆναι ὑμᾶς ἀπὸ τοῦ νοὸς
		2) Second undesirable action	μηδὲ θροεῖσθαι
		b. Causes which give rise to these actions	
		1) Means of transmission	
		a) First means	μήτε διὰ πνεύματος
		b) Second means	μήτε διὰ λόγου
		c) Third means	μήτε δι' ἐπιστολῆς
		2) Reputed source of authority	ὡς δι' ἡμῶν

1 Thessalonians	1 and 2 Thessalonians
παρακαλοῦντες ὑμᾶς…καὶ μαρτυρόμενοι εἰς τὸ περιπατεῖν ὑμᾶς ἀξίως τοῦ θεοῦ τοῦ καλοῦντος ὑμᾶς εἰς τὴν ἑαυτοῦ βασιλείαν καὶ δόξαν (2:12) μνημονεύοντες ὑμῶν	εἰς τὸ καταξιωθῆναι ὑμᾶς τῆς βασιλείας τοῦ θεοῦ (2 Thess. 1:5) εὐχαριστεῖν ὀφείλομεν…
τοῦ ἔργου τῆς πίστεως (1:3a)	ὅτι ὑπεραυξάνει ἡ πίστις ὑμῶν (2 Thess. 1:3)
	ὅταν ἔλθῃ ἐνδοξασθῆναι ἐν τοῖς ἁγίοις αὐτοῦ (2 Thess. 1:10a)
	χάρις ὑμῖν καὶ εἰρήνη ἀπὸ θεοῦ πατρὸς [ἡμῶν] καὶ κυρίου Ἰησοῦ Χριστοῦ (2 Thess. 1:2)
ἐρωτῶμεν δὲ ὑμᾶς ἀδελφοί (5:12a) ὁ κύριος…καταβήσεται ἀπ' οὐρανοῦ…ἔπειτα ἡμεῖς… ἁρπαγησόμεθα ἐν νεφέλαις εἰς ἀπάντησιν τοῦ κυρίου εἰς ἀέρα (4:16–17) τὸ μηδένα σαίνεσθαι ἐν ταῖς θλίψεσιν ταύταις (3:3a)	…ἀδελφοί, ἐρωτῶμεν ὑμᾶς καὶ παρακαλοῦμεν ἐν κυρίῳ Ἰησοῦ (1 Thess. 4:1) εἰς τὴν παρουσίαν τοῦ κυρίου οὐ μὴ φθάσωμεν… (1 Thess. 4:15) …καὶ ὁ θεὸς τοὺς κοιμηθέντας διὰ τοῦ Ἰησοῦ ἄξει σὺν αὐτῷ (1 Thess. 4:14b)
περὶ δὲ τῶν χρόνων καὶ τῶν καιρῶν, ἀδελφοί, οὐ χρείαν ἔχετε ὑμῖν γράφεσθαι (5:1)	ἄρα οὖν, ἀδελφοί, στήκετε καὶ κρατεῖτε τὰς παραδόσεις ἃς ἐδιδάχθητε εἴτε διὰ λόγου εἴτε δι' ἐπιστολῆς ἡμῶν (2 Thess. 2:15)

	3) Content of (false) message	ὡς ὅτι ἐνέστηκεν ἡ ἡμέρα τοῦ κυρίου
2:3	5. Summary of preceding exhortation: conclusion	μή τις ὑμᾶς ἐξαπατήσῃ κατὰ μηδένα τρόπον
	B. Proofs of the falsehood of the disturbing message	
	1. First proof: doctrinal tradition concerning necessary prior episodes	
	a. Introductory formula for traditional material	ὅτι
	b. Protasis of condition	
	1) Formula of negative condition	ἐὰν μὴ
	2) Necessary episodes	
	a) First episode	
	i) Action	ἔλθῃ
	ii) Subject of apocalyptic *topos*	ἡ ἀποστασία
	b) Order of action	πρῶτον
	c) Second episode	
	i) Action	καὶ ἀποκαλυφθῇ
	ii) Subject	
	(a) Demonological titles	
	(1) First title	ὁ ἄνθρωπος τῆς ἀνομίας
	(2) Second title	ὁ υἱὸς τῆς ἀπωλείας
	(b) Demonic actions	
2:4	(1) First action	ὁ ἀντικείμενος
	(2) Second action	καὶ ὑπεραιρόμενος
	(3) Object	ἐπὶ πάντα λεγόμενον θεὸν ἢ σέβασμα
	(4) Indication of consecutive action	ὥστε
	(5) Third action	αὐτὸν εἰς τὸν ναὸν τοῦ θεοῦ καθίσαι
	(6) Fourth action	ἀποδεικνύντα ἑαυτὸν ὅτι ἔστιν θεός
	c. Apodosis of condition (missing)	

ἡμέρα κυρίου ὡς κλέπτης ἐν νυκτὶ οὕτως ἔρχεται (5:2b) τὸ μηδένα σαίνεσθαι ἐν ταῖς θλίψεσιν ταύταις (3:3a)	τότε αἰφνίδιος αὐτοῖς ἐφίσταται ὄλεθρος ὥσπερ ἡ ὠδὶν τῇ ἐν γαστρὶ ἐχούσῃ, καὶ οὐ μὴ ἐκφύγωσιν (1 Thess. 5:3b)
καὶ ἀναμένειν	ἐν τῇ παρουσίᾳ
τὸν υἱὸν αὐτοῦ ἐκ τῶν οὐρανῶν	τοῦ κυρίου ἡμῶν Ἰησοῦ μετὰ πάντων τῶν ἁγίων αὐτοῦ (1 Thess. 3:13)
ὃν ἤγειρεν ἐκ [τῶν] νεκρῶν, Ἰησοῦν τὸν ῥυόμενον ἡμᾶς ἐκ τῆς ὀργῆς τῆς ἐρχομένης (1:10)	
αὐτὸς ὁ κύριος ἐν κελεύσματι, ἐν φωνῇ ἀρχαγγέλου καὶ ἐν σάλπιγγι θεοῦ, καταβήσεται ἀπ' οὐρανοῦ (4:16a)	

2:5   d. Rhetorical question: apocalyptic *topos* of "traditional" nature of apocalyptic scenario   οὐ μνημονεύετε ὅτι ἔτι ὢν πρὸς ὑμᾶς ταῦτα ἔλεγον ὑμῖν;

    2. Second proof: new doctrine concerning that which presently restrains ὁ ἄνομος

2:6   a. Introductory formula in opposition to preceding ἔτι   καὶ νῦν

        b. Subject: apocalyptic *topos*   τὸ κατέχον

        c. Instruction formula   οἴδατε

        d. Apocalyptic function of subject   εἰς τὸ

            1) Action   ἀποκαλυφθῆναι

            2) Subject of action   αὐτὸν

            3) Apocalyptic time of action   ἐν τῷ ἑαυτοῦ καιρῷ

        e. Confirmation of the above

2:7   1) Basis for the sequential series of apocalyptic acts   τὸ γὰρ μυστήριον ἤδη ἐνεργεῖται τῆς ἀνομίας

            2) The series of acts

                a) First episode: the present

                    i) Action and subject   μόνον ὁ κατέχων

                    ii) Action which serves as its temporal limitation   ἄρτι ἕως ἐκ μέσου γένηται

                b) Second episode: the future

2:8   i) Formula of sequential action   καὶ τότε

                    ii) Action   ἀποκαλυφθήσεται

                    iii) Subject   ὁ ἄνομος

                c) Third episode: temporal limitation of the above

                    i) Direct object of action   ὃν

                    ii) Subject of action   ὁ κύριος [Ἰησοῦς]

                    iii) First action   ἀνελεῖ τῷ πνεύματι τοῦ στόματος αὐτοῦ

                    iv) Second action   καὶ καταργήσει τῇ ἐπιφανείᾳ τῆς παρουσίας αὐτοῦ

1 Thessalonians	1 and 2 Thessalonians
περὶ δὲ τῶν χρόνων καὶ τῶν καιρῶν, ἀδελφοί, οὐ χρείαν ἔχετε ὑμῖν γράφεσθαι (5:1)	οἴδατε γὰρ τίνας παραγγελίας ἐδώκαμεν ὑμῖν διὰ τοῦ κυρίου Ἰησοῦ (1 Thess. 4:2)
ὑμᾶς δὲ ὁ κύριος πλεονάσαι καὶ περισσεύσαι τῇ ἀγάπῃ…εἰς τὸ στηρίξαι ὑμῶν τὰς καρδίας ἀμέμπτους ἐν ἁγιωσύνῃ (3:12-13a)	προελέγομεν ὑμῖν ὅτι μέλλομεν θλίβεσθαι, καθὼς καὶ ἐγένετο καὶ οἴδατε (1 Thess. 3:4b)
ἔμπροσθεν τοῦ κυρίου ἡμῶν Ἰησοῦ	ἔμπροσθεν τοῦ θεοῦ καὶ πατρὸς ἡμῶν
ἐν τῇ αὐτοῦ παρουσίᾳ (2:19b)	ἐν τῇ παρουσίᾳ τοῦ κυρίου ἡμῶν

	3. Third proof: ὁ ἄνομος will be manifest in demonic mimicry of Christ by reversal	
2:9	a. Subject (in contrast to the παρουσία just referred to in 2:8)	οὗ ἐστιν ἡ παρουσία
	b. Means of operation	κατ' ἐνέργειαν τοῦ Σατανᾶ
	c. Accompanying phenomena	
	1) First phenomenon	ἐν πάσῃ δυνάμει
	2) Second phenomenon	καὶ σημείοις
	3) Third phenomenon	καὶ τέρασιν
	4) Characterization of phenomena	ψεύδους
2:10	5) Fourth phenomenon	καὶ ἐν πάσῃ ἀπάτῃ ἀδικίας
	d. Indirect object	τοῖς ἀπολλυμένοις
	e. Reason	ἀνθ' ὧν τὴν ἀγάπην τῆς ἀληθείας οὐκ ἐδέξαντο εἰς τὸ σωθῆναι αὐτούς
	f. Eschatological consequence: God's "righteous judgment"	
2:11	1) Basis: the rejection of the saving truth by the lost	καὶ διὰ τοῦτο
	2) Action	πέμπει
	3) Indirect object: the lost	αὐτοῖς
	4) Subject	ὁ θεὸς
	5) Direct object	ἐνέργειαν πλάνης
	6) Purpose	εἰς τὸ
	a) Action (proper)	πιστεῦσαι
	b) Subject: the lost	αὐτοὺς
	c) Object (improper)	τῷ ψεύδει
2:12	7) Intended result	ἵνα
	a) Action (reflexive?)	κριθῶσιν
	b) Subjects	πάντες
	i) First characterization	
	(a) Action (improper)	οἱ μὴ πιστεύσαντες
	(b) Object (proper)	τῇ ἀληθείᾳ
	ii) Second characterization	
	(a) Action (proper)	ἀλλὰ εὐδοκήσαντες
	(b) Object (improper)	τῇ ἀδικίᾳ

	Ἰησοῦ μετὰ πάντων τῶν ἁγίων αὐτοῦ (1 Thess. 3:13)
	ἐν τῇ ἀποκαλύψει τοῦ κυρίου Ἰησοῦ
	ἀπ' οὐρανοῦ
	μετ' ἀγγέλων δυνάμεως αὐτοῦ ἐν πυρὶ φλογός
οὐκ ἔθετο ἡμᾶς ὁ θεὸς εἰς ὀργὴν ἀλλὰ εἰς περιποίησιν σωτηρίας διὰ τοῦ κυρίου ἡμῶν Ἰησοῦ Χριστοῦ (5:9)	διδόντος ἐκδίκησιν τοῖς μὴ εἰδόσιν θεὸν καὶ τοῖς μὴ ὑπακούουσιν τῷ εὐαγγελίῳ τοῦ κυρίου ἡμῶν Ἰησοῦ (2 Thess. 1:7b-8)
	αὐτὸς δὲ ὁ θεὸς τῆς εἰρήνης
τὸ εὐαγγέλιον ἡμῶν οὐκ ἐγενήθη εἰς ὑμᾶς ἐν λόγῳ μόνον	ἁγιάσαι ὑμᾶς ὁλοτελεῖς
ἀλλὰ καὶ ἐν δυνάμει καὶ ἐν πνεύματι ἁγίῳ καὶ [ἐν] πληροφορίᾳ πολλῇ (1:5) παραλαβόντες	καὶ ὁλόκληρον ὑμῶν τὸ πνεῦμα καὶ ἡ ψυχὴ καὶ τὸ σῶμα ἀμέμπτως
λόγον ἀκοῆς παρ' ἡμῶν	ἐν τῇ παρουσίᾳ τοῦ κυρίου ἡμῶν Ἰησοῦ Χριστοῦ τηρηθείη (1 Thess. 5:23)
τοῦ θεοῦ ἐδέξασθε οὐ	
λόγον ἀνθρώπων ἀλλὰ καθώς ἐστιν ἀληθῶς λόγον θεοῦ,	
ὃς καὶ ἐνεργεῖται ἐν ὑμῖν	
τοῖς πιστεύουσιν (2:13)	

	C. Description of an act of thanksgiving	
2:13	1. Subject	ἡμεῖς
	2. Particle of disjunction	δὲ
	3. Statement of obligation	ὀφείλομεν
	4. Thanksgiving formula	εὐχαριστεῖν
	5. One addressed in thanksgiving	τῷ θεῷ
	6. Appropriate time of thanksgiving	πάντοτε
	7. Object of thanksgiving	περὶ ὑμῶν
	8. Address	
	a. Title (as Christians)	ἀδελφοὶ
	b. Self-definition (as Christians)	ἠγαπημένοι ὑπὸ κυρίου
	9. Reason for thanksgiving: actions of God	ὅτι
	a. First action	
	1) Action	εἵλατο
	2) Object	ὑμᾶς
	3) Subject	ὁ θεὸς
	4) Time of action	ἀπ' ἀρχῆς
	5) Goal of action	εἰς σωτηρίαν
	6) Attendant virtues	ἐν
	a) First virtue	ἁγιασμῷ πνεύματος
	b) Second virtue	καὶ πίστει ἀληθείας
	b. Second action	
2:14	1) Indication of dependence of the second action on the first	εἰς ὃ [καὶ]
	2) Action	ἐκάλεσεν
	3) Object	ὑμᾶς
	4) Means	διὰ τοῦ εὐαγγελίου ἡμῶν
	5) Goal of action	εἰς περιποίησιν δόξης τοῦ κυρίου ἡμῶν Ἰησοῦ Χριστοῦ
	D. Conclusion	
2:15	1. Concluding formula	ἄρα οὖν
	2. Address	ἀδελφοί
	3. Actions to be taken	
	a. First action	στήκετε
	b. Second action	καὶ
	1) Action	κρατεῖτε
	2) Object	
	a) Object	τὰς παραδόσεις
	b) Source	ἃς ἐδιδάχθητε
	c) Means of transmission	
	i) First means	εἴτε διὰ λόγου
	ii) Second means	εἴτε δι' ἐπιστολῆς
	d) Source of authority	ἡμῶν

1 Thessalonians	1 and 2 Thessalonians	
	καὶ διὰ τοῦτο καὶ ἡμεῖς	
εὐχαριστοῦμεν τῷ θεῷ πάντοτε περὶ πάντων ὑμῶν (1:2a) ἀδελφοὶ ἠγαπημένοι ὑπὸ [τοῦ] θεοῦ	εὐχαριστοῦμεν τῷ θεῷ ἀδιαλείπτως (1 Thess. 2:13a)	εὐχαριστεῖν ὀφείλομεν τῷ θεῷ πάντοτε περὶ ὑμῶν ἀδελφοί (2 Thess. 1:3)
τὴν ἐκλογὴν ὑμῶν ὅτι τὸ εὐαγγέλιον ἡμῶν οὐκ ἐγενήθη εἰς ὑμᾶς ἐν λόγῳ μόνον ἀλλὰ καὶ ἐν δυνάμει καὶ ἐν πνεύματι ἁγίῳ καὶ [ἐν] πληροφορίᾳ πολλῇ (1:4-5) τὴν ἐκλογὴν ὑμῶν ὅτι τὸ εὐαγγέλιον ἡμῶν οὐκ ἐγενήθη εἰς ὑμᾶς ἐν λόγῳ μόνον (1:4-5a) διὰ τοῦτο παρεκλήθημεν, ἀδελφοί, ἐφ' ὑμῖν... ὅτι νῦν ζῶμεν ἐὰν ὑμεῖς στήκετε ἐν κυρίῳ (3:7-8)	ὅτι οὐκ ἔθετο ἡμᾶς ὁ θεὸς εἰς ὀργὴν ἀλλὰ εἰς περιποίησιν σωτηρίας (1 Thess. 5:9) ...ἀλλ' ἐν ἁγιασμῷ (1 Thess. 4:7) ἀνθ' ὧν τὴν ἀγάπην τῆς ἀληθείας οὐκ ἐδέξαντο (2 Thess. 2:10) εἰς τὸ πιστεῦσαι αὐτοὺς τῷ ψεύδει (2 Thess. 2:11b) εἰς τὸ περιπατεῖν ὑμᾶς ἀξίως τοῦ θεοῦ τοῦ καλοῦντος ὑμᾶς εἰς τὴν ἑαυτοῦ βασιλείαν καὶ δόξαν (1 Thess. 2:12) εἰς περιποίησιν σωτηρίας διὰ τοῦ κυρίου ἡμῶν Ἰησοῦ Χριστοῦ (1 Thess. 5:9) πάντες οἱ μὴ πιστεύσαντες τῇ ἀληθείᾳ ἀλλὰ εὐδοκήσαντες τῇ ἀδικίᾳ (2 Thess. 2:12) εἰς τὸ μὴ ταχέως σαλευθῆναι ὑμᾶς ἀπὸ τοῦ νοὸς μηδὲ θροεῖσθαι μήτε διὰ πνεύματος μήτε διὰ λόγου μήτε δι' ἐπιστολῆς ὡς δι' ἡμῶν (2 Thess. 2:2)	οὐ γὰρ ἐκάλεσεν ἡμᾶς ὁ θεὸς ἐπὶ ἀκαθαρσίᾳ (1 Thess. 4:7)

	E.	Intercessory prayer (by the author on behalf of the addressees)	
2:16		1. Invocation	
		a. Primary address	αὐτὸς δὲ
		1) Title (in respect to man)	ὁ κύριος ἡμῶν
		2) Name	Ἰησοῦς Χριστὸς
		b. Secondary address	καὶ
		1) Name	[ὁ] θεὸς
		2) Title (in respect to man)	ὁ πατὴρ ἡμῶν
		3) Aretalogy	
		a) First action	
		i) Action	ὁ ἀγαπήσας
		ii) Object	ἡμᾶς
		b) Second action	
		i) Action	καὶ δοὺς
		ii) Objects	
		(a) First object	παράκλησιν αἰωνίαν
		(b) Second object	καὶ ἐλπίδα ἀγαθὴν
		iii) Divine attribute demonstrated by these gifts	ἐν χάριτι
		2. Petitions	
		a. First petition	
2:17		1) Desired action	παρακαλέσαι
		2) Object	ὑμῶν τὰς καρδίας
		b. Second petition	
		1) Desired action	καὶ στηρίξαι
		2) Desired virtuous action	ἐν παντὶ ἔργῳ καὶ λόγῳ ἀγαθῷ
	V.	Exhortatio 3:1-13	
		A. Request for intercessory prayer by addressees on behalf of author	
		1. Request	
3:1		a. Introductory phrase indicating new section	τὸ λοιπὸν
		b. Desired action	προσεύχεσθε
		c. Address	ἀδελφοί
		d. Object	περὶ ἡμῶν
		e. Petitions of prayer	
		1) First petition	ἵνα
		a) Subject	ὁ λόγος τοῦ κυρίου
		b) Desired actions	
		i) First action	τρέχῃ
		ii) Second action	καὶ δοξάζηται

αὐτὸς δὲ
ὁ θεὸς

καὶ πατὴρ ἡμῶν
καὶ
ὁ κύριος ἡμῶν
Ἰησοῦς (3:11a)

αὐτὸς δὲ
ὁ θεὸς τῆς εἰρήνης (1 Thess.
5:23) ὁ κύριος τῆς εἰρήνης
(2 Thess. 3:16)

καὶ περικεφαλαίαν ἐλπίδα
σωτηρίας (5:8b)

κατὰ τὴν χάριν τοῦ θεοῦ ἡμῶν
καὶ κυρίου Ἰησοῦ Χριστοῦ
(2 Thess. 1:12)

εἰς τὸ στηρίξαι
ὑμῶν τὰς καρδίας (3:13a)
καὶ ἐπέμψαμεν Τιμόθεον...
εἰς τὸ στηρίξαι ὑμᾶς καὶ
παρακαλέσαι ὑπὲρ τῆς πίστεως
ὑμῶν (3:2)

ἀδελφοί,
προσεύχεσθε [καὶ]
περὶ ἡμῶν (5:25)

λοιπὸν οὖν,

ἀδελφοί (1 Thess. 4:1a)

ἀφ' ὑμῶν γὰρ ἐξήχηται
ὁ λόγος τοῦ κυρίου οὐ μόνον
ἐν τῇ Μακεδονίᾳ καὶ [ἐν τῇ]
Ἀχαΐᾳ, ἀλλ' ἐν παντὶ τόπῳ
ἡ πίστις ὑμῶν ἡ πρὸς τὸν

ὅπως ἐνδοξασθῇ τὸ ὄνομα τοῦ

	c) Comparison	καθὼς καὶ πρὸς ὑμᾶς
3:2	2) Second petition	καὶ ἵνα
	a) Subject (implied)	
	b) Desired action	ῥυσθῶμεν
	c) Threat to be avoided	ἀπὸ τῶν ἀτόπων καὶ πονηρῶν ἀνθρώπων
	f. Doctrinal basis of request	
	1) Negative characterization of humanity	οὐ γὰρ πάντων ἡ πίστις
3:3	2) Contrasting positive characterization of the Lord	πιστὸς δέ ἐστιν ὁ κύριος
	3) The Lord's actions on behalf of addressees in contrast to prayer request	
	a) Subject	ὃς
	b) First action	στηρίξει
	c) Object	ὑμᾶς
	d) Second action	καὶ φυλάξει
	e) Threat to be avoided	ἀπὸ τοῦ πονηροῦ
	2. Expression of confidence by the author	
3:4	a. Action	πεποίθαμεν δὲ
	b. Source of confidence	ἐν κυρίῳ
	c. Object	ἐφ' ὑμᾶς
	d. Expected behavior	ὅτι
	1) Object	ἃ παραγγέλλομεν
	2) Expected actions	
	a) Present action	[καὶ] ποιεῖτε
	b) Future action	καὶ ποιήσετε
	3. Epistolary prayer wish	
3:5	a. Divine subject	ὁ δὲ κύριος
	b. Desired action	κατευθύναι
	c. Direct object	ὑμῶν τὰς καρδίας
	d. Desired results	
	1) First result: theological	εἰς τὴν ἀγάπην τοῦ θεοῦ
	2) Second result: Christological	καὶ εἰς τὴν ὑπομονὴν τοῦ Χριστοῦ
	B. Exhortation against the ἄτακτοι	
3:6	1. Command formula	παραγγέλλομεν δὲ
	2. Those to whom the command is addressed	ὑμῖν
	3. Address	ἀδελφοί
	4. Basis of authority	ἐν ὀνόματι τοῦ κυρίου [ἡμῶν] Ἰησοῦ Χριστοῦ

1 Thessalonians	1 and 2 Thessalonians
θεὸν ἐξελήλυθεν (1:8)	κυρίου ἡμῶν Ἰησοῦ ἐν ὑμῖν, καὶ ὑμεῖς ἐν αὐτῷ (2 Thess. 1:12a)
Ἰησοῦν τὸν ῥυόμενον ἡμᾶς ἐκ τῆς ὀργῆς τῆς ἐρχομένης (1:10b)	
(2:15-16)	
πιστὸς ὁ καλῶν ὑμᾶς, ὃς καὶ ποιήσει (5:24)	
εἰς τὸ στηρίξαι ὑμῶν τὰς καρδίας ἀμέμπτους (3:13a)	παρακαλέσαι ὑμῶν τὰς καρδίας καὶ στηρίξαι ἐν παντὶ ἔργῳ καὶ λόγῳ ἀγαθῷ (2 Thess. 2:17)
οἴδατε γὰρ τίνας παραγγελίας ἐδώκαμεν ὑμῖν διὰ τοῦ κυρίου Ἰησοῦ (4:2) καθὼς παρελάβετε παρ' ἡμῶν τὸ πῶς δεῖ ὑμᾶς περιπατεῖν καὶ ἀρέσκειν θεῷ, καθὼς καὶ περιπατεῖτε, ἵνα περισσεύητε μᾶλλον (4:1) μνημονεύοντες ὑμῶν... τοῦ κόπου τῆς ἀγάπης καὶ	αὐτὸς δὲ ὁ θεὸς καὶ πατὴρ ἡμῶν καὶ ὁ κύριος ἡμῶν Ἰησοῦς κατευθύναι τὴν ὁδὸν ἡμῶν πρὸς ὑμᾶς (1 Thess. 3:11)
τῆς ὑπομονῆς τῆς ἐλπίδος τοῦ κυρίου ἡμῶν Ἰησοῦ Χριστοῦ (1:3)	
παρακαλοῦμεν δὲ ὑμᾶς, ἀδελφοί,	λοιπὸν οὖν, ἀδελφοί, ἐρωτῶμεν ὑμᾶς καὶ παρακαλοῦμεν ἐν κυρίῳ Ἰησοῦ

28 2 Thessalonians

	5. Command	
	a. Action desired	στέλλεσθαι ὑμᾶς
	b. Persons to be avoided	
	1) Religious designation	ἀπὸ παντὸς ἀδελφοῦ
	2) Characteristic actions	
	a) Positive description	ἀτάκτως περιπατοῦντος
	b) Negative description	καὶ μὴ κατὰ τὴν παράδοσιν ἣν παρελάβοσαν παρ' ἡμῶν
	6. Bases of command	
	a. First basis: example of Paul	
3:7	1) Instruction formula	αὐτοὶ γὰρ οἴδατε
	2) Substance of instruction	πῶς δεῖ μιμεῖσθαι ἡμᾶς
	3) Citation of Paul's example (tradition)	
	a) Negative examples	
	i) First negative example	ὅτι οὐκ ἠτακτήσαμεν ἐν ὑμῖν
3:8	ii) Second negative example	οὐδὲ δωρεὰν ἄρτον ἐφάγομεν παρά τινος
	b) Positive example	ἀλλ' ἐν κόπῳ καὶ μόχθῳ νυκτὸς καὶ ἡμέρας ἐργαζόμενοι
	c) Intention of actions	πρὸς τὸ μὴ ἐπιβαρῆσαί τινα ὑμῶν
3:9	d) Reason for actions	
	i) Negative reason	οὐχ ὅτι οὐκ ἔχομεν ἐξουσίαν
	ii) Positive reason	ἀλλ' ἵνα ἑαυτοὺς τύπον δῶμεν ὑμῖν εἰς τὸ μιμεῖσθαι ἡμᾶς
	b. Second basis: earlier instruction	
3:10	1) Time when previous instruction was given	καὶ γὰρ ὅτε ἦμεν πρὸς ὑμᾶς
	2) Action of instruction	
	a) Command formula	τοῦτο παρηγγέλλομεν ὑμῖν
	b) Content: command in the form of a community rule	ὅτι εἴ τις οὐ θέλει ἐργάζεσθαι μηδὲ ἐσθιέτω
	7. Necessity for exhortation: disobedience to earlier command	
3:11	a. Source of information	ἀκούομεν γάρ
	b. Content	
	1) Subject	τινας

νουθετεῖτε

τοὺς ἀτάκτους (5:14a)
ὅτι παραλαβόντες λόγον ἀκοῆς
παρ' ἡμῶν τοῦ θεοῦ ἐδέξασθε
οὐ λόγον ἀνθρώπων ἀλλὰ...λόγον
θεοῦ (2:13b)

ἵνα καθὼς παρελάβετε παρ' ἡμῶν
τὸ πῶς δεῖ ὑμᾶς περιπατεῖν καὶ
ἀρέσκειν θεῷ, καθὼς καὶ περιπατεῖτε,
ἵνα περισσεύητε μᾶλλον
(1 Thess. 4:1)

αὐτοὶ γὰρ οἴδατε, ἀδελφοί,
τὴν εἴσοδον ἡμῶν τὴν πρὸς
ὑμᾶς

καὶ ὑμεῖς
μιμηταὶ ἡμῶν ἐγενήθητε καὶ τοῦ
κυρίου (1 Thess. 1:6a)

ὅτι οὐ κενὴ γέγονεν (2:1)

μνημονεύετε γάρ, ἀδελφοί,
τὸν κόπον ἡμῶν καὶ τὸν μόχθον
νυκτὸς καὶ ἡμέρας
ἐργαζόμενοι
πρὸς τὸ μὴ ἐπιβαρῆσαί
τινα ὑμῶν (2:9)

δυνάμενοι ἐν βάρει εἶναι ὡς
Χριστοῦ ἀπόστολοι, ἀλλὰ
ἐγενήθημεν νήπιοι ἐν μέσῳ ὑμῶν
(2:7a)

καὶ γὰρ ὅτε πρὸς ὑμᾶς ἦμεν

προελέγομεν ὑμῖν... (3:4)

		2) Actions	
		a) General action	περιπατοῦντας ἐν ὑμῖν ἀτάκτως
		b) Specific actions	
		i) Action refrained from	μηδὲν ἐργαζομένους
		ii) Action indulged in	ἀλλὰ περιεργαζομένους
	8.	Specific exhortation to the ἄτακτοι	
3:12		a. Those addressed	τοῖς δὲ τοιούτοις
		b. Command formula	παραγγέλλομεν καὶ παρακαλοῦμεν
		c. Basis of authority	ἐν κυρίῳ Ἰησοῦ Χριστῷ
		d. Command	
		1) Desired primary action	ἵνα μετὰ ἡσυχίας ἐργαζόμενοι
		2) Desired secondary action	τὸν ἑαυτῶν ἄρτον ἐσθίωσιν
	9.	General concluding exhortation to the addressees at large	
3:13		a. Contrasting address	ὑμεῖς δέ, ἀδελφοί,
		b. Command in negative form	μὴ ἐγκακήσητε καλοποιοῦντες

VI. Peroratio 3:14-16
  A. Command for enforcing the content of the letter upon the congregation
    1. Hypothetical situation (protasis)

3:14	a. Hypothetical action	εἰ δέ τις οὐχ ὑπακούει
	b. Object	τῷ λόγῳ
	c. Basis of authority	ἡμῶν
	d. Source	διὰ τῆς ἐπιστολῆς
	2. Command (apodosis)	
	a. First step: note that person as a portent	τοῦτον σημειοῦσθε
	b. Second step: avoid him	μὴ συναναμίγνυσθαι αὐτῷ
	3. Intention	ἵνα ἐντραπῇ
3:15	4. Limitation	
	a. Negative limitation	καὶ μὴ ὡς ἐχθρὸν ἡγεῖσθε
	b. Positive limitation	ἀλλὰ νουθετεῖτε ὡς ἀδελφόν

  B. Intercessory prayer wish for the peace of the congregation
    1. First prayer wish

3:16	a. Invocation	αὐτὸς δὲ ὁ κύριος τῆς εἰρήνης

1 Thessalonians

παρακαλοῦμεν δὲ ὑμᾶς, ἀδελφοί,
νουθετεῖτε τοὺς ἀτάκτους
(5:14a)

λοιπὸν οὖν, ἀδελφοί,
ἐρωτῶμεν ὑμᾶς
καὶ
παρακαλοῦμεν
ἐν κυρίῳ Ἰησοῦ (4:1a)

καὶ φιλοτιμεῖσθαι ἡσυχάζειν
καὶ πράσσειν τὰ ἴδια καὶ
ἐργάζεσθαι
ταῖς [ἰδίαις] χερσὶν
ὑμῶν, καθὼς ὑμῖν παρηγγείλαμεν
(4:11)

1 and 2 Thessalonians

παρακαλοῦντες ὑμᾶς καὶ παραμυθούμενοι καὶ μαρτυρόμενοι
εἰς τὸ περιπατεῖν ὑμᾶς ἀξίως
τοῦ θεοῦ τοῦ καλοῦντος ὑμᾶς
εἰς τὴν ἑαυτοῦ βασιλείαν καὶ
δόξαν (1 Thess. 2:12)

ἄρα οὖν, ἀδελφοί, στήκετε καὶ
κρατεῖτε τὰς παραδόσεις ἃς
ἐδιδάχθητε
εἴτε διὰ λόγου

εἴτε δι' ἐπιστολῆς ἡμῶν
(2 Thess. 2:15)

παρακαλοῦμεν δὲ ὑμᾶς, ἀδελφοί,
νουθετεῖτε τοὺς ἀτάκτους,
παραμυθεῖσθε τοὺς ὀλιγοψύχους,
ἀντέχεσθε τῶν ἀσθενῶν, μακρο-
θυμεῖτε πρὸς πάντας (5:14)

αὐτὸς δὲ ὁ θεὸς τῆς
εἰρήνης ἁγιάσαι

ἐρωτῶμεν δὲ ὑμᾶς, ἀδελφοί,
εἰδέναι τοὺς κοπιῶντας ἐν ὑμῖν
καὶ προϊσταμένους ὑμῶν ἐν κυρίῳ
καὶ νουθετοῦντας ὑμᾶς, καὶ
ἡγεῖσθαι αὐτοὺς ὑπερεκπερρισσοῦ
ἐν ἀγάπῃ διὰ τὸ ἔργον αὐτῶν

εἰρηνεύετε ἐν ἑαυτοῖς (1 Thess. 5:12-13)

	b. Wish	δῷη
	c. Indirect object	ὑμῖν
	d. Direct object	τὴν εἰρήνην
	e. Extent of gift wished for	διὰ παντὸς ἐν παντὶ τρόπῳ
	2. Second prayer wish (liturgical)	ὁ κύριος μετὰ πάντων ὑμῶν

VII. Epistolary Postscript
3:17-18

3:17 A. A formula of epistolary authentication ὁ ἀσπασμὸς τῇ ἐμῇ χειρὶ Παύλου
B. Explanation ὅ ἐστιν σημεῖον ἐν πάσῃ ἐπιστολῇ· οὕτως γράφω
3:18 C. Final benediction ἡ χάρις τοῦ κυρίου ἡμῶν Ἰησοῦ Χριστοῦ μετὰ πάντων ὑμῶν

ὑμᾶς ὁλοτελεῖς (5:23a)

ἀσπάσασθε τοὺς ἀδελφοὺς
πάντας ἐν φιλήματι ἁγίῳ
(5:26)

ἡ χάρις τοῦ κυρίου
ἡμῶν Ἰησοῦ Χριστοῦ
μεθ' ὑμῶν (5:28)

On the basis of this analysis, we can now investigate the various parts of the letter in closer detail. This investigation is primarily concerned to clarify the argument and doctrinal content of the letter, as well as to provide an exegetical basis for the comparison of the letter with 1 Thessalonians. We shall proceed section by section. In our exegesis we will refer to "the congregation" to which 2 Thessalonians is addressed, but this does not imply a judgment as to whether the letter was directed to a specific congregation or not.

1. *Epistolary Prescript, 1:1-2*

The most striking characteristic of the prescript, of course, is its very close parallel to that of 1 Thessalonians (1:1). Trilling notes: "Das ist vor allem deshalb auffällig, weil Paulus im Präskript stets variiert. In seinen authentischen Briefen gleicht kein Text so stark einem anderen wie in unserem Fall."[4] The particular features of the addresses of 1 and 2 Thessalonians are the three named senders of the letter, the omission of Paul's title of "apostle", and the designation of the congregation as "the church of the Thessalonians"[5]. None of these considerations, however, has any bearing on the question of authorship in and of itself.

The form of address is of interest in comparison to those of the undisputed Pauline epistles[6]. Of these, Romans does not address an ἐκκλησία (πᾶσιν τοῖς οὖσιν ἐν Ῥώμῃ ἀγαπητοῖς θεοῦ), but those "loved of God", 1 and 2 Corinthians have τῇ ἐκκλησίᾳ τοῦ θεοῦ τῇ οὔσῃ ἐν Κορίνθῳ, Galatians has ταῖς ἐκκλησίαις τῆς Γαλατίας, Philippians has πᾶσιν τοῖς ἁγίοις ἐν Χριστῷ Ἰησοῦ τοῖς οὖσιν ἐν Φιλίπποις. Like 1 and 2 Corinthians, 1 and 2 Thessalonians have both an ethno-political and a religious designation, that is, as an ἐκκλησία located in a particular geographical location (ἐν Κορίνθῳ) or composed of a particular ethno-political group (Θεσσαλονικέων). Galatians is designated as an ἐκκλησία without a modifying clause tying it to God (as in 1 and 2 Corinthians) or indicating its participation "in God our Father and (the) Lord Jesus Christ" (as in 1 and 2 Thessalonians). This may have been because Paul felt the true affiliation of the Galatian church was in doubt, although elsewhere in Paul the use of ἐκκλησία is always specifically Christian[7]. In any event, the repetition in 2 Thessalonians 1:1 of the specific designation of the church as "the church of the Thessalonians" is itself not of particular significance (cf. 1 Cor. 1:2a,

---

[4] Trilling, *Der zweite Brief*, p. 35.
[5] Trilling, *Der zweite Brief*, p. 35.
[6] Milligan, *Thessalonians*, p. 4.
[7] Cf. Rom. 16:1, 4, 5, 16; 1 Cor. 11:16, 18, 22; Gal. 1:13, 22.

2 Cor. 1:1b), but the reproduction of the entire address is; it demonstrates a clear dependence, most probably a literary dependence.

The reading of 1 Thessalonians 1:1, ἐν θεῷ πατρὶ [ἡμῶν], is not well attested and is considered dubious, a result of assimilation to 2 Thessalonians 1:1[8]. The same is true of the longer reading of the ending of 1 Thessalonians 1:1, χάρις ὑμῖν καὶ εἰρήνη [ἀπὸ θεοῦ πατρὸς ἡμῶν καὶ κυρίου Ἰησοῦ Χριστοῦ], which is considered an expansion based on the salutations of the other Pauline letters and particularly that of 2 Thessalonians. However, according to the theory of deutero-Pauline authorship, 2 Thessalonians would be the earliest witness to the text of 1 Thessalonians, particularly in this prescript, where the parallel is so close. On that basis, then, we have included the longer reading in our parallel text of 1 Thessalonians[9].

Probably the greatest significance of this prescript derives from its association with 1 Thessalonians, which is not our present concern. Under either theory of authorship, the inclusion of Silvanus and Timothy as "co-senders" is not an indication that they were co-authors as well: "Der Brief ist eine persönliche Aussprache des Paulus, auch wo er 'wir' gebraucht."[10] This is obviously also true if the author is not Paul; the letter is still a personal statement.

The inclusion of what Betz has called "the usual epithets and polite compliments" in the address of the letter[11] indicates that the author believes the disruptions caused by the proclamation of the approach of the parousia (2:1-2) and the presence of the ἄτακτοι who disregard the traditional teachings (3:6) have not yet affected the faith of the majority of the readers[12]. However, the intention of the letter is specifically to preserve the readers "in good standing" by assuring their fidelity to the traditions they have inherited. The spiritual well-being of the readers is entirely dependent upon their reaction to the author's words in the letter.

2. Exordium, 1:3-4

The purpose of the *exordium*, or introduction, is to prepare the reader for what follows, so that he may give it proper attention. In 2 Thessalonians the *exordium* is provided by the traditional epistolary thanksgiving, in which the writer gives thanks for favors granted to himself or to the addressee. The

---

[8] Milligan, *Thessalonians*, p. 5; Dibelius, *An die Thessalonicher*, p. 2.
[9] von Dobschütz, *Die Thessalonicher-Briefe*, p. 234.
[10] Ibid., p. 57.
[11] Betz, *Galatians*, p. 40.
[12] We may compare Gal. 1:6-9; Betz, ibid., pp. 44-56.

thanksgiving is a recurring element in Paul's letters[13], the notable exception being Galatians. Properly speaking, in 2 Thessalonians we find not a thanksgiving but a description of an act of thanksgiving, since the language is descriptive rather than performative. This distinction is made clearer by the inclusion of ὀφείλομεν, which introduces the idea of obligation, and the liturgical phrase καθὼς ἄξιόν ἐστιν, which makes it clear that this obligation is of a religious nature[14]. Indeed, verse 3a gives the impression of a standard formula of thanksgiving, an impression strengthened by the awkward transition introduced by ὅτι[15]. Ὅτι introduces the reason for thanksgiving, when it properly should introduce the reason for the obligation.

The reason for thanksgiving is the "superabounding" of the faith of the readers and the increase of the love of each one of them for one another. The growth of these two virtues is apparently unchecked by the unrest the letter describes[16]. Both of these virtues are "interior", that is, they are in operation within the community without regard to the influence of those outside[17].

Rigaux notes that αὐτοὺς ἡμᾶς is set in some sort of apposition, although he is unable to give a satisfactory answer as to what the second term of the antithesis was[18]. We have set verse 4 into contrast with verse 3, showing the parallel between the two verses. The emphatic αὐτοὺς ἡμᾶς indicates the introduction of a contrasting phrase, in this case the contrast between the act of giving thanks for the readers to God, and the act of boasting about them before his churches. In both cases the language is descriptive rather than performative. The boast is not concerned with a "growth" of virtue, but merely with its display. This is an indication that the virtues in question are not "interior" but "exterior", that is, they are virtues that arise in contact with outsiders, specifically the unbelievers who persecute the congregation. Although ὑπομονή is a fitting virtue in face of persecution, πίστις is also displayed, here particularly the faithfulness which endures in persecution; this persecution appears to be a present reality (cf. 1:6).

The "boast" of the author is based on the virtue displayed by the readers in affliction and persecution, trials he will next associate with the end-times, the parousia, and the return made to both persecutor and persecuted (1:5-7). Θλῖψις and διωγμός are the lot of the Christian[19], but also a feature of the

---

[13] Cf. Rom. 1:8, 1 Cor 1:4-9, 2 Cor. 1:3-7, Phil. 1:3-11, 1 Thess. 1:2-10, Phlm. 4-7.

[14] Roger D. Aus, "The Liturgical Background of the Necessity and Propriety of Giving Thanks According to 2 Thes. 1:3," *Journal of Biblical Literature* 92 (1973): 422–38.

[15] von Dobschütz, *Die Thessalonicher-Briefe*, p. 236; von Dobschütz takes this as evidence that Paul was not a slave to epistolary formulae.

[16] Ibid., p. 237.

[17] Trilling, *Der zweite Brief*, p. 45.

[18] Rigaux, *St. Paul*, pp. 614–15.

[19] Cf. Rom. 5:3, 8:35, 12:12; 2 Cor. 1:4, 4:16-17; cf. Matt. 5:11-12, 13:21.

end-times[20]. The ὑπομονή is thus displayed in expectation of the end and is, as Trilling notes, the experiential equivalent of hope[21]. Although the major section of 2:1-17 deals with the "hope" of the parousia, the word itself appears only in 2:16 in association with "consolation". The author's concern is less with the theological virtue of hope and more with its practical result, steadfastness (cf. 1:11-12; 2:15-17; 3:3-5).

The contrast between the thanksgiving of 1:3 and the "boast" of 1:4 thus operates on several levels: the general and formulaic description of the thanksgiving[22] is paralleled by the unexpected description of the author's "boast" which is provoked by the readers' virtuous action in persecution (cf. 2 Cor. 8:1-5, 9:2). The "boast" here, since it is related to the expectation of the end, looks ahead to verse 1:10, where the events of the parousia and the glorification of the Lord by believers is connected to the belief provoked by the witness of the author. As we shall see, the author also anticipates acting as an intercessor on the congregation's behalf at the judgment (see below concerning 1:10). The "boast" before the churches of God is thus a foreshadowing of the author's later "boast" before God himself at the parousia. As a result, the present act of thanksgiving and the act of "boasting" are more closely related than is at first apparent.

3. Narratio, 1:5-12

The beginning of the narratio (1:5-12) is signalled by ἔνδειγμα, "example", which stands in accusative apposition to the whole preceding phrase (1:4) almost as a title. The eschatological orientation of both thanksgiving and "boast" is demonstrated through the development of the ἔνδειγμα into an "episode in the Last Judgment", which portrays the ultimate outcome of the present sufferings of the congregation. Jouette Bassler has argued that God's "righteous judgment" is demonstrated specifically by the experience of persecution, and links this idea with rabbinic *Leidenstheologie*[23]. Unfortunately, Bassler fails to differentiate between the idea of suffering as a means of punishing the sins of the good so that they many enjoy unalloyed reward in the future life (*Leidenstheologie* proper)[24] and the idea of suffering as discipline or "chastening" (as in Bassler's examples from Ps. Sol. 13:9-10, 2 Macc. 6:12-

---

[20] Cf. Dan. 12:1, Mark 13:19, Matt. 24:21, Rev. 7:14.

[21] Trilling, *Der zweite Brief*, p. 47.

[22] The general and inspecific nature of the thanksgiving leads Trilling to question whether a real congregation is in mind at all, ibid., p. 45.

[23] Jouette M. Bassler, "The Enigmatic Sign: 2 Thessalonians 1:5", *Catholic Biblical Quarterly* 46 (1984): 496–510.

[24] Ibid., p. 502.

16, 2 Bar. 13:3-10, 78:5)²⁵. This latter, of course, is a common idea in the Hebrew Bible (cf. Isa. 40:1-2, Job 33:19-30, Prov. 3:11-12) and the Septuagint (cf. Wis. 11:9-10, Bar. 4:5-29). We would suggest that this idea of suffering as chastisement is operative in 2 Thessalonians 1:5, especially since there is also the idea of "becoming worthy" of God's kingdom through suffering (εἰς τὸ καταξιωθῆναι...).

The purpose of the *narratio* is to present a "statement of facts" that will further the purpose of the author. Of course, in any rhetorical work the "statement of facts" is really a work of fiction, insofar as it is a presentation of past events (or in this case, future events) intended to substantiate a polemical point and designed to serve that single purpose. In Paul's report of his conflict with Cephas (Gal. 2:14) there is no mention of the outcome of the conflict, which suggests that Paul was unable to persuade Cephas²⁶. In the present case, the "statement of facts" describes the fate of the good and evil to remind the readers of the ultimate consequences of the moral decision the author asks them to make. Its inclusion provides the eschatological presupposition both for the *probatio* and the paraenesis of the *exhortatio*²⁷.

The "episode in the Last Judgment", which we have identified as the particular form taken by the ἔνδειγμα (1:5-10) has been isolated as a particular literary genre by Hans Dieter Betz²⁸. One of the features of this genre is that it is composed of and supposes knowledge of traditional material about the judgment; its function within a particular composition depends upon the readers' understanding of the process of judgment as an event²⁹.

The topic of the ἔνδειγμα, that is, the fact for which it is offered as evidence is "the righteous judgment of God." The ἔνδειγμα presents a preview of the final judgment, which will take place at the end of the age, when the Lord Jesus will be revealed (1:7). Although this act of judgment lies in the future, the outcome is already known because the salvation of the faithful forms an invariable part of the Judeo-Christian apocalyptic traditions upon which this letter draws. The author believes, and expects his readers to agree, that at the

---

[25] Ibid., pp. 503–5.

[26] On this passage, cf. Betz, *Galatians*, pp. 110–12.

[27] Goldstein, *Demosthenes*, p. 105: "Whatever extensive narrative may be present in *demegoriae* [i.e., deliberative rhetoric] is organized not to show that some particular action took place, but to remind the hearers of facts that will help them make a good decision."

[28] Hans Dieter Betz, "An Episode in the Last Judgment (Matt. 7:21-23)", *Essays on the Sermon on the Mount*, trans. Laurence L. Welborn (Philadelphia: Fortress Press, 1985), pp. 125–57.

[29] Ibid., p. 127; Betz cites P. Volz, *Die Eschatologie der jüdischen Gemeinde im neutestamentlichen Zeitalter* (Tübingen: J.C.B. Mohr [Paul Siebeck], 1934), p. 272. Among the Old Testament passages alluded to in 2 Thess. 1:5-10 are Isa. 2:10, 11, 19, 21; 66:4, 15; Jer. 10:25; Ps. 67:36 (LXX), 88:8 (LXX); see references in Nestle-Aland, *Novum Testamentum Graece*, 26th ed. (Stuttgart: Deutsche Bibelgesellschaft, 1979).

parousia these things will take place. The apocalyptic tradition provides the proof of "the righteous judgment of God"; the appeal to the reversal typical of the *lex talionis* (1:6) is a rhetorical device, since no one would question the "righteousness" of the law of retribution as a basis for God's actions. The use of the conditional εἴπερ here, which has led some commentators into complicated defenses of the author's intentions, is thus part of the rhetorical device: "If indeed it is righteous for God to repay (as of course it is)..." (1:6).

The "episode in the Last Judgment" is based on prophecies concerning God as judge, in this case drawing heavily from Isaiah 66. There are parallels in other apocalyptic materials as well[30]. Such parallels, of course, do not demonstrate dependence, but merely indicate that 2 Thessalonians lies within the apocalyptic tradition of the Judaism and Christianity of the first century A.D. As often happens in the use of these traditional materials in the New Testament, Jesus takes the place originally held by God. As Trilling points out, verses 3-7a have prepared the reader for a theocentric description of the end (since "the righteous judgment of God" is the event under discussion), but verses 7b-10 provide a Christocentric description[31]. It is the Lord Jesus who is revealed from heaven, inflicting vengeance (1:7b-8), and it is apparently he to whom 1:9 refers as "the Lord", from whose presence the wicked are banished. It is then Jesus again who is the subject of ὅταν ἔλθῃ... ἐν τῇ ἡμέρᾳ ἐκείνῃ (1:10). Jesus fills the role of eschatological judge, and God himself is nowhere in evidence.

The emphasis in this episode is upon the fate of the wicked. The initial emphasis was upon the acceptance of those who now suffer for the sake of the kingdom of God (1:5), and then upon the idea of recompense under the provision of the *lex talionis* (1:6). But in 1:8, the Lord Jesus is revealed "giving retribution" (διδόντος ἐκδίκησιν) specifically against the wicked, described in parallel structure: "those who do not know God and those who do not obey the gospel of our Lord Jesus Christ" (1:8). The idea of "disobedience" is thereby equated with ignorance of God; this crucial idea of "obedience" (cf. 3:14) is here given eschatological importance (cf. 2:15-17, 3:6-12). The retribution the evil, the disobedient, will suffer is indicated: "everlasting destruction away from the presence of the Lord and from the glory of his might" (1:9). Since the primary emphasis is on the work of retribution against those who have troubled the readers, the power of the Lord is emphasized as well (1:7b, 1:9b). In 1:10, the attention shifts again to the believers, but only insofar as they, unlike the wicked, are in the presence of the Lord at his revelation (cf. 2:1b). They form his coterie, but their adoration is presented in the passive voice, from the Lord's point of view: "When he comes to be

---

[30] There is a useful chart in Rigaux, *Saint Paul*, p. 624.
[31] Trilling, *Der zweite Brief*, p. 53.

glorified in [i.e. "among"][32] his holy ones and to be marvelled at in all those who believe...." In other words, the concern of the episodes appears to be, first, to depict the fate of the wicked, and second, to depict the strength and glory of the Lord at his appearing. In verses 6-10a the believers are only those who bear witness to the glory of the Lord; the idea of retribution has outweighed that of reward. It is true that the emphasis shifts back to the elect in verses 11-12, but these verses fall outside the strictly apocalyptic picture presented by the ἔνδειγμα; there the theme is primarily retribution against the wicked.

The cryptic reference ὅτι ἐπιστεύθη τὸ μαρτύριον ἡμῶν ἐφ' ὑμᾶς (1:10) appears to disrupt the orientation towards the future which is assumed in the episode from the Last Judgment. This is because the favorable judgment to be passed upon the readers at that time is somehow made dependent upon an action which was already past at the time of writing: "because our testimony concerning you was believed" (the propositional phrase ἐφ' ὑμᾶς is ambiguous). Von Dobschütz noted that τὸ μαρτύριον must refer either to the testimony of the author on the day of judgment or to his previous testimony in preaching; he then ruled out the former possibility on the basis of the past sense of the aorist passive[33].

This may be too hasty a judgment. The author certainly stands in solidarity with the congregation in this apocalyptic scenario, as he looks forward to God granting "to you who have been afflicted, rest *with us* in the revelation of the Lord Jesus from heaven..." (1:7).

This same verse, 1:7, marks the beginning of a ring composition which concludes in verse 1:10, the beginning and end are indicated by the time reference to the day of judgment (ἐν τῇ ἀποκαλύψει τοῦ κυρίου Ἰησοῦ and ἐν τῇ ἡμέρᾳ ἐκείνῃ). Both of these time references are tied to expressions of the author's solidarity with his readers, presumably within the apocalyptic framework; in the first case, rest "with us", and in the second, "because our testimony concerning you was believed." How then do we explain the use of the aorist passive? As has been previously stated, this narrative about the Last Judgment presents a future occurrence which is a fact accepted by both author and readers. It is this accepted fact which demonstrates "the righteous judgment of God." In dealing with this fact, the author can describe future certainties as past events; this is certainly not a novelty within apocalyptic literature[34].

The flexibility of the time sequence is further suggested by the time reference which follows, referring to the future day of judgment. This is the same

---

[32] von Dobschütz, *Die Thessalonicher-Briefe*, p. 251.
[33] Ibid., p. 252.
[34] Cf. the use of the aorist in Dan. 7-12 (LXX) and Rev. 14-21.

"day" on which the readers will receive rest "with us". The description of the day itself in verses 1:7b-10a carries no reference to author or readers; they reappear only in the reference to the author's testimony concerning the readers "on that day". This mention of the testimony is complicated by the fact that the preposition cannot be shown to render the meaning usually given in translation, "to you". Milligan considers it a unique usage,[35] while Frame cites 1 Maccabees 2:37 (LXX) for the meaning "over"[36]. Thus it is not clear whether the assumed subject of the passive verb ἐπιστεύθη is the readers (thus, "you believed our testimony to you," as most translations and commentators) or someone else (thus, "X believed our testimony concerning you"). If the latter is the case, as the commonly understood meaning of the preposition would suggest, the assumed subject must be Christ as the eschatological judge. The author would then, in the context of the Day of Judgment, offer his testimony as an advocate for the readers before the judgment seat of Christ. His solidarity with them would then be that of an advocate and mediator.

We find a similar idea in Paul's letters in 2 Corinthians 11:2, where Paul is responsible for presenting the congregation to Christ "as a pure bride to her one husband" and in 1 Thessalonians 2:19. The testimony of the author (or the author-as-Paul) will be "accredited" to the congregation in the eschatological judgment; since the present letter also contains this testimony in a preliminary form, the letter itself has an eschatological function. It is "pre-trial deposition" from the author testifying to the faith and steadfastness of the Thessalonians under persecution (1:4). The process of "testifying" had begun before the author wrote, continued in the letter, and would continue until the author appeared with the faithful before Christ the judge at the parousia. From this point of view, the use of the aorist passive is quite appropriate; the testimony has been believed, is believed, and will be believed by the Judge "on that day." Such an interpretation allows for a more natural understanding of ἐφ' ὑμᾶς as "on your behalf" and does not make the phrase an unexplained parenthesis, but rather a proper conclusion to the scene of the Last Judgment (cf. 1 Thess. 2:19-20, 3:13).

With this understanding of verse 1:10, we may see a direct connection to the report of a prayer of intercession which follows in verses 11-12. The prayer does not take place in these verses but is only reported, as was also the case with the thanksgiving of 1:3-4. Commentators are agreed in taking εἰς ὅ as "to which end," but fail to see any direct connection between verses 5-10

---

[35] Milligan, *Thessalonians*, p. 92.
[36] James Everett Frame, *A Critical and Exegetical Commentary on the Epistles of St. Paul to the Thessalonians*, International Critical Commentary (Edinburgh: T. and T. Clark, 1912), p. 237.

and 11-12. With the interpretation advanced above, the prayer the author offers is that the Thessalonians may indeed live up to his testimony given before Christ, "that our God may make you worthy of the call and fulfill every delight in goodness and work of faith in power" (1:11). The κλῆσις is then a future event, since the author is praying that the readers may be helped to gain acceptance at the judgment on the basis of his own testimony and their own behavior, which has been consistent with the author's instruction. As Trilling notes, such an understanding of κλῆσις is contrary to the normal usage of Paul (cf. 1 Cor. 1:26, 7:20), and he believes its use here indicates the work of a later author (cf. Eph. 1:18, 4:4; 2 Pet. 1:10), using words whose meanings had become vague[37]. This may be so, but of course the use of κλῆσις in itself is not determinative one way or the other. What is important is the sense of the present letter, and our understanding seems to require that κλῆσις refer to a future event.

The parallel action to this "making worthy" is to "fulfill every delight in goodness and work of faith in power" (1:11b). Since the concern is the status of the readers at judgment, the fulfillment must be of the human deeds of the readers. Von Dobschütz would attribute both "delight" and "work of faith" to God, making the point of the prayer the desire that God's delight in the goodness of men and his own work of faith might work "in power" in the readers[38]. It is difficult, however, to see what God's "work of faith" might be. The phrase recalls 1 Thessalonians 1:3, but also the mention of πίστις in persecution in 2 Thessalonians 1:4b. This is faithfulness which endures in persecution, and thus the visible manifestation of faithfulness under duress. This is at least part of the "work of faithfulness" which God is asked to fulfill. "Fulfill" is eschatological in this context, so the author is praying for the continued steadfastness of the readers under persecution. This steadfastness forms part of the author's testimony concerning the congregation. The final phrase, ἐν δυνάμει, attributes the efficacy of the prayer to the power of God at work in the faithful to bring about the desired virtues in them.

The reason for this prayer is revealed in the next verse: "so that the name of our Lord Jesus may be glorified in you, and you in him..." (1:12). Most recent commentators take this to refer to a present glorification of the Lord[39]. However, within the context of our understanding of the preceding two verses, it appears that this verse is a reference to 1:10, ὅταν ἔλθῃ ἐνδοξασθῆναι ἐν τοῖς ἁγίοις αὐτοῦ. The same verb is used in reference to the same person (the "name" and the person being the same), and the glorification is to take place among the same people, the "saints" or "holy ones"

---

[37] Trilling, *Der zweite Brief*, pp. 62–63.
[38] von Dobschütz, *Die Thessalonicher-Briefe*, pp. 253–57.
[39] Ibid., p. 257; Rigaux, *Saint Paul*, p. 641; Trilling, *Der zweite Brief*, p. 64.

being a title for "all who believe" (as in the parallel in 1:10b), including the readers. The reciprocity of the glorification and its operation through grace do not appear to rule out this interpretation[40]. To some extent, of course, this glorification has a present reality, but its primary reference is to the future parousia. That this reciprocal glorification is a result of the work of divine grace, even on the day of judgment (or especially on the day of judgment) should come as no surprise. The source of this grace is "our God and Lord Jesus Christ" (1:12b). As Trilling has pointed out, the title "God" for Christ is grammatically and text-critically clear, and should not be ruled out as the intention of the author[41]. This is especially significant in view of the way the figure of Christ predominates in the originally theophanous scene from the Last Judgment, and the parallel statements about God and Christ in exacting retribution (1:6, 1:8) and as the proper objects of devotion (1:8). It is perhaps best to accept the plain meaning of the text.

The intention of the ἔνδειγμα, then, is to demonstrate God's righteous judgment. This judgment is manifested by the vindication of his faithful ones at the judgment before Christ, and the condemnation of those who do not acknowledge God. The author himself provides testimony that the readers are faithful, and he and they will share in the kingdom of God for which they now suffer. The author prays that God may help them to remain faithful, so that they may prove his testimony to be true, and glorify Christ in the time of his coming, through divine grace. The author intends this ἔνδειγμα partly as a means of consoling his readers in their persecution, but also as a means of encouraging them to remain faithful.

4. Probatio, 2:1-17

The particular apocalyptic scenario presented by the second chapter of the letter will be discussed at length in another chapter. However, it is appropriate to examine at this time how that scenario fits into the composition of the letter as a whole, and this in turn may illustrate the meaning of this chapter.

This section is presented initially as an exhortation, signalled by the use of the technical term ἐρωτῶμεν. However, the exhortation is "doctrinal" rather than "ethical", that is, the author is not concerned with instilling a certain moral behavior (as Paul is in Romans 12) or even a particular attitude of mind (as in 1 Cor. 10:31-11:1); rather, he wishes the congregation to understand correctly a particular part of doctrine ὑπὲρ τῆς παρουσίας τοῦ κυρίου ἡμῶν Ἰησοῦ Χριστοῦ καὶ ἡμῶν ἐπισυναγωγῆς ἐπ' αὐτόν. To be more

---
[40] Contra Rigaux, Saint Paul, p. 641.
[41] Trilling, Der zweite Brief, p. 65.

exact, the author wishes his readers to adopt a certain attitude towards this doctrinal idea, that of steadfastness. This is expressed by the rejection of the opposite behavior: εἰς τὸ μὴ ταχέως σαλευθῆναι ὑμᾶς ἀπὸ τοῦ νοὸς μηδὲ θροεῖσθαι.

To be "shaken in mind" or "befuddled" is not so much an opposite of steadfastness as it is a result of its absence, just as to be "alarmed" or "in distress" is the result of an absence of faithfulness. It is those very virtues which the author has commended in the Thessalonians in the face of "persecutions and afflictions" which the readers must also exhibit in the face of doctrinal error. Just as the "persecutions and afflictions" are the first pangs of eschatological troubles, so it would appear that the attempts to "shake" the faithful from a proper understanding of the tradition they have received is a symptom of the eschatological apostasy to which the author will shortly refer (2:3).

What is the doctrine under attack? "The coming of our Lord Jesus Christ and our gathering together with him" (2:1b) both appear as topics of the discussion, although neither is properly speaking the topic of the *probatio*. It seems likely that the author regarded the two ideas of parousia and "gathering" as parts of a single unit, and synonymous with "the eschatological process"[42]. We find the two most closely associated, of course, in 1 Thessalonians 5:1-11 and 4:13-18, respectively, but they have also been linked already in 2 Thessalonians 1:10. It would appear that the author has the two sections of 1 Thessalonians in mind, and it is this doctrine of the whole chain of events associated with the parousia that he wishes his readers to understand correctly. Just what he conceives this chain of events to be is revealed in due course. The true topic of the *probatio*, however, is the refutation of the false proclamation, "The Day of the Lord is here!" (2:2b).

As we have said, the readers are called upon to hold steadfastly to this doctrine of the parousia. But as it is a point of doctrine, a "tradition", it must not only be maintained but interpreted correctly. Indeed, the disturbance the author fears stems not from a denial of the parousia, but from the misunderstanding of the eschatological process.

This reinterpretation has theoretically been conveyed by one or all of three means of communication. These three means by which this reinterpretation has been conveyed are by spirit, by word, or by letter ὡς δι' ἡμῶν. Many commentators take the phrase ὡς δι' ἡμῶν as applying to all three members of the preceding phrase[43], but it seems best in terms of grammar[44] and sense[45] to ascribe them to the last member alone. This reinterpretation of the parousia

---

[42] This idea will be more fully developed in chap. 3.

[43] So Milligan, *Thessalonians*, pp. 96–97; von Dobschütz, *Die Thessalonicher-Briefe*, pp. 267–68; Rigaux, *Saint Paul*, p. 653.

[44] Trilling, *Der zweite Brief*, p. 77.

[45] Rigaux, *Saint Paul*, p. 651.

has come about, then, through an ecstatic utterance ("spirit"), or through an authoritative pronouncement ("word"), or through a letter either written by or ascribed to Paul, since ὡς δι' ἡμῶν will admit either interpretation. It may be that what the author regards as a distortion of the doctrine of the parousia has come about through an incorrect interpretation of Paul's letters, specifically 1 Thessalonians. This theory will be examined in the fourth chapter.

The content of this reinterpretation of the parousia is ὡς ὅτι ἐνέστηκεν ἡ ἡμέρα τοῦ κυρίου. We should take ἐνέστηκεν in its usual sense and translate, "that the Day of the Lord is here"[46]. We are not now concerned with the meaning of this statement, either as understood by its proponents or as understood by our author. For the moment, it is enough that for the author the statement is both false and deceitful; thus the warning, μή τις ὑμᾶς ἐξαπατήσῃ κατὰ μηδένα τρόπον (2:3a). There are people in the congregation or in association with it who are proclaiming a message that the author regards as incorrect, and these people are deceiving the congregation. They are not opponents of the author in the same sense that the "Judaizers" were opponents of Paul, for both parties represent "Paul" as they understand him; the case is probably closer to that in Corinth, where some believers apparently regarded Paul's teaching as a form of wisdom (σοφία) that set them above their brothers (cf. 1 Cor. 2:1-5). But these people are opponents insofar as they represent an incorrect point of view that is leading the faithful astray, and the author must oppose them and their belief if he is to keep his readers faithful to the tradition as he understands it. Thus 2 Thessalonians, unlike 1 Thessalonians, was written at least in part to refute the beliefs of opponents.

This refutation is based on three proofs which describe (a) events which must take place before the Day of the Lord (2:3b-5), (b) the reason for the present delay of the Day (2:6-8), and (c) the manifest nature of the appearance of ὁ ἄνομος. The first of these is presented within a conditional sentence which is lacking its apodosis; it is usually assumed that the apodosis would make the Day of the Lord conditional on the previous coming of ἡ ἀποστασία. The coming of ὁ ἄνθρωπος τῆς ἀνομίας also involves his blasphemous actions described in 2:4. This first proof is concluded by a rhetorical question (2:5) which is intended to provide a "traditional" basis for this apocalyptic scenario.

The second proof is presented as new information, the καὶ νῦν standing in apposition to the preceding ἔτι ὢν πρὸς ὑμᾶς. There is a force that restrains ὁ ἄνθρωπος τῆς ἀνομίας until the appointed time of his appearing. Nevertheless, the "mystery of lawlessness" is already at work, and when the restraining one is removed, ὁ ἄνομος will be revealed, only to be destroyed by the Lord

---

[46] Cf. Milligan, *Thessalonians*, p. 97; von Dobschütz, *Die Thessalonicher-Briefe*, pp. 267–68; Rigaux, *Saint Paul*, p. 653.

at his coming. In the second proof, τὸ μυστήριον τῆς ἀνομίας and τὸ κατέχον are already at work; it is reasonable then to assume that in the first proof, ἡ ἀποστασία is at work in the present as well. The adverb πρῶτον modifies only ἔλθῃ ἡ ἀποστασία, giving the event of the ἀποστασία chronological priority over the appearance of the man of lawlessness. Since the apocalyptic drama as described in 2 Thessalonians 2:1-7 refers only to two periods, the present and the later time of crisis, we must assume that ἡ ἀποστασία belongs to the first of these, the present. Ἡ ἀποστασία refers to religious rebellion, but more specifically to a renunciation of one's faith or an abandonment of a religious loyalty. The ἀποστασία would then be at least in part the abandonment by Christians of their inherited traditions or the teachings of the apostolic leaders. As noted above, the author warns his readers against being "shaken in mind" or becoming upset, actions which we have understood as a result of a lack of steadfastness and faithfulness. These virtues are especially suited to the persecutions and tribulations of the end-times, and we have suggested that the attempt to "shake" the Thessalonians from the inherited tradition was a symptom of the present apocalyptic apostasy. Those in the congregation who maintained that "the Day of the Lord is present" are cast in the rôle of "apostates" whose work is part of the eschatological ἀποστασία. The author's words against such people also serve an eschatological function; they work against the ἀποστασία which is already present. Just as the letter serves an apocalyptic function as a testimony on the behalf of the congregation at judgment, so it also serves such a function as a measure against the spread of the apocalyptic ἀποστασία.

The third proof employed by the author to demonstrate that the Day of the Lord is not present is the manifest nature of the coming of the eschatological Antagonist, ὁ ἄνομος, the Lawless One. His demonic mimicry of Christ at his own parousia is performed through the activity of Satan, with the express purpose of deceiving those who have refused to believe the truth that might save them. However, their downfall is in reality a result of God's own act of will; he has sent a "strong delusion" upon them so that they might be judged and condemned. As is usual in apocalyptic literature, it is emphasized that it is God who is in control, and that evil forces operate only where God has given them leave to do so.

The description of an act of thanksgiving which follows (2:13-14) shifts the attention from those who are lost because God has allowed it to happen to those who are saved because God himself has called them. As in 1:3, ὀφείλομεν introduces the idea of obligation, and 2:13a has a very close parallel in 1:3a. In this case, however, the reason for thanksgiving is not the virtue displayed by the readers, but the work of God in calling them to salvation. As in 2:11-12, the emphasis is upon the fact that God is in control, in salvation as well as in condemnation. The ἡμεῖς δὲ appears to refer back in contrast to the last group mentioned, i.e., "all those who did not believe in the truth but took pleasure in unrighteousness" (2:12b). The author would certainly regard himself not as one of this group but as one of the saved, but the apparent parallel is not between the lost and the author, but between the lost and the readers. Trilling suggests that ἡμεῖς is an imitation of the renewed thanksgiving of 1 Thessalonians 2:13, because no personal note or specific situation is in mind within the present context, although both appear in 1 Thessalonians[47]. Whether this is the case or not, it is clear that the author sees himself as standing over against the readers; it is through "our gospel" that the call of God has come to the congregation. The author looks back to Paul's initial preaching of the gospel as it is presented in 1 Thessalonians 1:2-10, as a message ἐν δυνάμει καὶ ἐν πνεύματι ἁγίῳ καὶ ἐν πληροφορίᾳ πολλῇ because it is the vehicle of God's call. The real apposition, then, would be between the author and ὁ ἄνομος, the latter being a spreader of lies and of condemnation which is the vehicle of rejection by God (2:9-12). The Lawless One is a false prophet of Satan who brings ruin through lies to those rejected by God; the author represents the true apostle of Christ who brings salvation through the gospel to those chosen and called by God.

The choice of God has been ἀπ' ἀρχῆς[48], which may refer either to the beginning of the world or to the beginning of Paul's mission. Von Dobschütz, on the assumption of Pauline authorship, rejected the latter possibility because at the time the letter was supposedly written Paul's mission was already twelve years old; such a remark, he believed, would be appropriate only at a later time[49]. To some extent the interpretation of this phrase (and indeed, the choice of this phrase over the well-attested variant, ἀπαρχήν) is dependent upon a position in regard to authorship. However, because of the extra-historical point of view introduced by the apocalyptic scenario, we believe the reference here to be extra-historical as well, and take ἀπ' ἀρχῆς as referring to the beginning of the world[50].

God has called the faithful from the beginning εἰς σωτηρίαν, in contrast to the condemnation of the unbelievers (2:13b). This end is brought about by sanctification by the Spirit (taking the genitive as subjective), that is, by God's action on man; this action is in contrast to God sending a "force of delusion" (ἐνέργειαν πλάνης) upon the wicked. The sanctification is paired with πίστει ἀληθείας, "faithfulness in the truth", which is man's response to God;

---

[47] Trilling, Der zweite Brief, p. 119.
[48] The textual witness is divided between ἀπ' ἀρχῆς and ἀπαρχήν; on this point, cf. Trilling, Der zweite Brief, pp. 120–22.
[49] Cf. Phil. 4:15, ἐν ἀρχῇ τοῦ εὐαγγελίου; von Dobschütz, Die Thessalonicher-Briefe, p. 298.
[50] Cf. Mark. 13:19; Matt. 24:21; John 1:1, 15:27 et al.; Col. 1:18; 2 Pet. 3:4; 1 John 1:1, et al.; Rev. 3:14, 21:6, 22:13.

this action in turn is in contrast to the response of the wicked to the "force of delusion", which is sent εἰς τὸ πιστεῦσαι αὐτοὺς τῷ ψεύδει (2:11). The contrast between the fate of the unbelievers and that of the faithful congregation is now followed by the source of the latter's saving call, which stands in contrast to the "wicked deception" of ὁ ἄνομος, who has led the unbelievers astray. The believers were called "through the gospel", that is, through the truth originally brought by Paul, God's true apostle, with whom the author identifies himself. The goal of God's call is that the believers might "obtain the glory of our Lord Jesus Christ"; in view of the contrast with the fate of the lost, it is clear that this refers to the eschatological glory of Christ. The whole point of salvation here is entirely eschatological: God has called the faithful through the gospel preached by the apostle, so that they might avoid the fate of the wicked (exclusion from the Lord's presence and ἀπὸ τῆς δόξης τῆς ἰσχύος αὐτοῦ, 1:9) and share in the glory of Jesus Christ at his parousia (1:12). It should be recalled at this point that for our author, the parousia and ἡμῶν ἐπισυναγωγῆς ἐπ' αὐτόν are inextricably linked (2:1b); the apocalyptic end is clearly in the author's mind.

This apocalyptic end has a paraenetic consequence in the present, as indicated by the phrase ἄρα οὖν, and the address ἀδελφοί, which repeats the address used at the beginning of the description of the thanksgiving. This marks the beginning of the conclusion of the *probatio*, and forms an *inclusio* by means of its parallels with 2:2. The readers are called upon to "stand firm" (στήκετε) and to "hold to the traditions that you were taught" (κρατεῖτε τὰς παραδόσεις ἃς ἐδιδάχθητε); this stands in contrast to the behavior depicted in 2:2, that of being "quickly shaken in mind or excited", especially since the message which triggers this excitement (ὡς ὅτι ἐνέστηκεν ἡ ἡμέρα τοῦ κυρίου, 2:2c) has just been shown to be in contradiction to the "tradition". The source of this correct tradition is the teaching of the author (or the author-as-Paul), εἴτε διὰ λόγου εἴτε δι' ἐπιστολῆς ἡμῶν, just as the error is to be disregarded, no matter the means by which it is conveyed, μήτε διὰ πνεύματος μήτε διὰ λόγου μήτε δι' ἐπιστολῆς ὡς δι' ἡμῶν (2:2b). In this case, both "word" and "letter" have their source in the author, since he is presented as the guarantor of the congregation's salvation, which lies in their adherence to the "tradition". Milligan notes that the verb κρατεῖν with the accusative emphasizes that the "tradition" is a present possession of the readers[51]. This "tradition" is the anchor of the readers' faith, and adherence to it will guarantee their eschatological salvation. Since we have already seen that the author regards himself as the representative of the congregation before the eschatological judge, and as the bearer of "our gospel" which separates the believers from the unbelievers, this "tradition" must refer to the sum total of

---

[51] Milligan, *Thessalonians*, p. 107.

the author's teaching to his readers. The author (or the author-as-Paul) must be referring then not only to 1 Thessalonians but to the present letter as well, especially since this letter contains the "tradition" which is surest proof against the congregation being led astray by the error of 2:2c. All of the communication between the author or the author-as-Paul and the congregation, εἴτε διὰ λόγου εἴτε δι' ἐπιστολῆς ἡμῶν, that is, the whole body of doctrine, forms the "tradition" to which the readers must cling for their salvation at the end. (The author will later add the example of Paul to the substance of this tradition, 3:7-9.) The implicit rejection of this "tradition" being communicated διὰ πνεύματος suggests that the tradition is a formal body of doctrine not subject to charismatic alteration.

An intercessory prayer by the author on behalf of the readers concludes the *probatio* (2:16). The address of the prayer is presented in chiasmus, with both Christ and God represented by titles which define their relationship to the community of believers. The chiasmus draws the two figures together, but they are separated both by their respective functional titles (Christ as Lord, God as Father) and the aretalogy which characterizes God specifically in terms of his rôle as the originator of the apocalyptic drama. Ὁ ἀγαπήσας ἡμᾶς refers to the anterior love of God which provoked his past act of giving παράκλησιν αἰωνίαν καὶ ἐλπίδα ἀγαθήν. Both of these gifts are results of the certainty of eschatological salvation; this provides the inexhaustible comfort or consolation of the believers in persecution, and is the object of their "good hope". These gifts are given ἐν χάριτι, which is adverbial to the preceding participle[52], perhaps stressing the gratuitous nature of God's gift of salvation[53].

The action requested of God is that he may indeed comfort the hearts of the readers; since the comfort or consolation with which the letter is concerned is a result of a proper understanding of the apocalyptic scenario, this may be a request that the present letter may have its desired effect. In that case, von Dobschütz's suggestion that this phrase forms a chiasmus would indeed be correct[54]; the request would be that God might comfort the hearts of the readers in (by means of) every good word and establish them in (by means of) every good work. Both, ἔργον καὶ λόγος ἀγαθός, refer to the tradition. This "good work" is adherence to the tradition and, as we shall shortly see, avoidance of those who do not live in accordance with its moral component (3:6). The traditional doctrine brings consolation, and the practice of its paraenesis strengthens the faithful.

---

[52] von Dobschütz, *Die Thessalonicher-Briefe*, p. 303.
[53] Cf. Rom. 3:24, 4:16, 5:2; 1 Cor. 15:10; Gal. 1:6.
[54] von Dobschütz, *Die Thessalonicher-Briefe*, p. 303.

5. Exhortatio, 3:1-13

The intercessory prayer offered by the author on behalf of his readers is followed by a request for similar prayer on the author's behalf to be offered by his readers. Just as the description of a thanksgiving and an intercessory prayer concluded the *probatio* by pointing back to several of the points made, so this request for prayer points forward to several points to be raised in the following paraenesis. This section begins with a phrase more appropriate for a conclusion, τὸ λοιπόν. Milligan admits the term is "a colloquial expression frequently used to point forward to a coming conclusion", but continues, "in itself doing little more than mark the transition to a new subject in late Gk. where it is practically equivalent to an emphatic οὖν"[55].

The request for prayer has two petitions, the first in respect to "the word of the Lord" and the second in respect to the author's own safety. Both petitions, however, are really concerned with the author (or the author-as-Paul) as the apostle of God's word. To ask "that the word of the Lord may speed on and triumph" is to ask for the success of the apostle's mission. That the general mission of the church is not intended is demonstrated by the fact that this prayer is περὶ ἡμῶν, and that the request is that the word spread καθὼς καὶ πρὸς ὑμᾶς.

The translation of τρέχῃ καὶ δοξάζηται found in the RSV, "may speed on and triumph", points up the athletic metaphor at use here; the metaphor taken from the race track appears several times in Paul (cf. 1 Cor. 9:24-27; Gal. 2:2, 5:7; Phil. 2:16). There is also a reminiscence of 1:10, 12, where the glorification of the Lord "in" the faithful is in mind, although both the verb (ἐνδοξάζεσθαι) and the preposition (ἐν) are different. The congregation is taken as an example of the "successful" mission, this success being a prerequisite for the author's earlier prayer that the name of the Lord might be glorified "in" them (1:12).

The second petition is that the author may be delivered ἀπὸ τῶν ἀτόπων καὶ πονηρῶν ἀνθρώπων. Some commentators take the definite article as referring to a specific group of adversaries, i.e., the Jews[56]. One hesitates to draw this conclusion, although some definite group is in the author's mind; Trilling, for example, sees it as referring to the generic "adversaries" who opposed the mission of Paul the Wandering Herald and Persecuted Apostle as he was envisioned in the later church[57]. The justification for this request is "For faithfulness is not everyone's". Rigaux curiously believes that this statement has nothing to do with what has gone before, but is an interesting illustration

---

[55] Milligan, *Thessalonians*, p. 46.
[56] For example, Frame, *Thessalonians*, p. 292.
[57] Trilling, *Der zweite Brief*, p. 136.

Exhortatio, 3:1-13 51

of how Paul divided the world into two groups, believers and unbelievers[58]. However, the dichotomy Rigaux finds does not appear to be present in the author's mind. First of all, οὐ γὰρ πάντων ἡ πίστις does indeed explain the existence of "wicked and evil men", and second, the unfaithful are compared not with the faithful people, but with the faithful God, as in Romans 3:3-4: "For not all are faithful – but God is faithful." God's faithfulness is demonstrated in his anticipated action towards the congregation: he will strengthen them (as the author has requested in his own intercessory prayer of 2:16-17) and guard them ἀπὸ τοῦ πονηροῦ. Although this phrase may be either "from evil" or "from the Evil One", the ambiguity seems to be irresolvable[59]. However, it may be that the author has a specific "evil" in mind. As we noted, στηρίξει recalls 2:17, where the "strengthening" in question is "in (or by means of) every good word and every good work". There the reference is to adherence to the tradition delivered to the congregation by the author. So here, the author expresses his confidence that God will indeed "strengthen" and "guard" the congregation on the basis of the author's knowledge "in the Lord" that the congregation has done and will continue to do "the things which we command". The readers are safe from evil to the degree that they follow the instructions of the author in regard to doctrine and practice. Deviation from this tradition is the "evil" from which the author wishes God to protect his readers; their continual adherence to his commands gives him the confidence that God will do so. Trilling notes that both the apostle and the Lord stand over against the congregation and are in some way responsible for its good behavior[60]. This continues what Trilling perceives as the theme of apostolic mission and authority, but more specifically it is related to the idea of the author (or the author-as-Paul) as the representative of the congregation before the apocalyptic judge. He has handed over the tradition to his congregation, and their obedience to it will determine their standing at the judgment. The author's confidence in them is part of his testimony on their behalf (he is confident "in the Lord", πεποίθαμεν δὲ ἐν κυρίῳ ἐφ' ὑμᾶς), and another aspect of the apocalyptic function of the present letter itself.

The epistolary prayer wish of 3:5 is that the Lord "may direct your hearts", again recalling 2:17, where the wish is that God "may comfort your hearts". The desired object is τὴν ἀγάπην τοῦ θεοῦ, to be taken as an objective genitive, i.e., "God's love for us", and τὴν ὑπομονὴν τοῦ Χριστοῦ, which most commentators take as Christ's steadfastness which is somehow to be imitated by his followers[61]. God's love is thus joined with faithfulness under

---

[58] Rigaux compares Romans 1-3, *Saint Paul*, pp. 695-96.
[59] Ibid., p. 697.
[60] Trilling, *Der zweite Brief*, p. 137.
[61] Cf. the passion narratives; Rev. 1:9, 3:10; Mark 13:13 and pars.; Matt. 10:22.

duress, and faithfulness in turn has been joined with obedience to the author's commands.

Such a command follows. The emphasis on obedience to the author's instruction in the preceding section is further reinforced by the invocation of the name of the Lord Jesus Christ as the authority by which the author makes this command. Indeed, the substance of the command is concerned with the congregation's response to the author's (or the author's-as-Paul) previous commands, collectively regarded as "the tradition", ἡ παράδοσις. The readers are to keep away from any brother ἀτάκτως περιπατοῦντες, a way of life further defined as μὴ κατὰ τὴν παράδοσιν ἣν παρελάβοσαν παρ' ἡμῶν, "not according to the tradition that you received from us". Once again, obedience to the author's teaching is the point in question.

The usual translation of the phrase ἀτάκτως περιπατοῦντες is "those who live in idleness"[62], and this verse is thereby associated with 1 Thessalonians 5:14. However, Ceslaus Spicq has demonstrated that ἀτακτεῖν more properly means "to be disorderly"[63], as also taken by Milligan[64] and Rigaux[65]. The primary argument for translating this phrase "living in idleness" is the substance of 3:7-12, which deals with the refusal of the ἄτακτοι to work. However, this appears to be a deliberate attempt on the part of the author to denigrate those who do not obey the tradition. The most revealing remark about these people is μηδὲν ἐργαζόμενοι ἀλλὰ περιεργαζόμενοι (3:11b). Περιεργάζομαι, "to be a busybody", can refer specifically to those who meddle in spiritual or political matters which are none of their affair. This was the charge against Socrates, Σωκράτης ἀδικεῖ καὶ περιεργάζεται ζητῶν τά τε ὑπὸ γῆς καὶ οὐράνια (Plato, Apol., 19b). A similar charge appears to have been made in the political sphere against Demosthenes: εἰ μὲν γὰρ μὴ ἐχρῆν,... περιείργασμαι μὲν ἐγὼ περὶ τούτων εἰπών, περιείργασται δ' ἡ πόλις ἡ πεισθεῖσ' ἐμοί (Demosthenes, De Corona, 18.72). We would argue that the ἄτακτοι have not obeyed the tradition, and indeed have presented themselves as spiritual authorities. The author, after all, is attacking a real, albeit false, proclamation, and specifically chastises the ἄτακτοι for not following the tradition which is not only ethical but doctrinal as well (2:15, 3:6, 14). The instruction of 2:1-12, which is part of the "tradition" (3:14), will protect the readers from the deception of eschatological evil. Those who disregard the tradition are not only the victims of this evil (2:10-12), but also its agents (2:3a, 3:6, 14). False doctrine and "disorderly" behavior are related; the false prophets of "the Day of the Lord" are also those the author chastises

---

[62] So Frame, Thessalonians, pp. 298–99; Best, Thessalonians, p. 334.
[63] Ceslaus Spicq, "Les Thessaloniciens 'inquiets' étaient-ils des paresseux?", Studia Theologica 10 (1956): 1–13.
[64] Milligan, Thessalonians, pp. 152–54.
[65] Rigaux, Saint Paul, pp. 704–5.

for their behavior. It seems likely that these "busybodies" who claim spiritual authority have also claimed the right to be supported by the congregation. This was not uncommon (cf. 2 Cor. 12:11-18; cp. 3 Jn. 9-10), and the Didache gives instructions for examining prophets to ensure that they are genuine: "But whoever shall say in a spirit, 'Give me money, or something else', you shall not listen to him" (Did. 11. 12). Travellers likewise are not to impose on a congregation (Did. 12); the Christians were apparently well known for their generosity to those they felt possessed some special spiritual gift[66].

The author of 2 Thessalonians, then, is not simply denying a particular doctrine and correcting idleness; he is attacking a particular group of opponents on two fronts, on the basis both of their behavior and of their doctrine. Once their distinctive doctrine has been disproven and the basis of their spiritual authority thereby destroyed, the author is free to upbraid them for their behavior (3:12). They are not to claim special privileges, and the congregation is not to grant them any (3:6, 10, 14-15). Even if the ἄτακτοι were truly spiritual authorities, they should follow the example of their own spiritual leader, Paul, and work for their food (3:7-9). In reality they have no such authority, and should work in quietness (3:12)[67]. Only in this way can there be "peace" in the congregation (3:16), through obedience to the Pauline tradition (2:15, 3:6).

Of what is this "tradition" composed? The author first invokes his (or Paul's) example as somehow binding on the readers. As Trilling notes, the behavior of the apostle is here a measure of Christian self-realization by virtue of the obligation to imitate his example (δεῖ μιμεῖσθαι, cf. 1 Cor. 11:1)[68]. The substance of the example is presented first negatively (not an example of idleness, not one of eating food provided by others), then positively (working night and day in toil and labor), and its intention is made clear: not to be a burden to any one of the faithful. The reason for this behavior was ἵνα ἑαυτοὺς τύπον δῶμεν ὑμῖν εἰς τὸ μιμεῖσθαι ἡμᾶς, to provide an example for them to imitate. In other words, the behavior of the apostle was self-consciously part of the "tradition", τὴν παράδοσιν ἣν παρελάβοσαν παρ' ἡμῶν. The apostle's actions substantiate his words and are regarded by the author as binding for the congregation. His "image" serves as the *exemplum* for the faithful.

In this particular case, the example is reinforced by explicit instruction; the author refers to "when we were with you" as the time when a definite

---

[66] Lucian, *Peregrinus* 13.
[67] Hans Dieter Betz, "*De tranquilitate animi* (Moralia 464E–477F)", in *Plutarch's Ethical Writings and Early Christian Literature*, ed. idem, Studia ad Corpus Hellenisticum Novi Testamenti, vol. 4 (Leiden: E.J. Brill, 1978), pp. 206–8.
[68] Trilling, *Der zweite Brief*, pp. 145–46.

command was given. It was given in the form of a community rule: εἴ τις οὐ θέλει ἐργάζεσθαι μηδὲ ἐσθιέτω[69]. Therefore, in the case of the obligation to work, the "tradition" took the form both of the deeds of the apostle, which were intended to serve as an example for believers, and of an explicit command in the form of a community rule.

The author has in 3:4 expressed confidence in God's protection of the community because of their obedience to the author's commands, which form the tradition. In spite of this, the author has had to give a further command to the congregation, i.e., to keep away from those who have disobeyed the tradition and are "disorderly". It is worth noting the contrast between the way the author seeks to correct the doctrinal error and the way he corrects a moral error. In the former case, he offers the elaborate scenario of 2:3-12; here he depends on the authority of the apostle and of Jesus Christ (3:6, 12). He directly addresses the erring brothers and invokes the Lord Jesus Christ: παραγγέλλομεν καὶ παρακαλοῦμεν ἐν κυρίῳ Ἰησοῦ Χριστῷ (3:12). The author makes no attempt to base his command on the well-being of the community; it needs no justification other than the image of Paul which is part of the tradition. The argument consists of a process of command and reiteration of the command. The unity of the process is emphasized by the chiasmus formed by verses 3:6-12; the phrases and ideas of verses 3:6-8a recur in reverse order in 3:8b-12[70]. This having been said, the author turns back to the congregation at large (ὑμεῖς δέ, ἀδελφοί) and exhorts them to continue their own good behavior, expressed in good deeds: μὴ ἐγκακήσητε καλοποιοῦντες (cf. Gal. 6:9-10). The stress is not merely upon "work" but on the proper work of the believer: "doing good."

6. Peroratio, 3:14-16

The *peroratio* or *conclusio* summarizes the argument of the letter and attempts to persuade the readers to follow the course of action prescribed by the author. The *peroratio* is usually a reliable guide to the major concerns of the

---

[69] This rule has a long history, reflecting attitudes towards work in Judaism and the Hellenistic world; F. Hauck, *Die Stellung des Urchristentums zu Arbeit und Geld* (Gütersloh: C. Bertelsmann, 1921), pp. 38–62; idem, "Arbeit", in *Reallexikon für Antike und Christentum*, ed. T. Klauser, 11 vols. (Stuttgart: Hiersemann Verlag, 1950), 1:585–90; H.L. Strack and P. Billerbeck, *Kommentar zum Neuen Testament aus Talmud und Midrash*, 4 vols. (Munich: C.H. Beck, 1924), 2:745–47; 3:338, 604, 641–42.

[70] John C. Hurd, "Concerning the Authenticity of 2 Thessalonians", paper delivered to the Seminar on the Thessalonian Correspondence, annual meeting of the Society for Biblical Literature, Dallas, Texas, 19–22 December 1983, p. 16.

author, and presents the major points he wishes his readers to remember[71]. In 2 Thessalonians, the emphasis is once again on obedience to the tradition, i.e., "what we say in this letter" (3:14). The other major theme is "peace", which will be assured by such obedience (3:16).

The author has previously instructed his readers to keep away from those who do not live "according to the tradition that you received from us" (3:6b). That command is now reiterated (3:14): εἰ δέ τις οὐχ ὑπακούει τῷ λόγῳ ἡμῶν διὰ τῆς ἐπιστολῆς.... Τῷ λόγῳ ἡμῶν διὰ τῆς ἐπιστολῆς recalls both the possible source of the erroneous doctrine in 2:2 and the means by which the tradition had been taught to the congregation in 2:15. In the author's view it is possible to receive a tradition by word (that is, a definitive pronouncement on a given subject) or by letter (presumably containing a number of such pronouncements); again, "by spirit" is mentioned only in connection with the erroneous belief (2:2). The author appears to deny any validity to charismatic inspiration. The present case involves the definitive pronouncement (τῷ λόγῳ ἡμῶν) transmitted through a letter (διὰ τῆς ἐπιστολῆς), indeed, the letter at hand. Once again the author makes clear the authoritative and binding nature of the present letter itself as a part of the tradition he transmits to his readers. The hypothetical case εἰ δέ τις οὐχ ὑπακούει refers to the direct command to the ἄτακτοι to work quietly and eat their own food (3:11-12; cf. 3:6). If this corrective measure fails, if this definitive pronouncement which forms part of the inherited tradition is not heeded, the congregation is to take the action first mentioned in 3:6b. The readers are to regard the disobedient person as a portent and have nothing to do with him, with the intention that he may be ashamed of himself (3:15). This sense of σημειόομαι refers to regarding someone or something as a portent of greater meaning; in this case, the disobedience would presumably be an indication that the apocalyptic evil, ἡ ἀποστασία, was present in the congregation.

A limitation is placed on this exclusion, however; the man is not to be treated as an enemy, but warned (νουθετεῖτε) as a brother. This would appear to indicate that the ἄτακτοι are still to be regarded as members of the congregation, despite their false proclamation (2:2c) and their disobedience to the tradition (3:6-12). The direct command to the ἄτακτοι in 3:12 makes sense within this context, since presumably only those who recognized the author's authority (or the authority of Paul, whose persona the author adopts) would be likely to obey the command; this may explain why the command is given ἐν κυρίῳ Ἰησοῦ Χριστοῦ. However, in view of the severe attitude the author displays towards the ἄτακτοι elsewhere in the letter, we may properly ask whether the "limitation" on exclusion in 3:15 is sincerely meant. Trilling

---

[71] Aristotle, *Ars rhetorica* 3. 1419b–1420a; Quintillian, *Institutio oratoria* 6. 1. 1–2.

quite rightly has questioned the feasibility of such a mode of discipline[72]. The author has told his readers to keep away from (στέλλεσθαι) the "disorderly" (3:6) and not to associate with them (μὴ συναναμίγνυσθαι; 3:14b). He has labelled them as propagators of deception (2:3), themselves liable to deception (2:9-12) and God's judgment (2:12). The inclusion of 3:15 may well have been a conscious attempt to conform the instruction of 3:14-15 to that of 1 Thessalonians 5:14a. At best, the injunction of 2 Thessalonians 3:14-15 can refer only to those among the ἄτακτοι who are brought to repentance by the letter; the faithful are to correct such a penitent as a brother and to help him to reenter the community. However, since the ἄτακτοι presumably were as convinced of the validity of their understanding of the Pauline tradition as our author was of his, it seems unlikely that they would accept his interpretation of Paul or his commands in the persona of the apostle[73]. The lines of division have already been drawn.

This letter deals with two sorts of "error" that the author wishes to eliminate: doctrinal error and ethical error. The first error is dealt with in 2:1-12, and the "opposition" the author faces are those who spread the false belief that "the Day of the Lord is here". Such persons are "apostate", i.e., in rebellion against the authority of the tradition and the apostle. The author refutes the error by elaborating the apocalyptic scenario for the benefit of those who might otherwise become upset or shaken (2:2). We know of no other apocalyptic tradition quite like that of 2:1-12, and it may be presumed to be a synthesis of the author's own creation, although it is presented as Paul's. The second, ethical error is the subject of 3:6-15. The error of "disorderliness" stems from the same serious error of not "living according to the tradition that you received from us" (3:6b). Since the tradition is composed of the words and letters of the author (or the author-as-Paul), such disregard of the tradition is a refutation of the author's understanding of Paul. The author twice invokes Jesus Christ as he commands the congregation and then the disorderly to enforce obedience to the tradition. So there is opposition to what the author considers to be the right understanding of the tradition; it is a case of willful opposition to the tradition and the author as its guarantor, and the guilty parties are to be ostracized for the sake of their correction.

Once again we see how the author stands over against the congregation as

---

[72] Trilling, *Der zweite Brief*, p. 156. Trilling also notes that the context of the instruction gives the impression that the present letter will be ignored by the disorderly, and that the idea of correcting the one in the wrong as a brother and not an enemy is almost without parallel in the ancient church, ibid., pp. 153–54.

[73] Pseudepigrapha were rejected by a given group in Christian history almost exclusively on the basis of "unorthodoxy" as understood by that group; Lewis R. Donelson, *Pseudepigraphy and Ethical Argument in the Pastoral Epistles,* Hermeneutische Untersuchungen zur Theologie 22, Tübingen: J.C.B. Mohr, (Paul Siebeck), 1986, pp. 15–23 and notes.

its intermediary before God. He is the guarantor of the tradition which the congregation has received, and it is the observance of this tradition which guarantees the congregation's salvation on the day of judgment, a salvation which results from the author's advocacy on their behalf before the apocalyptic judge (1:7b, 10).

The *peroratio* ends with an intercessory prayer of the author on behalf of the congregation. The emphasis is on peace (αὐτὸς δὲ ὁ κύριος τῆς εἰρήνης δῴη ὑμῖν τὴν εἰρήνην), that is, the peace that will result from the "quiet work" of the idle and the elimination of the doctrinal error which has upset and "shaken" the readers. The proper appreciation of the author's (or the author's-as-Paul) rôle and of the tradition he imparts brings the peace of concord to the community. The intercession concludes with the liturgical prayer wish, ὁ κύριος μετὰ πάντων ὑμῶν: "The Lord be with all of you."

7. *Epistolary Postscript, 3:17-18*

A proper discussion of the epistolary postscript must entail the problems involved in the question of authenticity, and so will be dealt with at a later time. For the present, we may note that there is no greeting per se; the greeting consists of the mere mention of the idea of greeting (ὁ ἀσπασμός), that is, the language is descriptive rather than performative. The emphasis is not upon the act of greeting or the greetings conveyed, but rather upon the greeting as an authenticating mark within the epistle. In 1 Corinthians 16:21, the hand-written greeting follows a series of greetings and precedes a serious order of anathema. In Galatians 6:11, the hand-written greeting introduces the *recapitulatio* which restates the main points of the letter[74]. In Philemon 19, the greeting is part of a solemn promise of repayment. Therefore, the inclusion of a hand-written greeting in Paul (or at least such a greeting that calls attention to itself) is intended as some sort of authentication of what follows; it emphasizes that what follows comes from Paul himself. In 2 Thessalonians, on the other hand, the authentication serves as the entire greeting (as compared with the place of a similar phrase in 1 Corinthians 16:21 at the end of a series of greetings), and serves to authenticate not only what immediately follows, but the whole substance of the letter. This authenticating function is also made explicit: ὅ ἐστιν σημεῖον ἐν πάσῃ ἐπιστολῇ· οὕτως γράφω. Whatever we may say of Pauline practice, whether or not he always included a personally written note in his epistles, in the present instance the author has found it necessary to include not only a note, but an explanation as well. Such a

---

[74] Aristotle, *Ars rhetorica* 3. 1419b–1420a; Quintillian, *Institutio oratoria* 6. 1. 1–2; Betz, *Galatians*, p. 313.

signature should not be regarded as a guarantee against a pseudonymous author (cf. Col. 4:18); such "personal touches" were a common motif in Hellenistic pseudepigrapha[75].

The final benediction comes in 3:18, in what appears to be an expansion of the intercessory petition of 3:16b; in this case it is "the grace of the Lord Jesus Christ" rather than simply "the Lord", that is to be μετὰ πάντων ὑμῶν.

As we stated at the outset, the intention of this exegetical survey has been to explicate the argument and doctrinal content of the letter as revealed through the rhetorical analysis. The reader may feel that some points have been dealt with in too cursory a manner, but the limits of space and the avowed intention of this investigation have dictated that this survey be brief. Such points as are pertinent to other parts of our study will be dealt with at greater length in the proper place.

---

[75] This point is demonstrated by the illuminating survey by Donelson, *Pseudepigraphy*, pp. 7–66.

Chapter II

A Comparison of Material in 1 and 2 Thessalonians

Now that the preliminary work of analysis and exegesis has been done, we may investigate the relationship of 2 Thessalonians to 1 Thessalonians. As we said at the beginning of the first chapter, this question of relationship is secondary to the understanding of 2 Thessalonians as an independent letter, and should not influence the exegetical decisions made about the content of the letter. But once a preliminary exegesis has been completed, we may explore the relationship between 1 and 2 Thessalonians in two ways: first, in terms of the apparent appropriation of terminology and language from 1 Thessalonians in 2 Thessalonians, which necessarily involves a verse-by-verse comparison; and second, in terms of the major thematic content, properly understood, of the two letters.

There are several methods that have been employed to investigate the relationship between 1 and 2 Thessalonians, usually with the intention of settling the question of authorship. The method most commonly used by the commentators is what we may call parallel exegesis. That is, the text of 2 Thessalonians is interpreted in the light of 1 Thessalonians, with points of apparent agreement or disagreement noted by the commentator to produce a "weight of evidence" for one theory of authorship or another. Another method is less systematic and more likely to appear in articles or introductory texts. This concentrates on the vocabulary of the two letters and tends to invest evidence of varying applicability with equal value to support a particular theory. The various kinds of "evidence" from vocabulary are: (1) consistency or inconsistency of the vocabulary of 2 Thessalonians either with 1 Thessalonians or with the Pauline corpus as a whole; (2) apparent duplication of phrases from 1 Thessalonians in 2 Thessalonians; (3) the absence of "characteristic" Pauline vocabulary in 2 Thessalonians. A third argument often employed concentrates on the doctrinal content of the letters, especially the eschatological content of 2 Thessalonians 2, and finds the content of 2 Thessalonians either "Pauline" or "deutero-Pauline". These three major methods of comparison have been employed by scholars on both sides of the question of authorship, and the positions on both sides have become to a large extent "classic".

We do not intend to disavow these "classic" arguments altogether, since apart from exegesis, vocabulary, and doctrinal content we should have very little with which to make any sort of judgment about either of the letters. But our intention is rather to provide a sounder methodological foundation for the assessment of the relative value of the various sorts of "evidence" the letters offer. Part of this foundation is an independent analysis and exegesis of 2 Thessalonians. Another part is the attempt to discover how the author of 2 Thessalonians made use of 1 Thessalonians in the composition and argument of his own letter. The way 1 Thessalonians is utilized by the author of 2 Thessalonians should reveal his own understanding of the earlier letter.

We may easily see how this is the case. If the author of 2 Thessalonians was Paul, his conscious or unconscious references to the vocabulary and format of 1 Thessalonians should demonstrate how he attempted to reformulate the argument of the letter to respond to the new situation addressed in 2 Thessalonians. In other words, 2 Thessalonians would then be Paul's "re-thinking" of the pertinent sections of 1 Thessalonians and their re-statement to eliminate the problems the earlier letter had left unsolved. On the other hand, if the author of 2 Thessalonians was someone other than Paul, his conscious use of 1 Thessalonians shows that he felt the doctrinal material in that letter, properly understood and presented, was adequate to meet the situation he wished to address. In either case, as we have said, 2 Thessalonians reflects a particular understanding of 1 Thessalonians, and that understanding will be revealed only within the context of the later letter.

For this reason, we shall consider the use of 1 Thessalonians in each section of 2 Thessalonians as determined by our analysis. Our attention at this time will be given to wording and phrases in 2 Thessalonians that recall similar phrases in 1 Thessalonians, and to material in 1 and 2 Thessalonians that appears to allude to the thematic content of 1 Thessalonians. At the same time, we will point out any differences in the meaning of similar phrases or different emphases in similar content.

1. *Epistolary Prescript, 1:1-2*

This is the closest parallel between 1 and 2 Thessalonians. As we suggested in the first chapter, the exactness of the parallel strongly suggests a literary dependence. Wolfgang Trilling noted the peculiarities which set these two prescripts apart from those of the other letters in the Pauline corpus[1]: (1) the

---

[1] Trilling, *Der zweite Brief*, p. 35.

three named senders, Paul, Silvanus, and Timothy; (2) their designation of the congregation as "the church of the Thessalonians" (τῇ ἐκκλησίᾳ Θεσσαλονικέων); (3) the association of the recipients with God and Christ (ἐν θεῷ πατρὶ ἡμῶν καὶ κυρίῳ Ἰησοῦ Χριστῷ); (4) the omission of Paul's usual title of "apostle". The only differences between the two prescripts appear in well-attested variants: (1) ἐν θεῷ πατρὶ [ἡμῶν] (1 Thess. 1:1)/ ἡμῶν (2 Thess. 1:2); (2) [ἀπὸ θεοῦ πατρὸς κτλ.] (1 Thess. 1:1)/ ἀπὸ θεοῦ πατρὸς κτλ. (2 Thess. 1:2); (3) [... ἀπὸ θεοῦ πατρὸς ἡμῶν...] (1 Thess. 1:1)/ ἀπὸ θεοῦ πατρὸς [ἡμῶν] (2 Thess. 1:2). The presence of such variants, of course, indicates that a number of reliable witnesses include these readings, and it is commonly suggested that they were added by copyists who wished to bring the prescript of 1 Thessalonians into line with 2 Thessalonians and the majority of the Pauline letters (although this does not explain variant (3) above). But if 2 Thessalonians is not Pauline, as we said earlier, then the text of 2 Thessalonians in this close parallel is the earliest witness for the longer form of the prescript of 1 Thessalonians.

Of course, this parallel appears in a highly formulaic portion of the letters. It is a formula of salutation and serves exactly the same function in both letters. However, there is a similar situation behind the salutations of the letter of Paul to Corinth, and yet there are significant variations between them (1 Cor. 1:1-3, 2 Cor. 1:1-2). At the very least, we must acknowledge that the congruence of the two salutations in the Thessalonian letters is remarkable.

2. *Exordium, 1:3-4*

We also find a formulaic parallel between 1 Thessalonians 1:2a and 2 Thessalonians 1:3a, since both introduce the thanksgiving common to Hellenistic epistolography in general and to Paul's letters in particular. In this case, however, there is a significant difference; the formula in 2 Thessalonians includes the word ὀφείλομεν, which we have earlier identified as carrying liturgical overtones. This variation from the Pauline formula is important, for it indicates a change in the author's perspective from performative to descriptive language (see below).

The thanksgiving in 1 Thessalonians 1:3a is heavily overloaded, joining a particularly "practical" virtue (work, labor, steadfastness) to each of the "theological" virtues familiar to us from 1 Corinthians 13 (faith, hope, love). The overloaded phrase is "unloaded" in the parallel material of 2 Thessalonians 1:3-4. In those verses, the "practical" virtues are absent, leaving the "theological" virtues, with the exception that "steadfastness" replaces "hope": ὑμῶν τοῦ ἔργου τῆς πίστεως / ἡ πίστις ὑμῶν, καὶ πίστεως· καὶ τοῦ κόπου τῆς ἀγάπης / ἡ ἀγάπη· καὶ τῆς ὑπομονῆς τῆς ἐλπίδος / τῆς ὑπομονῆς ὑμῶν

(1 Thess. 1:3a, 2 Thess. 1:3-4). The general "practical" results of the theological virtues of 1 Thessalonians 1:3a are given a specific context in 2 Thessalonians 1:4. There "steadfastness" and "faithfulness" are specifically the virtues that are displayed in persecution (cf. 1 Thess. 2:14). This, of course, indicates that πίστις is no longer a "theological" but a "practical" virtue, a basic shift in the meaning of the word which will be examined at greater length below.

The cause for the obligation to give thanks in 2 Thessalonians 1:3b is in part ὅτι...πλεονάζει ἡ ἀγάπη ἑνὸς ἑκάστου πάντων ὑμῶν εἰς ἀλλήλους, recalling quite specifically the intercessory wish of 1 Thessalonians 3:12a, ὑμᾶς δὲ ὁ κύριος πλεονάσαι καὶ περισσεύσαι τῇ ἀγάπῃ εἰς ἀλλήλους καὶ εἰς πάντας.... The act of thanksgiving refers to the apparent fulfillment of the earlier intercessory wish for brotherly love. Does this indicate a passage of time, an acknowledgement of the efficacy of the earlier prayer, or does the author only wish to give that impression? There appears to be some significance in this thanksgiving for the fulfillment of the earlier prayer. Trilling notes that, although the love requested in 1 Thessalonians 3:12a is to abound "to one another and to all" (εἰς ἀλλήλους καὶ εἰς πάντας), the parallel in 2 Thessalonians 1:3b restricts that love to the members of the congregation (ἡ ἀγάπη ἑνὸς ἑκάστου πάντων ὑμῶν εἰς ἀλλήλους). This love is "brotherly" love only, without regard to those outside[2]. Von Dobschütz finds parallels to 2 Thessalonians 1:3b in 1 Thessalonians 2:11 (ἑνὸς ἑκάστου), 1 Thessalonians 1:2 (πάντων ὑμῶν), and 1 Thessalonians 3:12 (εἰς ἀλλήλους)[3]. The idea of such an amalgamation promotes the caricature of the "mechanical forgery", which denies any creativity to the pseudepigrapher. The formulation in 2 Thessalonians is in reality variation within a standard form, but what is significant is that this particular variation recalls 1 Thessalonians 3:12a so clearly.

The next verse, 2 Thessalonians 1:4, introduces the idea of the author "boasting" about the congregation "in the churches of God". Von Dobschütz admits that this appears to be a reversal of what Paul writes in 1 Thessalonians 1:7-9, that is, that others report to him the events surrounding the conversion of the Thessalonians. Von Dobschütz attempts to discount this discrepancy of boasting in 1 Thessalonians: the ones who boast about the Thessalonians to Paul are "those who believe in Macedonia and Achaia" and "everywhere" (1 Thess. 1:7); in 2 Thessalonians the author boasts "in the churches of God" (2 Thess. 1:4)[4]. This is of course a specious distinction; the two references are to the same group, that is, all believers gathered in the various churches of God throughout the field of mission. What is important here is the parallel idea of

---

[2] Ibid., p. 45.
[3] von Dobschütz, *Die Thessalonicher-Briefe*, p. 237.
[4] Ibid., p. 238.

the fame of the congregation. In 1 Thessalonians this fame is the result of its exemplary conversion, and in 2 Thessalonians the result of its virtue in persecution. In both cases the congregation is a source of "glory" (καύχησις) for the author (or the author-as-Paul), in 1 Thessalonians before the Lord Jesus at his parousia, and in 2 Thessalonians before "the churches of God".

3. Narratio, 1:5-12

The parallels to 1 Thessalonians in the ἔνδειγμα of 2 Thessalonians 1:5-10 are thematic. They draw upon the various references to the apocalyptic end in 1 Thessalonians, but also allude to the "beginning" of the Thessalonian congregation as described in 1 Thessalonians 1:4-10. This is because the two themes, that of beginning and of end, are connected. When one is "called", he or she is called to suffering (cf. 1 Thess. 1:5-6, 2 Thess. 1:5), to "worthiness" of the kingdom of God (1 Thess. 2:12b, 2 Thess. 1:5), and to steadfastness and hope in anticipation of the parousia of the Lord and subsequent vindication at judgment (1 Thess. 1:3b, 1:10; 2 Thess. 1:6-7a). The connection between the "call" (κλῆσις) and the judgment is made explicit in 2 Thessalonians, because for its author the κλῆσις retains its connotation of a legal summons into court, in this case the court of the eschatological judgment (2 Thess. 1:5-10, 11-12).

This means that the thematic parallels in 2 Thessalonians to the material in 1 Thessalonians that are related to the parousia and the beginnings of the congregation emphasize the eschatological orientation of the author of the later letter. The repeated reference by allusion to a relatively few verses of 1 Thessalonians that deal with the return of the Lord show how this idea has gained far greater importance in 2 Thessalonians. Indeed, as we have seen, the whole orientation of the letter is eschatological: it refers explicitly to the events of the parousia and the judgment in two of its major sections (2 Thess. 1:5-10, 2:2-12), it combats symptoms of the apocalyptic apostasy (2 Thess. 3:6-12), and itself serves an apocalyptic function[5].

This orientation towards the eschatological future stands in contrast to the orientation of 1 Thessalonians. In the first letter, Paul offers consolation to the congregation by looking back to the circumstances surrounding his mission to the Thessalonians and their response to it (1 Thess. 1:5-2:16). That the events of the "beginning" of the congregation are familiar to them is clear from the continual reference to their own knowledge of the events (cf. 1 Thess. 1:5b; 2:1, 2, 5, 9, 10, 11). Paul evokes three particular facts about his mission: (1) the Thessalonians received the true gospel from a true apostle,

---

[5] See the exegesis of 1:10, 2:6 in chap. 1.

that is, Paul himself (1 Thess. 1:5b, 2:1-12); (2) they then became imitators of Paul and of the Lord, thus becoming an example to others (1:6-7; 2:13-16); and (3) they have manifested particularly Christian virtues (1:3, 9-10; 3:6-8). These facts form a guarantee of salvation for the Thessalonians, despite their fears that the parousia will not include some of their number (4:13-18), or that they might not endure "the Day of the Lord" (5:1-11). It is these facts that allow the apostle to write εὐχαριστοῦμεν... εἰδότες, ἀδελφοί ἠγαπημένοι ὑπὸ [τοῦ] θεοῦ, τὴν ἐκλογὴν ὑμῶν (1 Thess. 1:4). He is sure of their election because they received the correct gospel from the correct person in the correct way, and have shown the correct behavior ever since.

The situation is quite different in 2 Thessalonians. In that letter, whatever consolation the author has to offer is based on a vision of the apocalyptic future, in which the readers will be rewarded in the presence of the Lord and their persecutors will be outcast forever. The author assumes the readers have no doubt about their own salvation, since he uses the fact of their future salvation as his proof of "God's righteous judgment" (2 Thess. 1:5-10). The longest section of his letter deals with a detailed scenario of the events which must precede the parousia, and the disciplinary problem with which he deals arises at least in part from an incorrect eschatological understanding. This difference in the orientation of the two letters will become clearer as we proceed with our analysis.

There is a parallel to 1 Thessalonians 4:5 in 2 Thessalonians 1:8a, a part of the description of the parousia of the Lord, 2 Thessalonians 1:7b-10. Both verses refer to "those who do not know God", with the reference in 1 Thessalonians being specifically to the Gentiles, τὰ ἔθνη. In 1 Thessalonians this group serves as a counter-example in an exhortation to observe that behavior which promotes "the will of God, your sanctification" (1 Thess. 4:3a). Obviously "those who do not know God" are unable to follow his will or to be sanctified. In 2 Thessalonians the shift is to an eschatological point of view, and "those who do not know God" are those who are subjected to the vengeance of the Lord at his coming. These people are by implication identified with those who afflict the faithful (2 Thess. 1:6) and those who are to be eternally rejected from the Lord's presence (2 Thess. 1:9). They serve not as a counter-example, but as a contrast to "his holy ones" (τοῖς ἁγίοις αὐτοῦ) and "those who have believed" (πᾶσιν τοῖς πιστεύσασιν), who will be eternally in the Lord's presence (2 Thess. 1:10). In other words, what was a religious and moral distinction between believers who suffer and unbelievers who persecute in 1 Thessalonians has become in 2 Thessalonians an example of eschatological dualism between the saved and the eternally lost.

One would expect as a result of the apocalyptic orientation of 2 Thessalonians that the similar material in 1 Thessalonians would be alluded to repeatedly. This is the case in the concluding eschatological formulae of 1 Thessalonians 1:10, 2:19, and 3:13. But surprisingly enough, the overtly apocalyptic material of 1 Thessalonians 4:13-18 is paralleled in 2 Thessalonians only in terms of its general subject matter in 2 Thessalonians 2:1, and in terms of its content in regard to the manner of the Lord's appearance at the parousia in 2 Thessalonians 1:7b-8a. This is because the point of interest in 2 Thessalonians is not the event of the parousia itself (in strict terms of the manner of the Lord's return), but rather its consequences: judgment (1:8b-10), and the destruction of the forces of evil (2:8b).

The idea that persists from 1 Thessalonians is that of the place of the faithful with the Lord at his coming. This is of course the subject of 1 Thess. 4:13-18, and it is apparent also in 1 Thessalonians 3:13. The same idea reappears in 2 Thessalonians 1:7b, 10, where we also see the faithful accompanying the Lord. We have said earlier that the emphasis in the ἔνδειγμα is upon the fate of the wicked; it is they who experience the judgment, and it is to them that the Lord will mete out vengeance and punishment (2 Thess. 1:8-9). The fate of the good stands out in muted contrast. In 1 Thessalonians, however, the whole concern is whether all the faithful, or only those living at the time of the parousia, will be united with the Lord at his coming (1 Thess. 4:15-17). Both of these themes are apocalyptic in nature, of course, since they deal with the supernatural events of the end. The important distinction, however, is the emphasis in 2 Thessalonians on judgment and the various supernatural phenomena which will accompany or precede it.

We return to a formulaic parallel in 2 Thessalonians 1:11-12. This is a standard feature of the contemporary epistolary style and of Paul's style in particular, a report of a prayer made by the author on behalf of the readers. As a result, we find close parallels to material in 1 Thessalonians. There is, for example, the formula of a prayer report in 1 Thessalonians 1:2, where it has its more usual place immediately following the expression of thanksgiving. The content of the prayer reported in 2 Thessalonians 1:11 is parallel to the content of an exhortation in 1 Thessalonians 2:11b-12, since both concern "becoming worthy" and God's act of "calling" the Thessalonians. This act of "calling" in both cases has an eschatological reference, but the perspective of the act of "becoming worthy" is different in the two letters. In 1 Thessalonians 2:11b-12, Paul recalls his behavior among the Thessalonians, how he exhorted them as a father does his children. The content of the exhortation is recalled as well, since it continues to be important instruction for the congregation. But whether in its original context at the foundation of the congregation or its context within the letter, this exhortation is concerned with the behavior of the congregation specifically in the present. The proper behavior is a means of "becoming worthy" now of the call, which is specifically a call "into his kingdom and glory" (1 Thess. 2:12). What the Thessalonians do in the present will make them worthy of their future entrance into the kingdom.

In 2 Thessalonians we have a "perpetual prayer" offered by the author on behalf of the congregation. This prayer is concerned with God's future action of "making worthy" those whom he calls. We have already determined that this call (κλῆσις) is in 2 Thessalonians a future (i.e., eschatological) event[6]. The author therefore prays that the readers may be enabled by God to gain acceptance at the judgment on the basis of the author's testimony. In other words, the exhortation for the present behavior of the congregation in 1 Thessalonians 2:11b-12 has become in 2 Thessalonians 1:11 a prayer for the (eschatological) action of God on behalf of the congregation. Both the author's testimony and the congregation's acceptance is based to some extent on the behavior of the congregation, but even this present behavior is the result of God's work among the faithful (2 Thess. 1:11). The attention in 2 Thessalonians has shifted from the action of the believers to the grace-filled action of God.

We may see this same phenomenon at work in relation to the ἔργον πίστεως (2 Thess. 1:11) and τοῦ ἔργου τῆς πίστεως (1 Thess. 1:3a), that is, we may again see this shift from a past to a future perspective. In 1 Thessalonians 1:3a, Paul recalls a specific past action of the Thessalonians, the work which is the practical result of the "theological" virtue of faith. We may call faith here a "theological" virtue because of its appearance in 1 Thessalonians 1:3 with love and hope, both with accompanying practical results. In 2 Thessalonians 1:11, the author also recalls a past action, but his desire is that God might "fulfill" a work of faithfulness, that is, bring it to its proper conclusion, eschatological salvation[7]. This work of faithfulness we have seen to be in part steadfastness in persecution, which the author wishes God to extend until the parousia.

It has become apparent, then, that in this prayer report some of the concerns expressed in 1 Thessalonians are picked up and given a specifically eschatological orientation in 2 Thessalonians. The attention of the author of the later letter is directed almost exclusively towards eschatological salvation at the judgment, which will be the result of the correct decision made in the present. The readers must conform to the "tradition" to gain salvation (2 Thess. 2:15), to "become worthy" of God's eschatological call.

As indicated in the analysis and exegesis in the first chapter, the secondary intention of the prayer reported in 2 Thessalonians 1:11-12 is the eschatological glorification of the Lord Jesus Christ (or of his "name"), a glorification previously referred to in 2 Thessalonians 1:10a. This idea of glorification confirms the eschatological perspective of 1 Thessalonians 1:11-12 and so also the "re-direction" of the material which has parallels in 1 Thessalonians.

---

[6] See the exegesis of 1:11-12 in chap. 1.
[7] Ibid.

There is in this "re-direction" an emphasis upon God's controlling part in bringing his chosen ones to salvation. However, the question of just who this God is remains ambivalent. The prayer of 2 Thessalonians 1:11 asks "that our God may make you worthy of his call", but the mutual glorification of the Lord Jesus Christ and the faithful is to be κατὰ τὴν χάριν τοῦ θεοῦ ἡμῶν καὶ κυρίου Ἰησοῦ Χριστοῦ. The source of grace is either both God and the Lord Jesus Christ, or, as we have argued above, the Lord Jesus Christ identified as "our God". In either event, the action desired by the prayer is controlled by God. This operation of grace recalls the variant addition to 1 Thessalonians 1:1b and the wishes for grace in other Pauline salutations (cf. Rom. 1:7b, 1 Cor. 1:3, 2 Cor. 1:2, Gal. 1:3).

4. Probatio, 2:1-17

In the previous chapter we found that the topic of the *probatio*, the proposition that "the Day of the Lord is present" (2:2), was presented in the form of a doctrinal exhortation[8]. The readers were warned to refrain from feelings of distress caused by an erroneous proclamation. We styled this a "doctrinal exhortation" because what was exhorted was not a behavior or even a moral attitude but a state of mind which could result only from a proper doctrinal understanding. That is, the author warns his readers not to be upset as a result of the erroneous proclamation (2:2) nor to allow anyone to deceive them (2:3a), that is, to compel them to believe what is false. He then combats the erroneous proclamation with new information about the apocalyptic scenario. Thus he combats a false doctrine ("the Day of the Lord is present") with a true doctrine ("that day will not come unless..."). The exhortatory nature of this presentation of the topic is signalled by the use of the technical term ἐρωτῶμεν in combination with the direct address ἀδελφοί. We may find a parallel in 1 Thessalonians at the beginning of the exhortatory section, 1 Thessalonians 5:12-22, ἐρωτῶμεν δὲ ὑμᾶς, ἀδελφοί (1 Thess. 5:12a). An amplified exhortatory phrase is found in 1 Thessalonians 4:1. There the exhortatory intention is made plain by the addition of παρακαλοῦμεν and the invocation of the Lord Jesus: ἀδελφοί, ἐρωτῶμεν ὑμᾶς καὶ παρακαλοῦμεν ἐν κυρίῳ Ἰησοῦ. As in these two cases, the author of 2 Thessalonians is trying in 2 Thessalonians 2:2 to promote a specific behavior, but as we have said, this behavior is now dependent upon a doctrinal understanding rather than virtue. He is trying to promote faithfulness to a doctrine instead of a specific exterior action. The parallels between 2 Thessa-

---

[8] See the relevant exegesis in chap. 1.

lonians 2:1 and 1 Thessalonians 4:1, 5:12 are thus formulaic rather than thematic; the exhortatory formula is retained, but its purpose is very different.

A very close thematic parallel follows as the author of 2 Thessalonians announces the point of doctrine which is the topic of the exhortation, τῆς παρουσίας τοῦ κυρίου ἡμῶν Ἰησοῦ Χριστοῦ καὶ ἡμῶν ἐπισυναγωγῆς ἐπ' αὐτόν. This is a clear reference to the events of the parousia as outlined in 1 Thessalonians 4:13-18, the main point of which was the gathering of believers, both living and dead, with the Lord at his coming. That it is specifically this idea as explained in 1 Thessalonians that is in the author's mind is shown by the fact that this "gathering together" is neither promoted nor challenged in the following exposition. The point at issue is whether or not "the Day of the Lord is present". We shall examine at length later the relationship between "the Day of the Lord" and the parousia as the author understood it, but we may say now that the parousia as a general topic included the event known as "the Day of the Lord", i.e., the latter was a part of the eschatological process. The author's addition of the idea of the "gathering together" in 2 Thessalonians 2:1b is the result of his acceptance of the idea promoted in 1 Thessalonians 4:13-18. He believed the "gathering together" to be an event not necessarily simultaneous with the parousia, as Paul would have it, but complementary to the parousia as a result of the judgment (cf. 2 Thess. 1:6-10). It is only after the punishment of the wicked that the Lord will be "glorified in his holy ones" and "marvelled at in all those who believe" (2 Thess. 1:10).

The author's concern is that his readers may not be "quickly shaken in conviction or upset" (2 Thess. 2:2a). That they be steady and obedient to the tradition (cf. 2 Thess. 2:15) is especially important in the face of persecution (2 Thess. 1:4) and of the religious rebellion (ἀποστασία). This concern recalls Paul's reasons for sending Timothy to the Thessalonians "to establish you in your faith and to exhort you", τὸ μηδένα σαίνεσθαι ἐν ταῖς θλίψεσιν ταύταις (1 Thess. 3:3). In both cases, the cause of the unrest the authors fear is some sort of affliction, in 1 Thessalonians the persecution which is the lot of the Christian, in 2 Thessalonians the false doctrine which is a symptom of the religious rebellion. It is the job of the figure of authority, whether Paul, Timothy as his representative, or the author of 2 Thessalonians, to do the work of exhortation as a means of "steadying" the congregation: εἰς τὸ στηρίξαι ὑμᾶς καὶ παρακαλέσαι ὑπὲρ τῆς πίστεως ὑμῶν (1 Thess. 3:2b). In both exhortations, there is a link to information that has been (at least so it is claimed) previously conveyed to the congregation. In 1 Thessalonians, the exhortation to steady the faithful in the face of persecution includes the reminder that they have been told of the inevitability of persecution (1 Thess. 3:3b-4). In 2 Thessalonians, the author poses a rhetorical question: οὐ μνημονεύετε ὅτι ἔτι ὢν πρὸς ὑμᾶς ταῦτα ἔλεγον ὑμῖν; (2 Thess.

2:5). Whether the congregation was indeed familiar with the scenario is another question. The primary difference between these two exhortations, however, is that 1 Thessalonians 3:1-5 refers to a past event whose successful result is a source of comfort to the apostle in his own afflictions; 2 Thessalonians 2:5 addresses a situation in the present whose outcome is very much in doubt.

The content of the disruptive proclamation, that "the Day of the Lord is present", and the warning against deception (2 Thess. 2:2b-3) stand in apparent contrast to 1 Thessalonians 5:1-2, where Paul expresses his assurance that the Thessalonians need no instruction about the "times and seasons" of the Day of the Lord. There is not necessarily a contradiction between the two letters on this point, however. The upshot of what the Thessalonians know about the "times and seasons", according to 1 Thessalonians 5:1-3, is that ἡμέρα κυρίου ὡς κλέπτης ἐν νυκτὶ οὕτως ἔρχεται. In other words, the Day of the Lord could come at any time. The false proclamation that the author of 2 Thessalonians combats is that the Day *has* come, presumably bringing with it the woes detailed in 1 Thessalonians 5:3. This position is not necessarily in opposition to that of 1 Thessalonians 5:1-3, but merely assumes that the "Day" has come. The contrast between 2 Thessalonians 2:2b and what follows and 1 Thessalonians 5:1-3 lies in the reaction of the author. Paul in 1 Thessalonians explains that the Day of the Lord is a matter which is no threat to the Thessalonians: "But you are not in darkness, brothers, for that day to surprise you like a thief... For God has not destined us for wrath, but to obtain salvation through our Lord Jesus Christ..." (1 Thess. 5:4, 9). The Thessalonians need not be upset over the prospect of the approach of the Day of the Lord, because their salvation from its wrath is assured πάντες γὰρ ὑμεῖς υἱοὶ φωτός ἐστε καὶ υἱοὶ ἡμέρας (1 Thess. 5:5a). In 2 Thessalonians, however, that author does not calm his readers by saying the advent of the Day of the Lord is of no concern to them. Rather, he sets about demonstrating that the Day has not yet come, and will not come for some time yet, because of the events which must necessarily precede it. The comfort offered lies not in the "readiness" of the congregation for the Day, but in the time remaining before the Day becomes a present reality. Part of this difference in approach, of course, may be attributed to the different situations which gave rise to the two letters. But for the moment our concern is with the literary relationship, and how the same thematic material is used to different effect in each of the letters.

The apocalyptic scenario of 2 Thessalonians 2:3b-12 finds few parallels in 1 Thessalonians, even within the eschatological sections of that letter. This is surprising in light of the fact that the eschatological material in both letters is concerned with the time of the Day of the Lord (1 Thess. 5:1-11, 2 Thess. 2:1-12) and the nature of the parousia (1 Thess. 4:13-18, 2 Thess. 1:5-10).

However, within the limits of these fairly general subjects, the two letters display different points of emphasis. 1 Thessalonians shows an interest in the apocalyptic "days" per se, whether the immediate result of the Lord's coming (1 Thess. 4:13-18) or the uncertainty of the time of the Day of the Lord (1 Thess. 5:1-11). 2 Thessalonians is concerned not only with the event of the parousia itself (2 Thess. 1:7b-8a) but also with the prelude to the parousia (2 Thess. 2:1-12) and its consequences in terms of judgment (2 Thess. 1:6-10).

The few parallels to 1 Thessalonians in the apocalyptic scenario appear first in the description of the characteristics and activities of ὁ ἄνθρωπος τῆς ἀνομίας, ὁ υἱὸς τῆς ἀπωλείας (2 Thess. 2:3b-4). Those characteristics stand in contrast to those attributed to Jesus in 1 Thessalonians 1:10, 4:16a, which describe Jesus in terms of his function (1:10), and the nature of his appearing (4:16a). The rhetorical question of 2 Thessalonians 2:5 has, as noted above, a parallel in 1 Thessalonians 5:1, but also in 1 Thessalonians 4:2, where Paul reminds his readers of instruction he has given them "through the Lord Jesus".

The contrast between the operation of evil forces as described in the apocalyptic scenario in 2 Thessalonians 2:1-2 and the description of various "good" forces in operation in 1 Thessalonians continues with the contrast between 2 Thessalonians 2:7a and the prayer of 1 Thessalonians 3:12-13a. The first speaks of the presence of evil even before the apocalyptic crisis: "For the mystery of lawlessness is already at work." The second is a prayer request for the working of love in holiness as a preparation for the parousia: "May the Lord make you increase and abound in love to one another and to all men, as we do to you, so that he may establish your hearts unblamable in holiness before our God and Father, at the coming of our Lord Jesus with all his saints." This latter verse presents the "positive" preparation for the revelation of Christ, in contrast to the "negative" preparation for the revelation of ὁ ἄνομος. This "mystery of lawlessness" of 2 Thessalonians 2:7a is of course associated with persecution; as we have said, θλῖψις usually has eschatological overtones[9]. It is this persecution which Paul has told the Thessalonians to expect and which they have already experienced (1 Thess. 3:4b). In this same verse we find the motif of a forewarning (προελέγομεν ὑμῖν) as a means of instilling steadiness of mind in time of trouble. This steadiness of mind entails maintaining a correct attitude based on sure doctrine, 1 Thessalonians 3:1-5; the forewarning and Timothy's visit both serve εἰς τὸ στηρίξαι ὑμᾶς καὶ παρακαλέσαι ὑπὲρ τῆς πίστεως ὑμῶν (1 Thess. 3:2b). This idea of forewarning of course also appears in the rhetorical question of 2 Thessalonians 2:5, but it is also related to the instruction concerning the various events leading up to the parousia, that is, the content of 2 Thessalonians 2. The author, by means of these instructions, prepares the congregation to stand fast

---

[9] See the exegesis of 1:3-4 in chap. 1.

when the anticipated events take place. For example, he prepares his readers for the apocalyptic θλῖψις by warning of the present reality of "the mystery of lawlessness" (2 Thess. 2:7a).

The mention of the parousia of the Lord in 2 Thessalonians 2:8b has thematic parallels in 1 Thessalonians 2:19 and 3:13. Both of these verses refer to the appearance of the believers before God or Christ at the judgment, a motif we have also found in 2 Thessalonians[10].

The rest of the apocalyptic scenario (2:9-12) finds its parallels in 1 Thessalonians primarily through the contrast between the fate of the evil (2 Thess. 2:10) and that of believers (1 Thess. 5:9), and the way God has worked in the evil (2 Thess. 2:11-12) and in the believers (1 Thess. 5:23), especially as exemplified by their reception of the gospel (1 Thess. 1:5, 2:13). We should note that 1 Thessalonians is concerned almost exclusively with the fate of the believers. 1 Thessalonians 4:13-18 addresses the problem of those believers who have died and their place in the parousia, while 1 Thessalonians 5:1-11 is concerned with the believers' status on the Day of the Lord. The only reference to the fate of non-believers comes in 1 Thessalonians 5:3, which is a general and possibly traditional formulation (cf. Matt. 24:39, Luke 21:34-35), and in 1 Thessalonians 2:16b, referring to the fate of the Jews.

In contrast to these two references to the apocalyptic fate of the unbelievers, 2 Thessalonians shows its primary interest in the punishment of the wicked, ἀνταποδοῦναι τοῖς θλίβουσιν ὑμᾶς θλῖψιν (2 Thess. 1:6)[11]. The reward of the believers still is a part of the scenario, but it is muted by comparison. Because of the difference in emphasis in the apocalyptic content of the two letters, the description of the fate of the wicked in 2 Thessalonians often appears to be drawn in deliberate contrast to the fate of the righteous in 1 Thessalonians. For example, the reassurance of salvation offered the readers in 1 Thessalonians 5:9, οὐκ ἔθετο ἡμᾶς ὁ θεὸς εἰς ὀργὴν ἀλλὰ εἰς περιποίησιν σωτηρίας, stands in contrast to the fate of those who reject the salvific truth in 2 Thessalonians 2:10, ἀνθ' ὧν τὴν ἀγάπην τῆς ἀληθείας οὐκ ἐδέξαντο εἰς τὸ σωθῆναι αὐτούς. Another example is the "power" of the gospel as preached to the Thessalonians (1 Thess. 1:5) in contrast to the ἐνέργεια πλάνης of 2 Thessalonians 2:11, or the way the Thessalonians' acceptance of Paul's message as originating with God (1 Thess. 2:13) stands in contrast to the rejection of the truth by those who choose unrighteousness (2 Thess. 2:12). This contrast of the wicked and the good points up the different perspectives of the two letters; 1 Thessalonians shows little interest in the fate of the wicked, while 2 Thessalonians vividly portrays that fate while paying comparatively little attention to the reward of the good.

---

[10] See the exegesis of 1:3-4, 10 in chap. 1.
[11] See the exegesis of 1:7a in chap. 1.

The prayer wish of 1 Thessalonians 5:23 expresses the proper state for the believer when the Lord comes, that is, a state of "peace" which is a result of thorough-going "holiness" (ἁγιασμός). We shall see that the attainment of this "peace" as a result of complete obedience is the desire of the author of 2 Thessalonians. The desired end is the same, but the paths believed to lead to it are different.

The second description of an act of thanksgiving (2 Thess. 2:13-17) follows the pattern established by the inclusion of a second thanksgiving in 1 Thessalonians 2:13-16, in contrast to the other Pauline letters. As in 1 Thessalonians 2:13, 2 Thessalonians 2:13 duplicates the thanksgiving formula of the first thanksgiving, 2 Thessalonians 1:3, and so includes the idea of the "obligation" of thanksgiving (ὀφείλομεν εὐχαριστεῖν). This is thus a parallel to 1 Thessalonians in regard both to structure (i.e., two thanksgivings) and to the wording of the thanksgiving formulae, insofar as the second thanksgiving in each letter reproduces the formula of the first. The repetition in 2 Thessalonians of the formula ὀφείλομεν + εὐχαριστεῖν indicates that this is a deliberately constructed phrase which has a specific meaning within the context of the letter; the author comments on the act of thanksgiving as a duty of the faithful, placing it within an ecclesiastical context.

The explanation of the basis for thanksgiving in 2 Thessalonians 2:13b-14 thematically recalls the narration of the events of the conversion of the Thessalonians in 1 Thessalonians 1:4-10. This passage in 1 Thessalonians is about τὴν ἐκλογήν of the Thessalonians, which is the result of the action εἵλατο ὑμᾶς ὁ θεὸς ἀπ' ἀρχῆς εἰς σωτηρίαν (2 Thess. 2:13b). In terms of language, this same section (2 Thess. 2:13b-14) recalls the consequences of the call. One is called εἰς σωτηρίαν (2 Thess. 2:13b, 1 Thess. 5:9) and ἐν ἁγιασμῷ πνεύματος (2 Thess. 2:13b, 1 Thess. 4:7). The call is linked to a particular way of life (περιπατεῖν) worthy of the one who calls (2 Thess. 2:14; 1 Thess. 2:12, 5:9).

The conclusion of the doctrinal discourse of the *probatio* of 2 Thessalonians includes a moral imperative: στήκετε καὶ κρατεῖτε τὰς παραδόσεις ἃς ἐδιδάχθητε (2:15). The behavior enjoined by this imperative is in 1 Thessalonians a present reality and a source of consolation to Paul in his trouble (1 Thess. 3:7-8). As we have seen, it is the virtue of "standing firm" which our author regards as necessary to the readers' salvation, and thus is the virtue he wishes his letter to instill in his readers (cf. chap. 1, p. 44). Στήκετε is joined to κρατεῖτε while the "proper" source of doctrine is contrasted with the "improper" source in 2 Thessalonians 2:1-2. This contrast is part of the *inclusio* which indicates the conclusion of the *probatio*. Στήκετε recalls the injunction of 1 Thessalonians 3:8, στήκετε ἐν κυρίῳ, "stand firm in the Lord". We may see a shift in thought between the two uses of the verb. In 2 Thessalonians, instead of the idea of adhering to some sort of fellowship with the Lord (since being "in" the Lord implies a spiritual participation not subject to empirical verification), we find adherence to a received tradition, an adherence which is demonstrated by public and private behavior. It is adherence to this tradition, as we have seen, which is the source of salvation in 2 Thessalonians.

The intercessory prayer of 2 Thessalonians 2:16-17 recalls 1 Thessalonians 3:11-13, a prayer with an eschatological orientation. However, the formula of 2 Thessalonians 2:16a reverses the order of 1 Thessalonians 3:11a: αὐτὸς δὲ ὁ κύριος ἡμῶν Ἰησοῦς Χριστὸς καὶ [ὁ] θεὸς ὁ πατὴρ ἡμῶν. This change reflects the general tendency in the letter to subordinate the Father to Christ (see below). 2 Thessalonians 2:17 appears to be an extension of 1 Thessalonians 3:13a, since it makes clear the object of στηρίξαι, just as 2 Thessalonians 2:15 illuminates the intention of στήκετε. The virtuous actions of "directing" and "standing fast" are related specifically to the tradition, which is what defines what constitutes "every good deed and word" (2 Thess. 2:17b). The author of 2 Thessalonians regards the "tradition" passed on to his readers as the sum total of Christian doctrine and moral instruction, and it is to this doctrinal and moral tradition that he wishes his readers to remain steadfastly loyal.

5. *Exhortatio*, 3:1-13

The request for prayer that begins the *exhortatio* (2 Thess. 3:1-5) has its most obvious parallel in a similar request in 1 Thessalonians 5:25, ἀδελφοί, προσεύχεσθε [καὶ] περὶ ἡμῶν. In contrast to this simple and formulaic prayer request, that in 2 Thessalonians has quite specific content; the prayer is solicited for a specific reason. The formula τὸ λοιπὸν... ἀδελφοί recalls λοιπὸν οὖν, ἀδελφοί (1 Thess. 4.1a), since both represent the beginning of a new section of the composition. The prayer request in 2 Thessalonians 3:1b, ἵνα ὁ λόγος τοῦ κυρίου τρέχῃ καὶ δοξάζηται καθὼς καὶ πρὸς ὑμᾶς, apparently refers to the way ὁ λόγος τοῦ κυρίου spread among the Thessalonians as described in 1 Thessalonians 1:5-8. Ὁ λόγος τοῦ κυρίου has this sense only in 1 Thessalonians 1:8 and 2 Thessalonians 3:1b; in 1 Thessalonians 4:15 it refers to a specific word, and Philippians 1:14 is textually uncertain (cf. Acts 12:24)[12]. The author asks for prayer for the progress of the word, and also ἵνα ῥυσθῶμεν ἀπὸ τῶν ἀτόπων καὶ πονηρῶν ἀνθρώπων (2 Thess. 3:2a). Such a prayer would of course be addressed to the Lord, Ἰησοῦν τὸν ῥυόμενον ἡμᾶς ἐκ τῆς ὀργῆς τῆς ἐρχομένης (1 Thess. 1:10b). As we have said previously[13], the eschatological evil is at work already in the person

---

[12] Trilling, *Der zweite Brief*, p. 134, n. 574.
[13] See the exegesis of 2:6 in chap. 1.

of those who oppose the author as the bearer of the tradition (cf. 2 Thess. 2:7). His prayer request is for rescue from these representatives of the eschatological evil, and it may be that Jesus as the eschatological "rescuer" (1 Thess. 1:10b) is specifically in mind in 2 Thessalonians 3:2[14]. The observation οὐ γὰρ πάντων ἡ πίστις (2 Thess. 3:2) may be applied at least in part to the Jews, especially if we take πίστις as "faithfulness" as elsewhere in the letter (see below). The Jews might be taken as a type of the political and religious rebellion the author calls ἡ ἀποστασία. Their opposition to the Judean church is seen by Paul as a type for all opposition to the spread of Christianity (1 Thess. 2:15-16), and some of the description of the opponents of God in 2 Thessalonians may be seen to apply to this characterization (cf. 2 Thess. 1:8, 2:10b-12).

The contrasting phrase, πιστὸς δέ ἐστιν ὁ κύριος (2 Thess. 3:3), is parallel to 1 Thessalonians 5:24, πιστὸς ὁ καλῶν ὑμᾶς, ὃς καὶ ποιήσει. The parallel is both literary and theological, since in both cases the intention is to provide a sure ground for confidence in the Lord's future actions on behalf of the congregation. In 2 Thessalonians 3:3, this future action is στηρίξαι ὑμᾶς καὶ φυλάξαι ἀπὸ τοῦ πονηροῦ. This is parallel to the prayer wish of 1 Thessalonians 3:11-13, especially 1 Thessalonians 3:13a, εἰς τὸ στηρίξαι ὑμῶν τὰς καρδίας ἀμέμπτους; again, this is a prayer wish with an explicitly eschatological setting, cf. 1 Thessalonians 2:19, par. 2 Thessalonians 2:8b (above).

The author expresses confidence in his readers' behavior, particularly in regard to ἃ παραγγέλλομεν. This is an apparent reference to paraenetic material such as that in 1 Thessalonians 4:1-12, and more specifically in 1 Thessalonians 4:2, οἴδατε γὰρ τίνας παραγγελίας ἐδώκαμεν ὑμῖν διὰ τοῦ κυρίου Ἰησοῦ. Paul has also expressed confidence in the Thessalonians' past behavior and its continuation into the future, cf. 1 Thessalonians 4:1b, καθὼς καὶ περιπατεῖτε, ἵνα περισσεύητε μᾶλλον. We find a similar thought in 2 Thessalonians 3:4b, [καὶ] ποιεῖτε καὶ ποιήσετε.

The prayer-wish of 2 Thessalonians 3:5 has two parallels in 1 Thessalonians. A similar prayer-wish in 1 Thessalonians 3:11 (which, as we have said above, has an eschatological setting) uses the same verb, κατευθύναι, in the non-moral sense that the Lord Jesus is asked to "direct our way to you". On the other hand, the two virtues the author requests for the Thessalonians, τὴν ἀγάπην τοῦ θεοῦ καὶ... τὴν ὑπομονὴν τοῦ Χριστοῦ (2 Thess. 3:5b), are found also in 1 Thessalonians 1:3. There these virtues are already possessed by the Thessalonians, and give rise to Paul's thanksgiving. In 2 Thessalonians 3:5b, the "practical" result of ἀγάπη, κόπος, is not present as it is in 1 Thessalonians 1:3. However, the "practical" result of "the hope of our Lord Jesus"

---

[14] The relationship of the phenomena associated with the apocalyptic scenario to the eschatological "wrath" will be examined in the third chapter.

(τῆς ἐλπίδος τοῦ κυρίου ἡμῶν Ἰησοῦ Χριστοῦ), ὑπομονή, is retained as τὴν ὑπομονὴν τοῦ Χριστοῦ, "the steadfastness of Christ". The shift is from steadfastness inspired by hope to the imitation of the steadfastness shown by Christ himself (cf. Mark 13:13 and pars.; Matt. 10:22; Rev. 1:9, 3:10). "Hope" appears in 2 Thessalonians only at 2 Thessalonians 2:16; on the whole, ὑπομονή has replaced it as its "experiential" equivalent[15].

The paraenetic material in 2 Thessalonians 3:6-13, which deals with the problems of οἱ ἀτάκτως περιπατοῦντες, finds abundant parallels in 1 Thessalonians. The subject as introduced in 2 Thessalonians 3:6 is paralleled both in formula and in subject matter in 1 Thessalonians 5:14a, which also deals with what action is to be taken in regard to οἱ ἄτακτοι. 2 Thessalonians has παραγγέλλομεν rather than παρακαλοῦμεν, in keeping with the later letter's emphasis on right doctrine and right behavior; one may compare 2 Thessalonians 3:12. The instruction of 1 Thessalonians 5:14a (νουθετεῖτε τοὺς ἀτάκτους) is different from, and to a certain extent contrary to, that of 2 Thessalonians 3:6; it is difficult to see how one can both "admonish" someone and yet "keep away" (στέλλεσθαι) from him at the same time[16]. There is an attempt to reconcile the two instructions in 2 Thessalonians 3:14-15 (μὴ συναναμίγνυσθαι αὐτῷ... ἀλλὰ νουθετεῖτε), but this does not remove the logical difficulties. Indeed, the modifications in 2 Thessalonians 3:15 of the instruction of 2 Thessalonians 3:14 may have been a conscious attempt to conform to the instruction of 1 Thessalonians 5:14a. The exhortatory formula in 1 Thessalonians 4:1 also has some affinities with 2 Thessalonians 3:6, and the "receiving" of the tradition in the latter verse seems to refer to the situation described in 1 Thessalonians 2:13b, παραλαβόντες λόγον ἀκοῆς παρ' ἡμῶν τοῦ θεοῦ ἐδέξασθε οὐ λόγον ἀνθρώπων ἀλλὰ καθώς ἐστιν ἀληθῶς λόγον θεοῦ. The author of 2 Thessalonians would certainly locate the time of the congregation "receiving" the tradition at the time of Paul's successful mission, a mission like the one 1 Thessalonians 2:13b describes.

Paul's first encounter with the Thessalonians is similarly recalled in 2 Thessalonians 3:7, specifically in regard to his behavior as an apostle. There is a verbal parallel between 2 Thessalonians 3:7 and 1 Thessalonians 2:1, αὐτοὶ γὰρ οἴδατε....ὅτι οὐ(κ).... The idea of an "imitation" of the author (or the author-as-Paul) appears in 1 Thessalonians 1:6a, although in 1 Thessalonians there is no idea of the obligation to imitate him as there is in 2 Thessalonians 3:7a, δεῖ μιμεῖσθαι ἡμᾶς (although cf. 1 Cor. 11:1)[17].

---

[15] Trilling, *Der zweite Brief*, p. 47.
[16] See the exegesis of 3:15 in chap. 1.
[17] See the exegesis of 3:6 in chap. 1.

We find a very close parallel in the expansion of this idea of imitation, between 2 Thessalonians 3:8 and 1 Thessalonians 2:9, which both speak of the author's (or the author's-as-Paul) behavior while a missionary. The verbal identity of νυκτὸς καὶ ἡμέρας ἐργαζόμενοι πρὸς τὸ μὴ ἐπιβαρῆσαί τινα ὑμῶν, as well as the similar phrases ἐν κόπῳ καὶ μόχθῳ / τὸν κόπον καὶ τὸν μόχθον strongly suggest a literary dependence between the two verses. There is, however, a difference in intention. In 1 Thessalonians, this example serves as part of the proof of Paul's status as a genuine apostle who is interested only in the good of the congregation, and is thus willing to set aside the perogatives of his office. In 2 Thessalonians, the example is offered as part of a self-conscious model of virtue for the Thessalonians to imitate, a part of the tradition which has been handed on to them[18]. Once again it appears that material in 1 Thessalonians has been re-interpreted to render new meanings in 2 Thessalonians. This shift in meaning is made clear in 2 Thessalonians 3:9 in comparison with 1 Thessalonians 2:7a: ἵνα ἑαυτοὺς τύπον δῶμεν ὑμῖν εἰς τὸ μιμεῖσθαι ἡμᾶς.

There is another, closer verbal affinity between 1 Thessalonians 3:4 and 2 Thessalonians 3:10 in regard to previous instruction from the author to the congregation: καὶ γὰρ ὅτε ἦμεν πρὸς ὑμᾶς προελέγομεν ὑμῖν / τοῦτο παρηγγέλλομεν ὑμῖν. Despite this similarity, the use of the phrase is different because the content of the previous instruction has changed. In 1 Thessalonians 3:4, Paul has forewarned the Thessalonians about the inevitability of persecution; in 2 Thessalonians 3:10, the author refers back to the previous imposition of a community rule appropriate to the situation addressed by the exhortation. In 2 Thessalonians 3:10, the emphasis once again is on "command" as the substance of the tradition; what has been commanded by the author must be obeyed.

The occasion for the exhortation is provided in 2 Thessalonians 3:11, the fact that there are in the congregation τινες περιπατοῦντες ἐν ὑμῖν ἀτάκτως, once again recalling the instruction of 1 Thessalonians 5:14a in regard to the "disorderly". The solemn instruction formula of 2 Thessalonians 3:12, with its two verbs and invocation of the Lord, recalls the general exhortation of 1 Thessalonians 4:11, "... aspire to live quietly, to mind your own affairs, and to work with your hands, as we charged you" (note again the reference to previous instruction; see 2 Thess. 3:10a, above). Both formula and instruction also find a parallel in 1 Thessalonians 2:11-12. There is the mention of previous instruction, the double verb (παρακαλοῦντες ὑμᾶς καὶ παραμυθούμενοι), and the eschatological context we believe to be present in 3:6-12 as well.

---

[18] Ibid.

6. Peroratio, 3:14-16

The intention of 1 Thessalonians 5:14, νουθετεῖτε τοὺς ἀτάκτους, finds its parallel in 2 Thessalonians finally in the *peroratio*, that is, the summation of the argument of the letter, in 2 Thessalonians 3:15. This verse places a theoretical limitation on the command to avoid the "disorderly" given in 2 Thessalonians 3:14. This is the third reference to an opposition party at work in the congregation, and so also the third parallel to 1 Thessalonians 5:14 (cf. 2 Thess. 3:6, 11). A problem that merits only passing reference in 1 Thessalonians has by the time of 2 Thessalonians developed into a real threat to the salvation of the congregation. This is because the "disorderly" represent real opposition to the author's spiritual authority and a doctrinal position that can only lead to unrest and undue excitement within the congregation. This is why the author seeks to compel obedience to the "tradition" he represents himself as upholding, cf. 2 Thessalonians 3:14. The reverse of this directive in 2 Thessalonians 3:14-15 in respect of the "disorderly" is the directive in respect to the leaders of the congregation in 1 Thessalonians 5:12-13, which also had "peace" as its intention, εἰρηνεύετε ἐν ἑαυτοῖς.

The emphasis on the idea of "peace" is demonstrated by 2 Thessalonians 3:16 as a summary of the letter's intentions. This intercessory prayer is overloaded. For example, the parallel in 1 Thessalonians 5:23a mentions ὁ θεὸς τῆς εἰρήνης without the additional wish for εἰρήνη found in 2 Thessalonians 3:16. There the invocation is changed to ὁ κύριος τῆς εἰρήνης, following the general tendency of the second letter to exalt Christ over God the Father. Not only does 2 Thessalonians 3:16 repeat εἰρήνη, but adds the intensive διὰ παντὸς ἐν παντὶ τρόπῳ. Thus the wish for sanctification in 1 Thessalonians 5:23a becomes explicitly a wish for "peace" from "the Lord of peace", peace being the result of the resolution of the various troubles within the congregation (cf. 2 Thess. 3:12).

7. Epistolary Postscript, 3:17-18

As we have noted earlier, the "greeting" of 2 Thessalonians 3:17 is merely a mark of authentication, much as it appears to be also in Colossians 4:18a. The greeting of 1 Thessalonians 5:26, however, is a genuine greeting to be handed on within the congregation not only verbally, but through the presumably liturgical exchange of the "holy kiss" (ἐν φιλήματι ἁγίῳ). The concluding benediction of 2 Thessalonians 3:18 has a close verbal parallel in 1 Thessalonians 5:28, the only difference between the two being the addition of πάντων in the second letter. This parallel is, of course, formulaic.

Now that we have examined at length the parallels between 1 Thessalonians and 2 Thessalonians, we may attempt to discover some of the significant points raised by those parallels. In the first place, we hope to have demonstrated that there are very significant similarities between the two letters, and that these similarities suggest some sort of dependence. It has been argued by John C. Hurd that the similarities between 1 and 2 Thessalonians are no greater than those between any other two Pauline letters; he cites for an example Romans 8:2-10 and Galatians 5:13-25[19]. This example, however, is not analogous to the situation in 1 and 2 Thessalonians, since these sections of Romans and Galatians share a common argument ("flesh" vs. "spirit") relative to a major point of Paul's theology. The similarities between 1 and 2 Thessalonians, on the other hand, are primarily formulaic, and the sections of each letter dealing with similar themes (e.g., the apocalyptic scenario) have few verbal or even thematic similarities. We may also remark the points the two letters have in common in contrast to the rest of the Pauline corpus (e.g., the appearance of two thanksgivings) and the high degree of similarity relative to the comparative lengths of the two letters (89 and 47 verses, respectively). John A. Bailey noted the similarity of structure and remarked, "The result is that the structure of 2 Thessalonians is at times unwieldy; the letter seems almost to have more form than content"[20]. It appears, then, that the author of 2 Thessalonians has used the framework of 1 Thessalonians and its specific "formulaic" vocabulary while shifting the emphasis of its content. The author has also utilized the "non-formulaic" vocabulary of 1 Thessalonians that is appropriate to the content of his own letter.[21] For this reason, both the similarities and the differences between the two letters are significant for understanding the relationship between the two.[22]

In the second place, we may now detect a pattern in the utilization of material from 1 Thessalonians in 2 Thessalonians, a pattern that may reveal

---

[19] Hurd, "Authenticity", p. 3–5.

[20] John A. Bailey, "Who Wrote II Thessalonians?", *New Testament Studies* 25 (1979): 132; Bailey cites in this regard R.J. Peterson, "The Structure and Purpose of Second Thessalonians", (Ph.D. dissertation, Harvard University, 1968), p. 46.

[21] Cf. 2 Thess. 3:3, 1 Thess. 3:13a; 2 Thess. 1:11b, ἔργον πίστεως, 1 Thess. 1:3a, τοῦ ἔργου τῆς πίστεως.

[22] Hurd argues that similarity is not a valid criterion for disputing the genuineness of the authorship, both because of the formulaic nature of the Hellenistic epistolary style and because every author repeats and modifies himself in his writings (Hurd, "Authenticity", pp. 4–5). However, the whole practice of pseudepigraphy involves the creation of verisimilitude; one way of accomplishing this is through the use of phrases or ideas found in an author's genuine work. This involves the reproduction of phrases as well as their modification. What is striking about the similarities between 1 and 2 Thessalonians is that they are often almost exact parallels of a sort not found elsewhere in Paul, and these do not occur

something of our author's intentions. This pattern may be demonstrated in the form of a table, showing the number of citations by allusion to each verse of 1 Thessalonians in 2 Thessalonians (see table 1). It may be seen from this table that some sections of 1 Thessalonians are referred to repeatedly in 2 Thessalonians, while others are referred to only once or not at all. The most frequently cited passages are as follows:

3:13: that he may maintain (στηρίξαι) your hearts blameless in holiness before our God and Father at the coming of our Lord Jesus with all his holy ones

1:10: and to await his son from the heavens, whom he raised from the dead, Jesus who saves us from the coming wrath

1:3: remembering your work of faith and labor of love and steadfastness of hope in our Lord Jesus Christ before our God and Father

4:1: For the rest, brothers, we ask and exhort you in (the) Lord Jesus, that just as you received from us how it is necessary for you to conduct yourself and to please God, just as you also have done, that you should do so more and more

1:5: because our gospel was not present among you in words only but also in power and in a holy spirit and in great conviction, just as you know what sort we were among you for your sake

2:12: exhorting and encouraging and bearing witness to you so that you might conduct yourselves in a way worthy of God, who calls you into his own kingdom and glory

These passages are alluded to from four to eight times in 2 Thessalonians.

The ideas conveyed in these passages are several: perseverance in holiness until the parousia (3:13, 2:12); the coming parousia and the "rescue" from wrath (1:10); the particular virtues of faith, love, and hope (1:3); conduct "worthy of God" (4:1, 2:12); and the gospel as word and power (1:5). We may further summarize the content of these key verses as (1) the events of the parousia, (2) conduct "worthy of God", and (3) the place of Paul as bearer of the gospel message and the guardian of the congregation's spiritual condition.

We may also see from this table that the "main matter" of 1 Thessalonians is hardly referred to in 2 Thessalonians. There are mostly incidental references to the *narratio*, 1 Thessalonians 1:5c-3:13, except for the eschatological references of 1:10, 2:12, 3:13, and the thanksgiving formula of 2:13. There are some thematic references to the early history of the congregation as described in 1 Thessalonians 1:6-7. There are more, but very selective, references to the

---

where similar themes are under discussion; indeed, this is where the fewest parallels are found (see table 1). What is significant in 1 and 2 Thessalonians is the peculiar combination of similarity and dissimiliarity between two such short letters; this is a peculiarity which even the defenders of Pauline authorship must acknowledge.

80   *A Comparison of Material in 1 and 2 Thessalonians*

Table 1: Allusions to 1 Thessalonians by Verse

Verse	Citations	Verse	Citations	Verse	Citations	Verse	Citations
1:1	1	2:14	0	4:3	0	5:7	0
2	3	15	1	4	0	8	1
3	5	16	1	5	1	9	3
4	2	17	0	6	0	10	0
5	4	18	1	7	2	11	0
6	2	19	2	8	thematic	12	2
7	3	20	0	9	0	13	1
8	1	3:1	0	10	0	14	3
9	1	2	1	11	1	15	0
10	7	3	2	12	0	16	0
2:1	1	4	2	13	0	17	0
2	0	5	0	14	1	18	0
3	0	6	0	15	1	19	0
4	0	7	1	16	3	20	0
5	0	8	1	17	2	21	0
6	0	9	0	18	0	22	0
7	0	10	0	5:1	2	23	3
8	0	11	2	2	1	24	1
9	1	12	2	3	1	25	1
10	0	13	8	4	0	26	1
11	0	4:1	5	5	0	27	0
12	4	2	2	6	0	28	1
13	3						

thematic and general content of 1 Thessalonians 4:1, to the parousia as described in 1 Thessalonians 4:16, to the contrast between the fate of the believers and the lost in 1 Thessalonians 5:9, and to the problem of the "disorderly", 1 Thessalonians 5:14. There are surprisingly few references to the eschatological material of 4:13-5:11, despite the fact that 2 Thessalonians has a highly eschatological orientation. The primary references are to the "mechanics" of the parousia as described in 1 Thessalonians 4:16 and to the doctrine of the faithful "joining" the Lord at his parousia in 1 Thessalonians 4:17. The references to the remainder of the letter (5:12-28) are formulaic, except for the blessing of 1 Thessalonians 5:23, which again has the eschatological reference to the parousia of the Lord Jesus Christ.

The parallels between the two letters are not necessarily such that the same or similar phrases appear in approximately the same place in both letters. When there are references of this sort, they are usually formulaic rather than thematic, e.g., 1 Thessalonians 1:1 and 2 Thessalonians 1:1-2; 1 Thessalonians 4:1 and 2 Thessalonians 3:1; 1 Thessalonians 5:23, 26, 28 and 2 Thessalonians 3:16-18. Other references are of two sorts. They may be verbal, that is, they may be repetitions of words or phrases in different contexts than those in which they appear in 1 Thessalonians. Examples are 2 Thessalonians 1:8 and 1 Thessalonians 4:5; 2 Thessalonians 1:11b and 1 Thessalonians 1:3a; 2 Thessalonians 2:13b and 1 Thessalonians 1:4-5a. If not verbal, the references may be thematic, that is, they may be allusions to similar ideas or contrasting ideas in different terms than those of 1 Thessalonians. Some examples of thematic parallels are 2 Thessalonians 1:4 and 1 Thessalonians 1:7; 2 Thessalonians 1:11a and 1 Thessalonians 2:12; 2 Thessalonians 2:2 and 1 Thessalonians 3:3a; 2 Thessalonians 2:13b-14 and 1 Thessalonians 1:4-5a.

The use or repeated use of selected material from 1 Thessalonians will indicate how the author of 2 Thessalonians understood that letter. Of course, the selection of material was also determined to some extent by the nature of the situation which gave rise to 2 Thessalonians. As our exegesis of the letter in the first chapter has demonstrated, this situation was the "opposition" which the author perceived to be at work against him in the congregation. This opposition was expressed in an erroneous doctrine about "the Day of the Lord" and in the agitation produced within the community by those who upheld this doctrine and claimed spiritual authority that challenged what the author calls "the tradition".

Both the parousia and the "disorderly" (οἱ ἄτακτοι) are subjects addressed by 1 Thessalonians, and we may ask what influence the treatment of these subjects in that letter had on the situation that the author of 2 Thessalonians addresses. In other words, were any of the problems addressed by 2 Thessalonians the result of reaction to 1 Thessalonians? The first problem is the erroneous doctrine concerning "the Day of the Lord", summarized in the statement, "the Day of the Lord is present" (2 Thess. 2:2b). The historical advent of "the Day of the Lord" is the topic of 1 Thessalonians 5:1-11, but this section emphasizes the unexpectedness, and hence the unpredictability, of its advent. The only indication of the time is ὅταν λέγωσιν, Εἰρήνη καὶ ἀσφάλεια, τότε αἰφνίδιος αὐτοῖς ἐφίσταται ὄλεθρος (1 Thess. 5:3a). The proclamation of 2 Thessalonians 2:2b is not necessarily inconsistent with the content of 1 Thessalonians 5:1-11. Presumably one might regard a given event as "sudden destruction" falling upon the wicked after assurances that all was well, and this could be understood as a sign that "the Day of the Lord is present". It should be noted that no connection is implied between the events of the parousia in 1 Thessalonians 4:13-18 and "the Day of the Lord" in 1 Thessalonians 5:1-11; readers of 1 Thessalonians would not necessarily, on the basis of that letter alone, expect the coming of Jesus and the "gathering" of the faithful to be an event connected with "the Day of the Lord" as such. Therefore, the absence of this event would not be a deterrent to the proclamation of 2 Thessalonians 2:2b. One of the problems of the eschatology of 2 Thessalonians is the author's understanding of the relationship between "the Day of the Lord" and the parousia.

The problem of the "disorderly" (οἱ ἄτακτοι, τινες περιπατοῦντες ἐν ὑμῖν ἀτάκτως) appears to have arisen in some form before the composition of 1 Thessalonians, since Paul addressed the problem briefly in 1 Thessalonians 5:14. However, it appears to have become a far more serious problem by the time of the composition of 2 Thessalonians. As we have seen, the author of 2 Thessalonians uses the epithet "disorderly" to refer to those who had set themselves up as spiritual authorities competent to discern the "signs of the times". These people did not work for a living, but expected the support of the congregation as its spiritual leaders by charismatic appointment (i.e., διὰ πνεύματος). It is possible that they cited the sorts of ideas in 1 Thessalonians 5:12-13, 19-20 in support of their claims of support, if they knew 1 Thessalonians. Certainly 1 Thessalonians is not hostile to a claim of charismatic leadership or inspiration; the caution of 1 Thessalonians 5:21, πάντα δὲ δοκιμάζετε, would not necessarily be associated particularly with claims of spiritual inspiration, as in 1 John 4:1a, δοκιμάζετε τὰ πνεύματα εἰ ἐκ τοῦ θεοῦ ἐστιν. For this very reason, we may assume that the "disorderliness" present in the congregation at the time Paul wrote 1 Thessalonians was not of the sort found there when 2 Thessalonians was written. If Paul had believed such to be the case, he would have been unlikely to write the commendatory words regarding the freedom of the spirit and prophecy in 1 Thessalonians 5:19-20. Indeed, we may not even assume that the same group of people is addressed by the admonitions in the letters. Rather, the author of 2 Thessalonians has identified a certain group of people in the congregation as τινες περιπατοῦντες ἐν ὑμῖν ἀτάκτως (2 Thess. 3:11a). He has chosen to identify this group with those Paul singles out for admonition from the congregation at large in 1 Thessalonians 5:14. This is a deliberate use of a phrase borrowed from 1 Thessalonians to address a new situation in the later letter. The problem of the "disorderly" in 2 Thessalonians, however, did not arise from or in reaction to 1 Thessalonians; we may not even assume they knew it. Rather it would appear to have arisen from the belief among some members of the congregation that they were endowed with special spiritual insight.

We may say, then, that the problems addressed in 2 Thessalonians, although they are also addressed in some way in 1 Thessalonians, did not arise in reaction to that letter. However, the author of 2 Thessalonians felt it was necessary to write his own letter because the new situation was not adequately addressed by the content of 1 Thessalonians, for whatever reason. On the other hand, the author chose to follow the structure and allude to the language of 1 Thessalonians as a means of rectifying the new situation. As we have seen, 2 Thessalonians resembles its predecessor most closely in structure and formulaic language, which is for the most part unrelated to content. Indeed, even when there has been a coincidence in subject matter, the author has not chosen to refer to the apparently pertinent material of 1 Thessalonians, except in the most general way. Rather, he has chosen to make his points by repeated reference to selected portions of 1 Thessalonians, and no reference to most of the rest of the letter. As we have seen, the three themes represented by the verses of 1 Thessalonians used most often by the author of 2 Thessalonians are (1) the events of the parousia, (2) conduct "worthy of God", and (3) the place of Paul (or in 2 Thessalonians, the author-as-Paul) as bearer of the gospel message and guardian of the congregation's spiritual well-being.

The author of 2 Thessalonians, then, has made selective use of the content of 1 Thessalonians to make his own points, and has modelled the structure of his letter upon that of the earlier letter. But given that this use of 1 Thessalonians is now apparent, the very need for the composition of a new letter indicates the earlier letter was somehow insufficient; why then use the old letter as a model for the new?

If Paul is the author of 2 Thessalonians, we may rule out the possibility that he consciously used a copy of 1 Thessalonians as a model for 2 Thessalonians. The composition of the later letter was occasioned either by the misinterpretation of the first letter, its failure to address the problems in the congregations properly, or the fear that such a misinterpretation or such a failure might come about. Paul would have no reason to use a "failed" letter as a model for a second letter intended to supplement it. We may compare the situation in Corinth. If the author of 2 Thessalonians was Paul, then, the allusions to 1 Thessalonians must be unconscious and a result of dealing with similar material and following a standard epistolary structure. But we have already seen that the parallels are fewest in the sections of the two letters which deal with eschatology and the time of "the Day of the Lord", where, under this theory of Pauline authorship, they should be most plentiful. On the other hand, the parallels in structure (e.g., the two thanksgiving formulae, 1 Thess. 1:2, 2:13; 2 Thess. 1:3, 2:13) and phrasing (e.g., 1 Thess. 1:1, 2 Thess. 1:1-2) are particularly striking in view of the length of the two letters involved. If 1 Thessalonians is an "eccentric" letter in comparison with the rest of the Pauline correspondence, the reproduction of so many of those "eccentric" elements in the forty-seven verses of 2 Thessalonians argues strongly against this happening as a result of unconscious self-plagiarism.

If the author was someone other than Paul, however, the use of the pattern of 1 Thessalonians was at least in part a conscious means of appropriating the name and authority of Paul for the author's own work. His use of 1 Thessalonians must then be explained by the appropriateness of its subject matter, by its use by the "disorderly" opponents to promote their own eschatological doctrine, or by some other such theory. We shall address this problem in the fourth chapter.

Similarity to Paul's other letters alone is not a sufficient ground for rejecting his authorship of 2 Thessalonians. What is revealing, rather, is the form the similarity takes (e.g., formulaic and structural rather than thematic) and the differences — thematic, literary, and theological — that are also present in 2 Thessalonians.

This question of the differences or apparent differences between 1 and 2 Thessalonians has been a major field of argument over the last century. Both proponents and opponents of Pauline authorship have offered arguments based on points of similarity and contrast, but these arguments are of several types. There is misinterpretation of evidence, often based on subjective reactions. For example, there is the argument that 2 Thessalonians lacks the "personal warmth" of 1 Thessalonians, based on the phrase εὐχαριστεῖν ὀφείλομεν (2 Thess. 1:3), or the opposite argument that it is full of warmth, since the author refers to the readers as ἀδελφοί. Both terms, of course, are church language and devoid of "emotional" content. Another erroneous argument is based on a mechanical idea of consistency. In this case, every deviation from a "standard" Pauline formula is regarded as evidence for another author. A counter-argument is based upon a false idea of pseudepigraphy, and argues that a forger would not feel himself to be at liberty to change Pauline formulae, but that Paul himself would. A similar argument in the case of 2 Thessalonians is the supposed difficulties raised by the authentication formula of 2 Thessalonians 3:17, either for Paul (since he nowhere else so authenticates his letters)[23] or for another author (since no one other than Paul would know that he always added a personal greeting in his own hand to his letters)[24]. Finally, there are various arguments based on the psychology of a forger or of Paul, none of which are acceptable in either historical or literary criticism.

In an effort to provide a more solid foundation for our own theory of authorship, we shall deal not with particular bits of evidence, but with major tendencies in 2 Thessalonians, as revealed by our analysis and exegesis of the letter, as well as by our comparative study of 2 and 1 Thessalonians. In this way, we hope to consider 2 Thessalonians as a whole, and the intentions of its author in composing it.

The first of these major tendencies is a strong emphasis upon the apocalyptic future. This involves not only the doctrinal material of the second chapter, which includes a detailed apocalyptic scenario, but the orientation of the entire letter. For example, there is the "scene from the Last Judgment" which serves as an ἔνδειγμα to introduce the *probatio*. It looks to the apocalyptic future to demonstrate "God's righteous judgment" (2 Thess. 1:5-10). There is also the role of the author (or the author-as-Paul) as the apocalyptic mediator

---

[23] Bailey, "Who Wrote II Thessalonians?", p. 138.
[24] Hurd, "Authenticity", pp. 18–19.

on the congregation's behalf before the judgment seat of Christ[25]. We also find the emphasis on the fate of the wicked (2 Thess. 1:8-9, 2:10-12), specifically within the apocalyptic framework. Finally, there is the apparent apocalyptic function of the letter itself, both as "witness" to the Thessalonians as a sort of "pre-trial deposition" and as a weapon against the apocalyptic ἀποστασία[26].

All this stands in contrast to the eschatological orientation of 1 Thessalonians, which looks forward to the parousia as the culmination of God's election (the κλῆσις; cf. 1 Thess. 1:10, 2:12, 3:13). The "doctrinal" content of 4:13-18 deals with the apocalyptic scenario of the parousia only in verses 16-17, and that of 5:1-11 only in verses 2-3. The primary intention of both these sections in 1 Thessalonians is exhortatory. This is made clear by 1 Thessalonians 4:18, ὥστε παρακαλεῖτε ἀλλήλους ἐν τοῖς λόγοις τούτοις and by 1 Thessalonians 5:11, διὸ παρακαλεῖτε ἀλλήλους καὶ οἰκοδομεῖτε εἰς τὸν ἕνα, καθὼς καὶ ποιεῖτε. Eschatological material forms less than one-fourth of the content of 1 Thessalonians (twenty verses out of eighty-nine) and more than one-third of the content of the much shorter 2 Thessalonians (eighteen verses out of forty-seven). As to the compatibility or lack of the same between the eschatological viewpoints of the two letters, this will be examined at length in the next chapter.

A second major tendency is the exaltation of the figure of Christ and the consequent eclipse of the Father in 2 Thessalonians[27]. The most striking example is found in 2 Thessalonians 1:12b, where Christ is called "God": κατὰ τὴν χάριν τοῦ θεοῦ ἡμῶν καὶ κυρίου Ἰησοῦ Χριστοῦ. The absence of the definite article before κυρίου renders the phrase ambiguous, but as noted in our exegesis in chapter 1, the most appropriate interpretation grammatically is to take both τοῦ θεοῦ ἡμῶν and κυρίου as referring to Christ. There is also a consistent trend of replacing θεός with κύριος in 2 Thessalonians as compared with 1 Thessalonians, e.g., 2 Thessalonians 2:13, 1 Thessalonians 1:4; 2 Thessalonians 3:16, 1 Thessalonians 5:23[28]; 2 Thessalonians 3:3a, 1 Thessalonians 5:24[29]. We may also note the shift from attention to God in 2 Thessalonians 1:5-7a to the Lord in 2 Thessalonians 1:7b-10 in the description of the Last Judgment, including the ascription of theophanous language to Christ

---

[25] See the exegesis of 1:10 in chap. 1.
[26] See the exegesis of 1:10, 2:6 in chap. 1.
[27] This point has been made by several commentators and other scholars, e.g., Herbert Braun, "Zur nachpaulinischen Herkunft des zweiten Thessalonicherbriefes", *Gesammelte Studien zum Neuen Testament und Seiner Umwelt*, 2: *durchgesehene und ergänzte Auflage* (Tübingen: J.C.B. Mohr [Paul Siebeck], 1967), p. 209; Bailey, "Who Wrote II Thessalonians?", p. 139.
[28] Cf. also 1 Cor. 14:33; 2 Cor. 13:11; Rom. 15:33, 16:20; Phil. 4:9.
[29] Cf. also 1 Cor. 1:9, 10:13; Bailey, "Who Wrote II Thessalonians?", p. 139.

(cf. Isa. 66:15, 2:10, 19, 21). There is the reversal of order of the Lord and God in 2 Thessalonians 2:16 (cf. 1 Thess. 3:11), and ὁ κύριος μετὰ πάντων ὑμῶν, 2 Thessalonians 3:16b (cf. Phil. 4:9b, 2 Cor. 13:11b).

A third major tendency of 2 Thessalonians is the strong emphasis upon "the tradition" (ἡ παράδοσις) as the object of obedience in the *exhortatio* (2 Thess. 3:1-13). Παράδοσις appears twice in 2 Thessalonians (2:15, 3:6), but elsewhere in Paul's genuine letters only in Galatians 1:14 (in reference to Jewish tradition, τῶν πατρικῶν μου παραδόσεων) and in 1 Corinthians 11:2. 1 Corinthians also has the only use in Paul of παραδίδωμι in the sense of "handing on" instruction, 1 Corinthians 11:2, 23, 15:3. In 1 Corinthians 11:2 what is passed on is the tradition, something of a tautology (παρέδωκα ὑμῖν τὰς παραδόσεις). In 1 Corinthians 11:23, it is an account of the Last Supper that is handed on, and in 15:3, an account of the resurrection appearances of Christ. In both of these cases, what is handed on is a major gospel (i.e., "historical") incident pertinent to the basic κήρυγμα (i.e., the resurrection) or liturgical practice (i.e., the Last Supper). In both 1 Corinthians 11:23 and 15:3, Paul has received the information which he imparts from others, so that he is a link in the tradition's chain of transmission. This might well be expected to be true also of 1 Corinthians 11:2, that is, that "tradition" there too refers to this sort of "foundation" tradition, "historical" incidents which serve as a basis for belief or practice. It might be argued, however, that the content of the discourse of 11:2-16 should be construed as one of the "traditions" to which Paul refers, and that this would be inconsistent with our interpretation of Paul's use of παράδοσις. However, Paul himself explicitly labels the practice in the churches in regard to headcoverings as συνήθεια, that is, a custom or habit (cf. 1 Cor. 8:7). Such matters of church practice were not part of the παράδοσις as Paul understood it.

Therefore, we may say that the use of παράδοσις in 2 Thessalonians, where it is a major theme, is inconsistent with Paul's use of the term in 1 Corinthians, where it is specifically related to the historical events in the life of Jesus. In 2 Thessalonians, παράδοσις refers to the author's (or the author's-as-Paul) commands, examples, and instructions[30]; to some extent, the apostle is the basis for the παράδοσις in 2 Thessalonians in the same way Jesus is the basis for the παράδοσις in the genuine Pauline epistles.

Coupled with this emphasis on tradition is the repeated use of the verb παραγγέλλω, "I command", in 2 Thessalonians 3. This same verb appears in 1 Corinthians 7:10, referring to a command of the Lord given through Paul (τοῖς δὲ γεγαμηκόσιν παραγγέλλω, οὐκ ἐγὼ ἀλλὰ ὁ κύριος), and also in 11:17, in reference to the following instructions that are intended to correct abuses of the Lord's Supper. In 1 Thessalonians, the verb appears in 4:11 in

---

[30] See the exegesis of 3:6-16 in chap. 1.

reference to several things Paul has commanded (καθὼς ὑμῖν παρηγγείλαμεν), including, interestingly enough, the need to live quietly, to mind one's own affairs, and to do manual labor. The noun, παραγγελία, appears in Paul only in 1 Thessalonians 4:2, οἴδατε γὰρ τίνας παραγγελίας ἐδώκαμεν ὑμῖν, which introduces the exhortations.

In 2 Thessalonians, we find four instances of παραγγέλλω. Three of these instances refer explicitly to the παράδοσις of working for one's own keep (2 Thess. 3:6, 10, 12). The last of these is joined with παρακαλοῦμεν and the command is given ἐν κυρίῳ Ἰησοῦ Χριστοῦ. This is the solemn exhortation to the "disorderly" to live in quiet self-sufficiency. The fourth reference is more general, πεποίθαμεν δὲ ἐν κυρίῳ ἐφ' ὑμᾶς, ὅτι ἃ παραγγέλλομεν [καὶ] ποιεῖτε καὶ ποιήσετε (2 Thess. 3:4). Again, the reference is to the παράδοσις which guarantees the congregation's salvation.

Therefore, the παράδοσις in 2 Thessalonians is whatever the author (or the author-as-Paul) commands, and it is conveyed through word or letter (2 Thess. 2:15, 3:14). It is the basis for the congregation's status at the parousia[31]. In 1 Thessalonians, by way of contrast, the status of the congregation at the parousia depends upon ἁγιωσύνη (1 Thess. 3:13); indeed, the congregation is called in holiness (1 Thess. 4:7). This is not only holiness in contrast to δικαιωσύνη, but also in contrast to ὑπακοή, the primary concern in 2 Thessalonians (cf. 2 Thess. 3:14).

Connected to this concern with obedience to a tradition in 2 Thessalonians is the connotation of the key word πίστις in the letter. The word appears five times, in 2 Thessalonians 1:3, 4, 11; 2:13; and 3:2b. The last of these, 3:2b, appears as the first term of a contrast completed in 3:3a: οὐ γὰρ πάντων ἡ πίστις, πιστὸς δέ ἐστιν ὁ κύριος.... The contrast is obviously between men and God, i.e., God is faithful, but faithfulness is not everyone's. Πίστις here should be interpreted "faithfulness". "Faithfulness" is, of course, also in contrast to ἀποστασία understood as rebellion or disloyalty to one's political or religious superior. Forcing someone to apostasize is the intention of persecution; one persecutes the members of a religious group in the hope they will prove disloyal to their religion or their god. This was the intention, for example, of the persecution of the Jews under Antiochus Epiphanes, and of the Christians under Trajan[32]. For this reason, it is also appropriate to interpret πίστις as "faithfulness" in 2 Thessalonians 1:4, the more so since it is joined to ὑπομονή in the context of persecution (ἐν πᾶσιν τοῖς διωγμοῖς ὑμῶν καὶ ταῖς θλίψεσιν αἷς ἀνέχεσθε). Milligan rejects this "passive" sense of πίστις here on the grounds that it is rare in Paul, and on the basis of the active sense in

---

[31] Ibid.
[32] Cf. 1 Macc. 1:41-51, 2:15-18; 2 Macc. 6:1-9; Pliny, *Ep.* 10. 97.

the immediately preceding verse, 2 Thessalonians 1:3[33]. However, since the sense of "faithfulness" seems entirely defensible in 2 Thessalonians 1:4, we may see whether this sense is consistent with the intention of 2 Thessalonians 1:3 as well. The difficulty is that πίστις indicates a possession, "faith", and a virtue, "faithfulness", or, to put it another way, an "interior" disposition and an "exterior" basis of action.

Much the same may be said of ἀγάπη or its English equivalent, "love". In 2 Thessalonians 1:3, the ἀγάπη for which the congregation is commended is an active virtue, ἡ ἀγάπη ἑνὸς ἑκάστου πάντων ὑμῶν εἰς ἀλλήλους, rather than "love" as a theological virtue (cf. 1 Cor. 13:13). Because of the implied parallel with πίστις, we might reasonably interpret this too as an active virtue with an exterior object, i.e., "faithfulness". "Faithfulness" expressed in obedience to the tradition is of course the primary virtue in 2 Thessalonians. For this reason, we may take ἔργον πίστεως ἐν δυνάμει as "work of faithfulness in power", complementing "resolve of goodness" as an active virtue which gives rise to practical results.

In 2 Thessalonians 2:13, the Thessalonians are said to be chosen for salvation ἐν ἁγιασμῷ πνεύματος καὶ πίστει ἀληθείας. Again we have parallel construction, which means the two genitives should be taken in the same way. If we take them as genitives of the efficient cause[34], the parallel phrase would be rendered, "in sanctification by the Spirit and faith by the truth". The second half of this phrase, however, the part with which we are concerned, makes no great sense. If we take the genitives as objective, we render the phrase, "santification having the spirit for its object, and faithfulness having the truth as its object". This makes good sense, whether we take πίστις as "faith" (thus, "belief in the truth") or "faithfulness" (thus, "loyalty to the truth"). Indeed, this phrase stands in contrast to the preceding verse, which speaks of πάντες οἱ μὴ πιστεύσαντες τῇ ἀληθείᾳ ἀλλὰ εὐδοκήσαντες τῇ ἀδικίᾳ (2 Thess. 2:12). Here, πιστεύω is contrasted with εὐδοκέω, "to be pleased with, take delight in". This notion of pleasing oneself with unrighteousness (cf. Rom. 1:32) contrasts not with believing in the truth, but with remaining loyal to the truth, being faithful to it despite the attractions of wickedness. This sense of πιστεύω is operative in 2 Thessalonians 2:11 as well, where God sends a "power of deception" to the wicked εἰς τὸ πιστεῦσαι αὐτοὺς τῷ ψεύδει. The ruin of the wicked is that they are faithful not to the truth, but to a lie.

The emphasis in the letter on obedience, on command, and on the tradition which the congregation has received, compels us to understand πίστις in all five occurrences in 2 Thessalonians as "faithfulness". "Faith" is directed to-

---

[33] Milligan, *Thessalonians*, p. 87.
[34] Ibid., p. 107.

ward a tradition, an instruction, or a religion. Of course, this sense of πίστις is out of keeping with its most common meaning in Paul. Indeed, it is difficult to see how Paul's thought could develop from concern with πίστις as "faithfulness" to a tradition, even in persecution, to a concern with πίστις as "faith" in the Lord Jesus Christ as that which brings the believer δικαιωσύνη. But it is "faithfulness" which is the opposite of the rebellion of the ἀποστασία, and so must be the meaning of πίστις in 2 Thessalonians.

The last of the major tendencies in 2 Thessalonians which set it apart from 1 Thessalonians is its use of "descriptive" rather than "performative" language. What is active and stylistically vivid in 1 Thessalonians is removed one step and rendered reflective in 2 Thessalonians. For example, the "performative" phrase εὐχαριστοῦμεν τῷ θεῷ in 1 Thessalonians 1:2, 2:13 is replaced by the "descriptive" liturgical phrase εὐχαριστεῖν ὀφείλομεν in 2 Thessalonians 1:3, 2:13. 2 Thessalonians 1:11-12 describes the prayer the author offers on behalf of the Thessalonians, but the prayer is not "performed" as it is in 1 Thessalonians 1:2, μνείαν ποιούμενοι ἐπὶ τῶν προσευχῶν ἡμῶν. As mentioned above, the "greeting" of 2 Thessalonians 3:17 is not a "greeting" in the proper sense, but rather a comment upon the epistolary habit of greeting, ὁ ἀσπασμὸς τῇ ἐμῇ χειρί. We may contrast the real command of greeting in 1 Thessalonians 5:26, which includes a specific action of greeting among the Thessalonians, the "holy kiss". This tendency of the author of 2 Thessalonians to step back from his writing and comment, in effect, upon what he is doing as a letter writer, sets 2 Thessalonians apart from 1 Thessalonians and the other genuine Pauline epistles.

We may now examine the epistolary postscript at greater length. As we said in the first chapter, the greeting of 2 Thessalonians 3:17 is a self-conscious mark of authentication, intended to validate the entire contents of the letter. The σημεῖον is either the signature Παύλου or the autographic addition as a whole. Although Paul sometimes added an explicit autograph to his letters (cf. 1 Cor. 16:21, Gal. 6:11, Phlm. 19), in each case it fulfilled a specific function, a function other than mere authentication (cf. Gal. 5:2)[35]. Therefore we cannot assume that Paul made some sort of addition in his own hand to every one of his letters. The practice would be purposeless unless it were made explicit in the text of the letter, since the great majority of those whom Paul addressed were listeners rather than readers; a note made personal only by the handwriting in which it was added would be as invisible to them as to us. We therefore cannot assume that those who received his letters would expect an autographic note.

The presence of a similar autographic greeting in Colossians, however, is of interest. Like the greeting in 2 Thessalonians, this "greeting" has no function

---

[35] See the exegesis of 3:17 in chap. 1.

within the letter other than to provide an autographic addition. Like the greeting in 2 Thessalonians, it merely serves to authenticate the letter as a whole. We therefore have the interesting possibility that other pseudepigraphers were familiar with the same σημεῖον as the author of 2 Thessalonians, if indeed Colossians is pseudonymous. Paul's practice of including a personal note in his letters must therefore have been well known, if not a cliché of the apostle's legend. Hurd writes, "The audacity of 2 Thessalonians 3:17 from the pen of anyone but Paul must be taken as evidence for the genuineness of the letter"[36]. In fact, a survey of the practice of pseudepigraphy in the Hellenistic world indicates that "audacity" in the pursuit of verisimilitude was common. "Personal" notes and references appear regularly[37]. However, the inclusion of the "signature" in 2 Thessalonians 3:17 does make the author's intentions clear: he wished his letter to be accepted as the work of Paul himself.

The self-conscious authentication provided by the postscript is further support for the conclusion we must now draw. We have found five major tendencies in 2 Thessalonians which set it apart, despite a host of similarities, from 1 Thessalonians. These are: (1) the strong emphasis throughout the letter upon the apocalyptic future; (2) the exaltation of the figure of Christ and the consequent eclipse of the Father; (3) the strong emphasis on the "tradition" as the basis for salvation and a consequent use of commands by the author to enforce the tradition; (4) the use of πίστις throughout the letter in the sense of "faithfulness" to the tradition; and (5) the shift from "performative" language in 1 Thessalonians to "descriptive" language in 2 Thessalonians, representing a self-consciousness best exemplified by the postscript of 2 Thessalonians 3:17. These tendencies not only set 2 Thessalonians apart from 1 Thessalonians, but from the other genuine Pauline epistles as well, without even taking into account the peculiar apocalyptic scenario of 2 Thessalonians. Therefore, it appears we must attribute the letter to some author other than Paul. In the following two chapters we shall attempt to discover more of the author's particular world-view and his intentions in writing, and thereby to discover the place of 2 Thessalonians within the Pauline tradition.

---

[36] Hurd, "Authenticity", p. 19.
[37] Donelson, *Pseudepigraphy*, pp. 7–66.

Chapter III

The Eschatology of 2 Thessalonians

In the previous two chapters, we analyzed the structure and argument of 2 Thessalonians and then compared this structure and argument with that of 1 Thessalonians. However, we gave comparatively little attention to the eschatological content of 2 Thessalonians. Although we mentioned the heightened apocalyptic interest as one of the "trends" indicating deutero-Pauline authorship, at that time we neither investigated the apocalyptic material itself nor indicated how the particular approach to eschatology in 2 Thessalonians might indicate an origin in the thought of the second Christian generation. It is to this work that we must now turn. In this chapter we shall investigate the nature and function of the eschatological material in 2 Thessalonians, and in the last chapter we shall see how this material helps to identify the *Sitz im Leben* of the letter, and its place in the Pauline tradition.

The second chapter of 2 Thessalonians is usually considered by commentators to be the most important portion of the letter. It contains what we have styled an "apocalyptic scenario" which includes elements unique in New Testament eschatology. The problems of its interpretation are rendered more difficult by its incomplete or awkward sentences, obscure references to matters apparently understood only by the author and the congregation, and a muddled chronology of the events it portrays. These problems are all the more vexing since the chapter is usually believed to bear the burdens of the author's intention in writing; he is assumed to have written the letter specifically to dampen apocalyptic expectation in the congregation by narrating a series of events which must take place before the second advent of the Lord Jesus. Like almost every example of apocalyptic thought in the New Testament, the second chapter of 2 Thessalonians has been examined or discounted according to the doctrinal interests of the scholars who have studied it, and despite a good deal of scholarly consensus, there is much that remains obscure. At the very least, all would agree that the apocalyptic scenario in 2 Thessalonians 2 is unique among those letters attributed to Paul.

As provocative as the second chapter might be, however, both from an exegetical and a doctrinal standpoint, it must not be considered in isolation from the rest of 2 Thessalonians. Indeed, it is only within the context of the letter as a whole that the second chapter may be properly understood. The reasons for this must be plainly evident. As our rhetorical analysis has shown, the apocalyptic scenario fills a particular function as part of the argument of the letter in its entirety. It is presented as "proof" that the Day of the Lord has not yet come, and thus serves to undermine the spiritual authority of the ἄτακτοι as it establishes and validates the authority of the author. This authority in turn enables him to establish order and "peace" in the congregation, which is the intention of the letter[1]. Thus the apocalyptic scenario is not the primary content of the letter. Nor is it the only eschatological portion of the letter; the ἔνδειγμα, which introduces it in verses 1:5-10, is also an expression of the author's eschatology, however traditional its content. The eschatological material is intended to serve a particular function within the letter, a function which is not necessarily the same as that which such material might serve in another context, or in isolation.

In addition, we must consider the relationship between the eschatological material of 2 Thessalonians and that of 1 Thessalonians 4:13-5:11, which should serve to clarify the intention of the former. Since we have seen that 2 Thessalonians is a "commentary" on some of the content, particularly the eschatological content, of 1 Thessalonians, we must discover to what extent the one provoked the composition of the other.

We shall proceed by first reviewing the main points of our earlier exegesis of 2 Thessalonians 1:5-10, the ἔνδειγμα of the *narratio*. We shall then investigate the apocalyptic scenario of the second chapter in a verse-by-verse exegesis, keeping in mind the place of the scenario within the letter. Last we shall deal at greater length with several ideas introduced in the scenario, as a means of further explicating and validating our exegesis.

We have previously analyzed 2 Thessalonians 1:5-10 in terms of its function within the letter's argument. In this particular case, the ἔνδειγμα belongs to a specific literary genre, the "episode in the Last Judgment"[2]. One of the features of this genre is that it is composed of and supposes knowledge of traditional material about the judgment; its function within a given composition depends upon the audience's understanding of the process of judgment as an event. In the case of 2 Thessalonians 1:5-10, parallel material may be found in Isaiah 2:10, 19, 21; 66:15-16; Jeremiah 10:25; Zechariah 14:5; Psalms 79:5-7. These are all references to God sitting in judgment, but in 2 Thessalonians 1:5-10, the role of judge is filled by Christ. As noted earlier, this shift in the traditional material is underlined by the theophanous language used in connection with Jesus Christ[3]. It should be kept in mind that Jesus is not always

---

[1] See our discussion of the *peroratio* in chap. 1.
[2] Betz, *Essays*, pp. 125–27.
[3] See our exegesis of 1:6-8 in chap. 1.

depicted as judge in the New Testament, but often appears in the role of intercessor for humanity before God as judge[4]. In the scene in 2 Thessalonians 1:5-10, the role of intercessor is filled by the author on the congregation's behalf (2 Thess. 1:7a, 10b)[5].

The primary point of this scene from the Last Judgment is the reversal of fortune for the good and the wicked. Initially "the righteous judgment of God" is demonstrated by the assurance that the members of the congregation will be made worthy of the kingdom of God, although this assurance is to some extent unstated. It is assumed that this is the nature of the requital, and this is the proof of "the righteous judgment of God" (1:5). This point is emphasized by the rhetorical conditional, "If it is indeed right for God to give back affliction to those who afflict you, and to you who are afflicted, rest with us..." (1:6-7a). This reversal of fortune seems to require the present suffering of the faithful, since this is what renders them worthy of the kingdom: they suffer for its sake (1:5b). There are actually two ideas at work here: first, the idea of becoming "worthy of the Kingdom" through suffering for it[6], and second, the different but related idea of receiving the opposite of one's present lot in the world to come[7]. However, neither idea appears in the scene itself; there both the characterizations of the wicked and the good and their respective fates are different. In the scene proper, the wicked are "those who do not know God and those who do not obey the gospel of our Lord Jesus", which is not directly relevant to their punishment of "eternal destruction from the face of the Lord and from the glory of his might" (2 Thess. 1:9). In the same way, the good are "his holy ones" and "those who believed", but their reward is not directly related to this characterization. In other words, the scene proper is not directly relevant to the point the author appears to be making; the specific situation of the persecuted and their persecutors gives place to the much more general idea of the good and wicked in general. This would seem to support our contention that the scene proper (1:7b-10) is composed of traditional material without consideration of the details for its use within the letter. This is not to say that the author has taken over written material from some other literary source, but that the traditional nature of the material is more responsible for its form here than the specific use for which the author included it.

Granted, then, that the material in "the scene from the last Judgment" is traditional, this fact should not prevent us from considering it as part of the author's eschatological schema. As mentioned above, such material is useful

---

[4] E.g., Betz's interpretation of Matt. 25:31-46, *Essays*, pp. 142–48.

[5] See our exegesis of these passages in chap. 1.

[6] Cf. Matt. 10:16-22, 34-39 and parallels; Matt. 5:10-12 and parallels; Rom. 5:3-5; 2 Cor. 1:3-7, 11:23-33; 1 Thess. 1:4-7, 2:14, 3:3-4; Rev. 2:9-11, 3:8-13, 6:9-11, 7:13-17.

[7] Cf. Matt. 5:4, 19:30, 20:16; Luke 13:30; Matt. 20:25-28 and parallels; Mark 10:31; Luke 6:21, 25-26, 16:25; James 5:1-6.

precisely because it is well known to both author and reader, and it is not necessary to fill in all the details of the scene in order for it to be understood. But this means that its validity as a vision of the future is accepted by both the author and, by implication, his readers. Therefore it is legitimate to include the scene of 1:7b-10 (and indeed, all of 1:5-10) in our consideration of the eschatology of 2 Thessalonians.

It is clear that Jesus, rather than God himself, is the eschatological judge in this scene, and that the role of intercessor for the congregation is filled by the author-as-Paul (1:8b-9; 10b). Reward and punishment are conceived of specifically in terms of proximity to the Lord (i.e., Jesus), with the ideas of "destruction" (ὄλεθρος) and, implicitly, blessedness a result of that proximity (cf. 1:9). Recompense, then, is a result of the Lord Jesus accepting someone into, or rejecting someone from, his presence[8]. As remarked above, the specific situation of persecutor and persecuted is generalized into a universal dualism between evil and good, whose respective fates are destruction and, again implicitly, blessing. This shift to a dualistic point of view is a typical trait of apocalyptic literature, which envisions all of humanity divided into only two camps, the damned and the saved[9].

The parousia, according to this scene, will be manifested with traditional theophanous phenomena (1:7b-8a), and its consequences will be universally felt. Its primary purpose is judgment (1:8b-9), more specifically the judgment of the wicked, and the glorification of the Lord by the faithful (1:10). The abiding metaphor for the scene is forensic, since it speaks of judgment, punishment, righteousness, and retribution.

We may see, then, that there is little in this scene of judgment which we do not find elsewhere in the New Testament, and that the most notable feature is probably the primacy of Jesus as the judge who is described in theophanous terms. This scene then serves as the background against which the more elaborate action of the apocalyptic scenario of the second chapter is acted out. We will do well to bear this scene of the Last Judgment in mind as we proceed to the second chapter, as our author undoubtedly intended us to do.

In view of the great amount of attention that has been devoted to 2 Thessalonians 2:1-12 by the commentators and other scholars, and the wide variety

---

[8] Matt. 7:21-23, 13:36-43, 25:1-13, 31-46; Luke 13:23-30, 23:42-43; Rom. 5:1-2, 8:31-39; 1 Cor. 15:21-28; Phil. 1:19-23; 1 Thess. 4:15-18.

[9] David Syme Russell, *The Method and Message of Jewish Apocalyptic* (Philadelphia: Westminster, 1964), pp. 266–71; John J. Collins, "Towards the Morphology of a Genre", in *Apocalypse: The Morphology of a Genre*, ed. idem, Semeia 14 (Missoula, Mont.: Scholars Press, 1974), pp. 1–9; Harold H. Rowley, *The Relevance of Apocalyptic*, 3d ed. (London: Lutterworth Press, 1963), pp. 174–75; Paul D. Hanson, *The Dawn of Apocalyptic* (Philadelphia: Fortress, 1975), pp. 396–97.

of theories advanced about its different points, it seems wisest to proceed with a systematic exegesis of the passage. This will necessarily entail some repetition of points raised in the first chapter and dealing with rather involved identifications and interpretive exposition in the course of a verse-by-verse exegesis, but the only alternative appears to be dealing with such things separately, and therefore to a certain extent out of context. The author, after all, dealt with these matters in the order which he felt would lead most easily to their proper understanding, and we may best proceed by following his lead. There will be certain points which will require further investigation, and these will be examined after the exegetical work proper.

After the introductory example of "the scene from the Last Judgment" in the ἔνδειγμα (1:5-10), there follows what appears to be an exhortatory section. There is the formula ἐρωτῶμεν δὲ ὑμᾶς, followed by the direct address, ἀδελφοί. However, the behavior enjoined on the readers is not a moral behavior, but rather one linked to a perception of a point of doctrine. That is, the readers are exhorted not to be "quickly shaken from your convictions" and not to be upset. However, such an "exhortation" does not depend upon the moral decision of those addressed. Rather, if they are not to be upset or moved from their convictions, it must be because they know that those convictions are correct; they must be persuaded of the truth of what they believe, and the falsity of any attack on that belief. But this is not a moral problem; it is a problem of doctrinal understanding. The intention of the exhortation is to forestall disquiet of mind (i.e., an interior disposition) caused by a false proclamation by proving that the proclamation is indeed false. It is not a moral exhortation, in spite of the formula, but a doctrinal exhortation, that is, a command to adhere to the tradition as the author presents it.

The exhortation appears to introduce the subject of the *probatio*, ἡ παρουσία τοῦ κυρίου ἡμῶν Ἰησοῦ Χριστοῦ καὶ ἡμῶν ἐπισυναγωγὴ ἐπ' αὐτόν. However, the "gathering together" does not enter into the question as developed in the rest of the chapter. Rather, as we discover in the second verse, the subject of the *probatio* is the denial of the false proclamation, ἐνέστηκεν ἡ ἡμέρα τοῦ κυρίου. To what then does ἡ παρουσία κτλ. refer? It is the subject of the *probatio* in the more general sense of the sort of problem being investigated. That is, the *probatio* deals with some part of the eschatological process which will culminate in the parousia and the events associated with it. The inclusion of ἡμῶν ἐπισυναγωγή in this context, where it is not relevant, indicates that this whole idea of παρουσία and ἐπισυναγωγή has become a dogmatic *locus*, a traditional way of referring to the events of the end. We may see the origin of this *locus* in the Pauline tradition in 1 Thessalonians 4:13-18, where the idea is fully developed, apparently for the first time. We find the same idea in Mark 13:27 (including the verb ἐπισυνάγω) and Matthew 24:31. It also appears to be behind the description of the Lord being glorified by the saved in 2 Thessalonians 1:10, where οἱ ἅγιοι and πάντες οἱ πιστεύσαντες presumably refer to the redeemed faithful. We may see then how the "live" topic of the "gathering together" of the faithful in 1 Thessalonians 4:13-18 has become an accepted way of referring to the eschatological process in general, whether or not the specific idea is actually present. This is a part of the result of Paul's writings becoming a "tradition".

In brief, then, the first verse of the second chapter introduces the general subject of the *probatio* by means of an exhortation formula. But the exhortation is concerned with a traditional doctrinal *locus* rather than genuine moral instruction. Already we may see how our author considers doctrine and ethics to be inextricably intertwined.

The second verse makes clear the real subject of the *probatio*: the denial of the false proclamation concerning the Day of the Lord. The exhortation introduced in the previous verse provides the subject by negation, since only the disproof of a disturbing message can effectively remove the disquiet it may cause. The exhorted behavior depends upon a correct doctrinal understanding, and since only the author is able to provide that understanding, the exhorted behavior really depends upon him, and not those he addresses. Their desired action is a passive one, that of accepting his explanation as a faithful interpretation of the "tradition" both parties share.

What is of immediate interest is the false proclamation, ἐνέστηκεν ἡ ἡμέρα τοῦ κυρίου. The emphasis by position is upon the verb, ἐνίστημι (cf. 2 Cor. 6:2); therefore, the emphasis is on the arrival, rather than upon what has arrived. We may translate, "It has come, the Day of the Lord" (cf. Luke 4:21). The emphasis upon "arrival" suggests that this is a real proclamation, and the author's slightly deprecating reference to it by use of ὡς ὅτι indicates that this was in fact the proclamation of the "disordered" element in the congregation. The author is, after all, attempting to prove a negative, which suggests that his opponents were promoting the positive message within the congregation. But if this is so, we must discover just what was meant by those who preached that "the Day of the Lord is here".

The term "the Day of the Lord" is a common one in the books of the prophets. Although there is some dispute over the origins of the term[10], it was apparently already a familiar concept before its use by Amos. In Amos 5:18-20, the prophet refutes the popular conception of the *yôm YHWH* as a day of deliverance for Israel by asserting, "it is darkness, not light" (Amos 5:18c, cf.

---

[10] Sigmund Mowinckel, *He That Cometh*, trans. G.W. Anderson (New York/Nashville: Abingdon Press, 1954), proposes that the term originated in the cult, specifically in the New Year's festival; Gerhard von Rad, "The Origin of the Concept of the Day of Yahweh", *Journal of Semitic Studies* 4 (1959): 97–108, finds the term's origins in the idea of the holy war.

20a). It is a day when the Lord will show his wrath against his enemies, both among the nations and among his own people (Ezek. 7:1-27, Zeph. 1:7-18). Sometimes the term is applied to specific historical events in the past (cf. Lam. 1:12, 2:1, 21-22), but most often it refers to a future event (Isa. 2:12-17, 13:1-22, 34:1-17, 61:1-3; Ezek. 30:1-9; Obad. 15-21). In the descriptions of the Day of the Lord, the Lord is depicted as taking vengeance, showing his wrath, and exacting punishment against the wicked. The Lord is thus making a judgment against them, but the emphasis is decidedly upon the execution of that judgment through punishment. It is not surprising that the Day of the Lord formed a major part of the developing eschatology of the post-exilic prophets (Joel 1-4, Zech. 14:1-21, Mal. 3:13-4:6). Although this was a day of wrath, it also offered an occasion for repentance (Zeph. 2:1-3, Joel 2:12-17), with the offer of a blessing afterwards (Joel 2:18-32).

The term is rare in the pseudepigraphic literature[11], in part perhaps because of the increasing belief in the sanctity of the name of God, although this would not explain its absence in Greek works, for example. Other terms began to take its place[12], most notably "day of judgment"[13], which emphasizes the purely forensic aspect of judgment and punishment. This shift in terminology, however, also reflects a change in the concept it describes, and the day of judgment is thus a different eschatological concept than the Day of the Lord. The use of the latter term by Paul and his contemporaries would appear to be derived from its use in the Old Testament rather than from any pseudepigraphical apocalyptic work, simply because the term does not appear in the later works. It is reasonable, therefore, to regard "the Day of the Lord" as a technical term which refers specifically to the "day" when God will manifest his wrath upon the unbelieving nations and upon those among his own people who have proven unfaithful.

The apparent distinction in the Jewish literature between "the Day of the Lord" and "the day of judgment" should alone dissuade us from assuming that the message of the "disorderly" was "the parousia of Jesus Christ is here". The author of 2 Thessalonians has already described the parousia of Christ in the forensic terms of "the scene from the Last Judgment" in 1:5-10, but also in

---

[11] I have found it only in 2 Enoch (J) 18:6, in the translation by Francis I. Andersen in *Old Testament Pseudepigrapha*, vol. 1: *Apocalyptic Literature and Testaments*, ed. J.H. Charlesworth (Garden City, N.Y.: Doubleday and Co., 1983). 2 Enoch is preserved in Slavonic and is dated by Andersen to the late first century of the Christian era, and so cannot be cited as an influence on Paul or his early followers.

[12] Among these were "day of tribulation", Test. Levi 5:5, 2 Esdras 16:74, 1 Enoch 98:10; "day of destruction", 1 Enoch 98:10; "your day", 2 Baruch 48:47, 49:2; "day which Israel trusts", Test. Dan 6:4; "day of the Mighty One", 2 Baruch 55:4-8; and numerous references to "those days" and "last days".

[13] Cf. Test. Levi 1:1, 3:2, 3; 2 Esdras 7:38, 102, 104, 113, 12:34; 1 Enoch 97:3, 98:8, 10, 99:15.

theophanous terms familiar from the Old Testament. As explained above, the author assumed that the traditional material used to describe the parousia and subsequent judgment represented a common ground for both his readers and himself. This means that he believed that he shared with them a conception of the parousia as "the day of judgment": the advent of Christ would be manifest and unmistakable[14], judgment would be passed in a heavenly tribunal, and finally punishment and reward would be meted out (1:8-10).

This conception of the parousia, which the author believed he shared with his readers, is simply not compatible with the proclamation of the ἄτακτοι. The very fact of their proclamation indicates that the Day of the Lord was present in some "hidden" way, so that only the spiritually perceptive could discern its presence. The identification of a present, historical reality with a "mythic" concept such as the Day of the Lord indicates that its "mythic" quality has become overshadowed by its historical manifestation. The fall of Jerusalem to the Babylonians could be described as "the Day of the Lord" in Lamentations 1:12, 2:1, 21-22 because this was a means of understanding its theological meaning for God's people[15]. The same is true of the proclamation of the ἄτακτοι, except that it defines the present as a particular episode in the eschatological drama, manifested in present historical reality. The parousia, however, is not subject to this sort of metaphorical application to the present. It is, according to our author, manifest and unmistakable, the consummation of history rather than an event within history. The parousia is more closely related to the forensic conception of the day of judgment than to the military conception of the Day of the Lord. Nor are these merely different metaphors for the same idea, such as the manifestation of judgment. The Day of the Lord, as we have seen, can be understood as being manifested in history; the judgment which follows the parousia of the Lord Jesus Christ, by virtue of its essential meaning as the consummation of history, cannot.

The message of the "disorderly" appears to have been an example of what David Aune styles the "salvation-judgment oracle"[16], insofar as it announces the historical arrival of a particular stage in the apocalyptic drama. The very act of proclamation assumes that some sort of human response is necessary; the presence of the Day of the Lord is a "crisis" to which the hearers are called to react. What this reaction should be would be determined by one's understanding of what "the Day of the Lord" was, that is, by what sort of historical crisis it was believed to represent.

We must make our meaning clear. It must be recalled that the ἄτακτοι in

---

[14] We may compare Mark 13:24-27, Matt. 24:27-28, and Luke 17:24.

[15] A. Joseph Everson, "The Days of Yahweh", *Journal of Biblical Literature* 93 (1974): 329–37.

[16] David Aune, *Prophecy in Early Christianity and the Ancient Mediterranean World* (Grand Rapids, Mich.: William B. Eerdmans Publishing Co., 1983), pp. 93, 118–21, 322–23.

proclaiming this message, were not announcing a future event, but an interpretation of the present: "This time in which we now live is the apocalyptic Day of the Lord." It is in this sense that the crisis designated by the term "the Day of the Lord" was "historical"; it was used to refer to the very time in which the message was proclaimed. This understanding of the present as the apocalyptic "Day" requires an adjusted perception of the present on the part of those who accept the proclamation, i.e., a human response. As we have indicated, this response would be determined by one's understanding of the "crisis" that "the Day of the Lord" represented. However, from the admonition the author of 2 Thessalonians gives in 2:1-2, it would appear that the response of at least some of those who heard the message was distress and confusion. The message that they were indeed experiencing the time known as "the Day of the Lord" brought them neither peace nor comfort[17].

This is not to say that "the Day of the Lord" was understood by the Pauline congregations as an "historical" rather than a "mythic" event[18], but only that their own present history was being given its "true" significance by its identification with the "mythic" concept of "the Day of the Lord". Borrowing a phrase from Hebrews 9:9a, we may say the phrase is παραβολὴ εἰς τὸν καιρὸν τὸν ἐνεστηκότα; it equates the "mythic" with the "historical".

Therefore, the Day of the Lord, as far as those who preached its presence were concerned, was an "historical" event rather than an "a-historical" or "mythic" one, that is, it represented an event in history which would demand some sort of human response. The parousia of Christ, on the other hand, is presented as an "a-historical" or "mythic" event, since it will require no human response; by the time of the parousia, all fates will have been decided, and no prophet will have to announce that it has arrived.

We have proceeded in this evaluation of the meaning of the proclamation, "the Day of the Lord is here", on the assumption that the "opposition" to the author of 2 Thessalonians represented by the ἄτακτοι also regarded itself as Pauline[19]. However, it may be that the ἄτακτοι were inspired by another tradition, or that they exploited some element in the Pauline tradition of which we are unaware. Therefore it is possible that the proclamation, "the

---

[17] We may perhaps compare their reaction with the sorrow of Baruch upon hearing about the judgment of "the day of the Mighty One", 2 Bar. 55:4-8.

[18] Our use of these terms is drawn from their use by Frank Moore Cross in *Canaanite Myth and Hebrew Epic* (Cambridge, Mass.: Harvard University Press, 1973).

[19] This assumption seems reasonable, since the author apparently regards them as members of the Pauline congregations (3:1-5, 15) and admonishes them in Paul's name (3:12). In addition, the use of 1 Thessalonians as a model for the letter and the reference to a letter "as if from us" (2:2b) make it likely that a "misinterpretation" of Paul's teaching was involved in the preaching of the ἄτακτοι, perhaps a misinterpretation of 1 Thessalonians. If these people recognized Paul as an authority, of course, they were to that extent "Pauline".

Day of the Lord is here", reflected a radical reinterpretation of the Day of the Lord as somehow equivalent to the parousia of Christ. Such a reinterpretation would most likely be gnostic or proto-gnostic in character[20]. But this seems to us unlikely, in view both of the Pauline model for 2 Thessalonians and the author's assumption that he and his readers shared a common understanding of the terms they employed. Moreover, we shall see that the proclamation announcing the presence of the Day of the Lord is comprehensible and may be supported by exegesis when conceived of in the terms we have outlined above, as a crisis in history that demands a human response.

Now that we have examined how the preachers of this message interpreted it, we shall investigate how the author of 2 Thessalonians understood it. We may begin by looking at the nature of his response to the proclamation. He dismisses it as false, a source of deception (2:2-3a). He outlines an apocalyptic scenario of various events which will culminate in the parousia of Christ (2:3b-4, 6-8). He refers to previous instruction concerning this scenario (2:5). What does this form of argument tell us about the way he perceived the false proclamation of the ἄτακτοι?

First of all, the author did not understand the proclamation as meaning that the parousia of Jesus Christ was present. If he had, he would not have presented the traditional material of the "scene from the Last Judgment" as mutually acceptable, since that material depicts a manifest and unmistakable advent of Christ. If he believed the proclamation concerned the parousia, he would have argued from its manifest nature, pointing out that the various events associated with the parousia had not taken place. Even if he might not have argued in this way, he assuredly would not have assumed that he and his readers understood the same terms in the same way. But he makes just this assumption and his argument proceeds from that point. Instead, he argues in part from the manifest nature of the coming of the apocalyptic Antagonist (2:8-9).

Moreover, the author accepts the congregation's disquiet over the message of the false proclamation. He apparently agrees that, if the Day of the Lord were indeed present, it would be a reasonable cause for concern and anxiety. He does not offer παράκλησις in anticipation of the Day of the Lord, as Paul does in 1 Thessalonians 5:1-11, to the effect that its advent is of concern only for the wicked, since the good will be saved. Our author instead accepts that the Day of the Lord is a cause for concern, and seeks to disprove the contention that it is present and thus a cause for immediate concern. He would thus appear to understand the proclamation in the same way as those who pro-

---

[20] This position is supported by Walter Schmithals, *Paul and the Gnostics*, trans. John E. Steely (Nashville, Tenn.: Abingdon Press, 1972), pp. 123-218.

claimed it: as a message of an immediate historical crisis which, if true, demanded a response from the members of the congregation.

What then was the meaning of the proclamation ἐνέστηκεν ἡ ἡμέρα τοῦ κυρίου, as understood by the ἄτακτοι who proclaimed it and our author who attempts to disprove it? If we rule out, as we have, the equation of "the Day of the Lord" with the parousia of Jesus Christ, we must find some other possible meaning and test its suitability to the situation in the Thessalonian congregation as we understand it. Since both the author and his readers share the Pauline tradition, it seems most appropriate to look for the meaning of "the Day of the Lord" and related terms in the genuine epistles of Paul, and see if these are consistent with our understanding of the terms as used in the Jewish literature.

Paul uses a series of related phrases which all speak of a "day" belonging to the Lord Jesus Christ. His use of these phrases has led many scholars to assume that "the Lord" of "the Day of the Lord" is necessarily Jesus Christ, especially since Paul elsewhere refers to Jesus simply as "the Lord"[21]. But "the Day of the Lord", as we have seen, is a technical term in the Judeo-Christian tradition, and we must be careful to determine its exact use in Paul. The phrases which Paul employs to refer to a "day" of Jesus Christ are variants of ἡ ἡμέρα (τοῦ) (κυρίου) (ἡμῶν) (Ἰησοῦ) (Χριστοῦ). In 1 Corinthians 1:8, we find ἐν τῇ ἡμέρᾳ τοῦ κυρίου ἡμῶν Ἰησοῦ [Χριστοῦ] in association with τὴν ἀποκάλυψιν τοῦ κυρίου ἡμῶν Ἰησοῦ Χριστοῦ in 1:7. The idea in this passage is of the presentation of the congregation before the eschatological judge, either Jesus Christ or God, on the "day". In 2 Corinthians 1:14, we find the phrase ἐν τῇ ἡμέρᾳ τοῦ κυρίου [ἡμῶν] Ἰησοῦ. Here the reference is to the intended outcome of the apostle's instruction, mutual pride "on the day of the Lord Jesus". Once again, the idea is of the presentation of the congregation before the judge at the parousia. A similar phrase appears in Philippians 1:6, ἄχρι ἡμέρας Χριστοῦ Ἰησοῦ. The thought here is of God bringing the good work begun in the Philippian congregation to completion "at the day of Christ Jesus". The idea is of the status of the congregation at the time of judgment, when God's work in the congregation will be completed. Again in Philippians 1:10, we find the phrase εἰς ἡμέραν Χριστοῦ, in the wish that the congregation may be "pure and blameless" (εἰλικρινεῖς καὶ ἀπρόσκοποι) for the "day of Christ". The status of the congregation at its presentation at judgment is once again in mind. A slight change is found in the third use of a similar phrase in Philippians 2:16, εἰς ἡμέραν Χριστοῦ. The apostle is the one who is in mind here, but his status at judgment depends on the spiritual health of his congregation, which is proof that we "did not run in

---

[21] Cf. Rom. 14:6, 8-9, 16:3-13; 1 Cor. 2:8, 4:4-5, 6:13-14, 15-17; 2 Cor. 10:7-8, 12:8-9; Gal. 1:19; Phil. 2:29, 3:1, 4:4-5, 10; 1 Thess. 1:6, 4:15-17; Phlm. 20.

vain or labor in vain". In all of these instances, the idea is not just of the parousia, nor just of the judgment, but specifically of the status of the congregation at its presentation for judgment or, in Philippians 2:16, how their status will effect the standing of the apostle, i.e., it will determine whether or not he "labored in vain". It would appear, then, that this series of phrases naming the "day" of Jesus Christ has a very specific place in Paul's thought; it is the "day" when his congregations are presented before the eschatological judge as the fruits of Paul's labor, and, implicitly, accepted into the kingdom. We have found this same idea in operation in 2 Thessalonians, specifically with the "day" of the revelation of the Lord Jesus from heaven (2 Thess. 1:7, 10b). It would appear that our author was familiar with this concept of "the Day of the Lord Jesus" in Paul and knew exactly what it meant[22]. We may compare it with the term in the Pseudepigrapha, "day of judgment".

A similar phrase in Paul is ἡμέρα ὀργῆς καὶ ἀποκαλύψεως δικαιοκρισίας τοῦ θεοῦ, which appears in Romans 2:5. This phrase introduces a long description of how God "will render to every man according to his works", reward to the good, but "wrath and fury" to the wicked. The description culminates with another time reference, ἐν ἡμέρᾳ ὅτε κρίνει ὁ θεὸς τὰ κρυπτὰ τῶν ἀνθρώπων κατὰ τὸ εὐαγγέλιόν μου διὰ Χριστοῦ Ἰησοῦ (Rom. 2:16). The description emphasizes the "wrath and fury" attendant on God's judgment, and this of course is in keeping with its place in the argument of the letter. This "day of wrath" is essentially a theocentric vision of the final judgment.

It is difficult to classify 1 Corinthians 5:5 among these phrases speaking of a "day", since a major variant includes the name of Jesus along with the title "Lord": ἐν τῇ ἡμέρᾳ τοῦ κυρίου [Ἰησοῦ][23]. The thought behind the passage is of punishment; by means of his presence in the congregation by spirit (τοῦ ἐμοῦ πνεύματος!), Paul commands that the man guilty of incest be delivered to Satan "for the destruction of the flesh, that his spirit may be saved in the day of the Lord Jesus" (1 Cor. 5:5). This is a notoriously difficult

---

[22] Cf. the excursus in Jörg Baumgarten, *Paulus und die Apokalyptik*, Wissenschaftliche Monographien zum Alten und Neuen Testament 44 (Neukirchen: Neukirchener Verlag, 1975), pp. 64–65. Baumgarten fails to differentiate between ἡμέρα κυρίου (Ἰησοῦ) and ἡμέρα κυρίου.

[23] Most of the texts have some identification of κύριος with Jesus. The reading κύριος alone appears in Codex B and the Chester Beatty Papyrus (P[46]), and is the reading in both the Nestle-Aland (26th ed.) and the United Bible Society texts. Metzger writes, "The reading that best explains the origin of the other readings is κυρίου, well attested by early and important manuscripts and Fathers" (Bruce M. Metzger, *A Textual Commentary on the Greek New Testament* (New York: United Bible Societies, 1971), p. 550.) We would argue, however, that both ἡμέρα κυρίου and ἡμέρα κυρίου Ἰησοῦ and its variants are technical terms in Paul, and some thought should be given to the meaning of the term in context.

verse[24], but the idea seems to be that the destruction of the man's body (by death?) will result in the saving of his soul on "the day". The assumption appears to be that the man, cleansed by the destruction of his body, will be presented together with the whole congregation on the day of judgment. The whole church is to be presented, and the whole church is to be accepted (cf. 2 Cor. 11:2, Phil. 1:9-11; cf. Rom. 8:14-17).

The only clear reference in Paul to ἡμέρα κυρίου appears in 1 Thessalonians 5:2, αὐτοὶ γὰρ ἀκριβῶς οἴδατε ὅτι ἡμέρα κυρίου ὡς κλέπτης ἐν νυκτὶ οὕτως ἔρχεται. Paul makes no explicit connections between ἡ παρουσία τοῦ κυρίου in 1 Thessalonians 4:15b and ἡμέρα κυρίου in 5:2. There appears, however, to be some sort of "temporal" connection between them, since the progression of the exposition is from the parousia and the "gathering together" in 4:15-18 and the idea of "times and seasons" in 5:2. What are the characteristics of the Day of the Lord according to Paul? First, it will come "like a thief in the night" when all is declared to be well (1 Thess. 5:2b-3a). It may appear that this description is qualified by 1 Thessalonians 5:4, where the apostle tells his readers that they are not in the dark, ἵνα ἡ ἡμέρα ὑμᾶς ὡς κλέπτης καταλάβῃ. However, in view of the use of this same metaphor elsewhere (Luke 12:39-40, Rev. 3:3, 16:15), we may say that the metaphor of "the thief in the night" is used primarily to express the way the Day of the Lord will overtake the unwary (cf. Luke 12:39-40, Rev. 3:3). Paul shows his awareness of this metaphor by assuring the Thessalonians that they will not be taken unaware by the advent of the Day, but this is because their behavior at all times as "sons of the day" prepares them for it. This does not mean that they know when the Day of the Lord will come, but rather that they know they do not know[25]. Paul assures them that they will be prepared for it when it comes; the metaphor is shifted in order to sustain it.

The second characteristic of the Day of the Lord is related to the use of the metaphor of the thief in the night in 1 Thessalonians 5:4, that is, that the "wrath" of the Day is intended for the wicked and not for the faithful (1 Thess. 5:4-7). This leads to the third point, that the faithful can best prepare for the Day of the Lord, whenever it may come, by being wakeful and sober. More specifically, they are to "put on the breastplate of faith and love, and for

---

[24] Cf. Hans Conzelmann, *1 Corinthians. A Commentary on the First Epistle to the Corinthians*, trans. James W. Leitch, Hermeneia (Philadelphia: Fortress, 1975), pp. 97-98; see also the remarks on this verse by Adela Yarbro Collins, "The Function of 'Excommunication' in Paul", *Harvard Theological Review* 73 (1980): 251-63, and those of Archibald Robertson and Alfred Plummer, *A Critical and Exegetical Commentary on the First Epistle of St. Paul to the Corinthians*, 2nd ed. (Edinburgh: T. and T. Clark, 1914), pp. 99-100.

[25] This acknowledgement of the limits of one's knowledge stands in contrast to the presumption of the wicked, who often act against their knowledge, cf. Rom. 1:21, 32, 2:1-2, 17-24, 10:19-21; cf. 1 Cor. 3:16, 5:6, 6:2, 3, 9, 15, 16, 19.

a helmet the hope of salvation" (1 Thess. 5:8). The fourth characteristic of the Day of the Lord is thus that it involves warfare of some sort, since it is the opposite of εἰρήνη καὶ ἀσφάλεια as proclaimed by the wicked (1 Thess. 5:3a), and the faithful prepare by donning "spiritual armor" (1 Thess. 5:8). The overriding metaphor for the Day of the Lord in 1 Thessalonians is military, just as that for the parousia is forensic. This military metaphor is maintained in the non-apocalyptic version of this description of the Day of the Lord in Romans 13:11-14, even though the intention there is paraenetic; Paul still calls his readers to "put on the armor of light", Romans 13:12b.

Although Paul's use of ἡμέρα κυρίου in 1 Thessalonians 5:2 appears to be the source for its use in 2 Thessalonians 2:2, this does not necessarily mean that either the "disorderly" or the author of the letter understood the term in the same way as Paul. From what we have seen of Paul's use of this and related terms, we may make the following observations: (1) Paul spoke of the Day of the Lord Jesus Christ, when believers would be presented and accepted before the eschatological judge, presumably Christ. Paul's main concern in relation to this "Day" was that his congregation might be presented as he puts it in 2 Corinthians 11:2, "as a pure bride to her one husband". The spiritual purity of the congregation "on that Day" assured Paul that his work was not in vain (Phil. 2:16). The parousia was to be the consummation of human history and endeavor. The author of 2 Thessalonians was fully aware of Paul's use of this term, and himself refers to the "day", which he quite properly equates with the parousia (2 Thess. 1:7, 10). (2) Paul writes in Romans 2:5-16 of a "day of wrath" when God's righteous judgment will be revealed. It is conceived of primarily in terms of punishment for the wicked, although the good will be rewarded according to their deserts. This is a theocentric eschatology, with the emphasis on God's wrath. (3) "The Day of the Lord" appears in 1 Thessalonians 5:2. It is a day of wrath for the wicked, and will come suddenly, like a thief in the night, just when all appears to be peace and security (1 Thess. 5:3). It is no threat to the good, although to endure they must put on "spiritual armor" (1 Thess. 5:4-8).

We may see that these three really represent two "days", one the "day" of the Lord Jesus, the parousia, and the other a "day" of wrath against the wicked, which the good, with proper spiritual armament, will survive, to find a blessing afterwards. These two different "days" represent the failure of Paul to integrate fully the Old Testament idea of "the Day of YHWH" and of God as the eschatological judge with the Christian idea of collective acceptance of the congregation (and collective rejection of the wicked) on "the Day of Jesus Christ". It would be improper to force a false harmony on these two different concepts by arguing, for example, that the faithful perceive "the Day" as salvation and reward, while the wicked perceive it as wrath and punishment. The only concession Paul himself made to such a harmonization was that

"God has not destined us for wrath, but to obtain salvation through our Lord Jesus Christ" (1 Thess. 5:9; cf. 1 Thess. 1:10). But this is not to say that the process of "wrath" and the process of "salvation" are one and the same. This only indicates that "wrath" is not the final end of the faithful, not that "wrath" is really "salvation" for them. The fact that Paul uses the terms about "the Day of the Lord Jesus Christ" in one very particular way, and uses "the Day of the Lord" and "the day of wrath" in another particular way should dissuade us once and for all from confusing the two. The independent development of the concept in the Old Testament of "the Day of the Lord" on the one hand and of Jesus as the eschatological savior on the day of judgment on the other (cf. 1 Thess. 1:10) demonstrates the integrity of each concept. Each stands independently in Paul's thought because he failed to integrate them; rather, he restricted his exposition of the day of the Lord's wrath to his earliest and latest extant epistles. Elsewhere he speaks of his congregations' acceptance on the Day of the Lord Jesus Christ. How he felt "the Day of the Lord" as a day of wrath and of judgment was associated with the parousia we cannot say. There was some sort of association between them, but exactly what it was remains unknown[26].

Therefore, on the basis of the evidence from both the Old Testament and Paul's own use of the concept of the Day of the Lord, which was in turn based on that of the Old Testament, the readers might reasonably conclude that the Day of the Lord, which was to be part of the eschatological process, was a day of wrath. It was a necessary prerequisite to the parousia of Jesus Christ. But this idea provoked uneasiness both by the prospect of the wrath of God against the wicked being unleashed, and by the uncertainty over whether the steadfastness of the faithful to the tradition was sufficient to carry them through to the time of blessing. The author of 2 Thessalonians shares the belief that the Day of the Lord is a day of wrath that will precede the parousia of Christ. His scenario in 2 Thessalonians 2:1-12 is intended not only to demonstrate that the Day of the Lord has not yet arrived, but also to provide a sequence of events which include and extend from the present to the return of the Lord Jesus at the parousia.

---

[26] We should also make mention in this regard to 1 Cor. 15:20-28. Here Paul describes the events of the end in the light of the order of resurrection. Christ has risen as the firstfruits of resurrection, and those who belong to him will rise at his parousia (1 Cor. 15:23). Then comes the end, when Christ will deliver the kingdom to the Father (1 Cor. 15:24a). Before this, Christ will have destroyed "every rule and every authority and power"; when will this take place? The decisive triumph over the enemies of God occurred at the crucifixion (cf. 1 Cor. 2:6-8; see on this verse Conzelmann, *1 Corinthians*, pp. 269–75). The last enemy, death, is destroyed by the resurrection (1 Cor. 15:26). This is a description of the parousia through the use of military rather than forensic metaphors, but it still refers explicitly to the "a-historical" end, rather than the military conception of the Day of the Lord.

This scenario is presented in a tightly woven series of events in 2:3-10. Questions arise almost immediately after the warning against deception in 2:3a. What follows is the protasis of a conditional sentence, ἐὰν μὴ ἔλθῃ κτλ., without an apodosis to complete the sentence. Since the apodosis is not stated, we must assume it is the most obvious possibility, to wit, "the Day of the Lord has not come"[27]. The author is thus presenting a series of events, on the understanding that until these take place, the Day of the Lord has not yet come.

The first two of these events are ἡ ἀποστασία and the revelation of ὁ ἄνθρωπος τῆς ἀνομίας. Since we are dealing with a "chronological" series of events, at least insofar as these events must proceed in a certain order before the process culminates in the parousia, we may properly ask what the "temporal" relationship is between these two events. Since the adverb πρῶτον modifies the verb ἔλθῃ, and the second verb, ἀποκαλυφθῇ, is separated from the first verb and the adverb by the conjunctive καί, grammatically the adverb modifies only ἔλθῃ. The sense of πρῶτον, "first", is such that it appears to mean both that this event must precede the Day of the Lord, and that it must also precede the revelation of the Antagonist, ὁ ἄνθρωπος τῆς ἀνομίας. This means that ἡ ἀποστασία is not the result of the false signs of ὁ ἄνομος, described in 2:9-10, but that ἡ ἀποστασία leads up to the appearance of the Antagonist. Indeed, ἡ ἀποστασία is presented as parallel to the operation of τὸ κατέχον and τὸ μυστήριον τῆς ἀνομίας (2 Thess. 2:6-7), both phenomena active in the present; in the same way, the revelation of ὁ ἄνθρωπος τῆς ἀνομίας is temporally parallel to the removal of ὁ κατέχων and the appearance of ὁ ἄνομος. As we have seen in the first chapter[28], ἡ ἀποστασία in the sense both of religious and political rebellion, is already at work in the congregation in the activity of οἱ ἄτακτοι, who are spreading a false doctrine and rebelling against the authority of the author[29]. Not only is ἡ ἀποστασία operative in the present, it is at work in the Pauline congregations. The author thus interprets the present activity of rebellion in the

---

[27] Charles H. Giblin, *The Threat to Faith: An Exegetical and Theological Re-examination of 2 Thessalonians 2*, Analecta Biblica 31 (Rome: Pontifical Biblical Institute, 1967), pp. 122–39, reconstructs the apodosis as "the judgment of God will not have been executed against the powers of deception, removing them once and for all" (p. 135). This reconstruction is based both on the assumption of Pauline authorship and on the belief that the author did not wish to create a "timetable", but rather a set of circumstances for the parousia. However, under our exegesis, a "timetable" is what is required, since the author wishes his readers to understand where their own time fits into the eschatological process. This is quite separate from the point that the readers would most naturally understand the unstated apodosis as "the Day of the Lord will not come...."

[28] See our exegesis of 2:3 in chap. 1.

[29] von Dobschütz, *Die Thessalonicher-Briefe*, p. 281.

congregation as a part of the eschatological deception (2:3a), and demonstrates how the present fits into the apocalyptic schema.

We have already touched upon the figure of the Antagonist, who is given three different titles in 2:3b and 8a. What is the significance of these various apocalyptic titles? In the case of ὁ ἄνθρωπος τῆς ἀνομίας, we may see a connection with τὸ μυστήριον τῆς ἀνομίας in 2:7, uniting the two different "chronologies" of the events of the schema. The second title, ὁ υἱὸς τῆς ἀπωλείας, is taken by most commentators to refer to the destruction which is his inevitable fate[30], but there is also the idea of an "embodiment" of destruction; cf. John 17:12, 6:70. This second title is thus in reality an indication of the fate of the Antagonist, and follows immediately upon his identification by his first title, ὁ ἄνθρωπος τῆς ἀνομίας. By the same token, the introduction of the third title, ὁ ἄνομος, is also immediately followed by a description of the Antagonist's ultimate fate as ὃν ὁ κύριος ἀνελεῖ κτλ. (2:8b). It cannot be an accident that the two primary titles of the Antagonist (the titles which refer to his lawlessness) are both immediately followed by the affirmation of his destruction. For the author, the surest fact about this lawless figure is that he will be destroyed by Christ at his parousia. The intrusion of this information in 2:8b further obscures an already complicated chronology of events.

The distinction between the two primary titles of the Antagonist, ὁ ἄνθρωπος τῆς ἀνομίας and ὁ ἄνομος, may be a subtle difference between a person who is characterized by lawlessness, and one who is the embodiment of lawlessness. The latter title, ὁ ἄνομος, appears to refer not to one who is lawless, that is, one who disregards the law which he should obey, but one who is without law, as the Gentiles were without the law according to Jewish tradition (cf. Rom. 2:12-16). However, if the title ὁ ἄνομος were intended by the author to refer to the Gentile origins of the Antagonist, we should expect this title to be associated with the description of the blasphemy in the Temple in 2:4 rather than the false signs of 2:9-10. Committing blasphemy in the Temple was, after all, a prerogative of pagan rulers.

In the case of the description in 2:4, the apparent model for the figure of ὁ ἄνθρωπος τῆς ἀνομίας is Antiochus IV Epiphanes of Syria. We find a description of his career in Daniel 11:36-37; 1 Maccabees 1:20-24, 41-50, 54-59; and 2 Maccabees 5:11-21, 6:1-6, as well as Josephus, *Antiquities* 12:5-6. Antiochus made a definite impression upon the sensibility of the Jews, and it is not surprising if his own infamous career lies behind that of the Antagonist, especially since he had already become a part of the apocalyptic tradition in Daniel. That the Antagonist is not an exact replica of Antiochus does not mean that the Syrian king is not to some extent in the author's mind. There

---

[30] Milligan, *Thessalonians*, p. 99, who compares υἱὸς θανάτου οὗτος in 1 Sam. 20:31, meaning "he must die".

may also be a reminiscence of Caligula in the description, since he desired to have a statue of himself placed within the sanctuary of the Temple in Jerusalem[31]. Although the statue was never actually placed there, this was because of chance, and certainly not because Caligula thought better of the idea. He claimed to be an incarnation of Zeus during his lifetime[32], as Antiochus was also reputed to have done[33]; and, like Antiochus "Epimanes", Caligula was popularly considered to be mad.

The Antagonist, depicted in 2:3-4 preeminently as a rebel, opposes πάντα λεγόμενον θεὸν ἢ σέβασμα. Here again the blasphemous claims of the pagan rulers seem to be in mind, the more so since σέβασμα may recall the Roman emperor's honorific title of Σεβαστός, "Augustus". We may compare the use of the word in Wisdom 14:20, although the idea of "reverence" in σέβασμα is secondary to that of "worship", that is, it usually refers to something that is worthy of worship. However, we know that the emperors received divine honors from their foreign subjects as early as the reign of Augustus, and sometimes claimed them explicitly, as appears to have been the case with Caligula[34]. It is fitting, then, that the culmination of the act of rebellion comes when the Antagonist seats himself in the Temple of God and proclaims himself to be a god. The Temple was of course God's "dwelling", and the Antagonist thus usurps God's place. This is the goal of the political rebel, to overthrow the monarch and to set himself up in his stead. The blasphemous claim of the Antagonist, ὅτι ἔστιν θεός, "that he is a god", would mean that the Antagonist was an incarnate god of some sort, rather than God himself.

This claim of divine status introduces the theme, which recurs throughout the scenario, of the Antagonist's demonic mimicry of Christ. He does many of the things that Christ is supposed to do. This theme should not be confused with the reversal of Christ's attributes in the Antagonist, such as his self-exaltation in contrast to Christ's humility. Rather, this demonic mimicry consists of similar acts or characteristics of Christ and the Antagonist; the contrast then lies in the nature of these characteristics (good in Christ vs. bad in the Antagonist) and/or their source (God in the case of Christ vs. Satan in the

---

[31] Josephus, *Ant.* 18. 261–309, *Bell. Jud.* 2. 185–203; Tacitus, *Hist.* 5. 9.

[32] Josephus, *Ant.* 19. 4–5, 11; Suetonius, *Vita Calig.* 22. 2–4, 33.

[33] Cf. the analysis of the character of Antiochus IV by David Syme Russell, *The Jews from Alexander to Herod*, New Clarendon Bible, Old Testament vol. 5 (Oxford: Oxford University Press, 1967), pp. 31–35; for his coins bearing the titles νικηφόρος and θεὸς ἐπιφανής, see N.K. Rutler, *Greek Coinage*, Shire Archaeology (Aylesbury, England: Shire Publications, 1983), pp. 46–47.

[34] "Der Kaiserkult", Martin Persson Nilsson, *Geschichte der Griechischen Religion*, vol. 2, 2nd ed. (Munich: C.H. Beck, 1961), pp. 384–95.

case of the Antagonist). The Antagonist's imitation of Christ is the very essence of his deception (cf. 2:9). Although the exterior acts are similar, the interior disposition is totally opposed to that of Christ; this is why diligence against deception is so important (2:3a).

We have accepted the usual identification of ὁ ναὸς τοῦ θεοῦ as "the Temple of God", the Jerusalem Temple. This is in keeping with the reminiscences of Antiochus IV in the portrait. Although, as Frame notes[35], neither Antiochus nor Caligula actually entered the sanctuary to make their blasphemous claims, we must bear in mind that they serve only as a pattern for the Antagonist in this passage; since he represents apocalyptic evil, his offense will accordingly be that much greater, the ultimate blasphemy.

The next verse, 2:5, poses a question: οὐ μνημονεύετε ὅτι ἔτι ὢν πρὸς ὑμᾶς ταῦτα ἔλεγον ὑμῖν. This question may either be a rhetorical device intended both to "authenticate" the letter as a product of the apostle's hand, and to validate the apocalyptic scenario by claiming that it formed a part of Paul's teaching, or a genuine historical reference to Paul's preaching in the congregation. As we have seen, the author is attempting to present systematically or "chronologically" an eschatological system that Paul did not fully develop or integrate. It is therefore not the case that Paul had explained the apocalyptic scenario to the congregation during his mission. The congregation's apparent ignorance of the eschatological process also indicates that they had not previously been instructed in "these things"; ταῦτα is a technical term for the content of such eschatological teaching (cf. Mark. 13:4, 29, 30; Luke 21:36; Rev. 22:8, 16, 20).

What then is the intention of this question? If, as we have suggested above, it is intended to authenticate the letter and validate its contents, how can this be accomplished by reference to a non-existent teaching of Paul? To answer this question, we must consider the nature of Paul's eschatological instruction in his congregations. It would appear that Paul's original teaching was that Jesus would return very soon as eschatological judge. This created problems when members of his congregations died before the parousia had occurred (cf. 1 Cor. 15:12-58; 1 Thess. 4:13-18). At such times he was required to offer further instruction, including such matters as the nature of the resurrection body (1 Cor. 15:35-50) and the manner in which the faithful will join Christ at the parousia (1 Cor. 15:51-55; 1 Thess. 4:15-17); that this is new instruction is indicated by the formula οὐ θέλομεν δὲ ὑμᾶς ἀγνοεῖν, ἀδελφοί, in 1 Thessalonians 4:13. In 1 Corinthians 15:51, Paul refers to such instruction as μυστήριον; this is "secret" instruction, not intended for all ears, even the ears of all believers. Apocalyptic teaching by nature is esoteric, and it would be

---

[35] Frame, *Thessalonians*, p. 257.

readily credible to the readers of 2 Thessalonians that this "secret teaching" had been offered to the congregation by Paul, and yet they themselves remained ignorant of it.

Indeed, the author is employing a common device, in which the apocalyptic teaching that addresses the author's contemporary situation is presented as a "secret teaching" of a great authority of the past[36]. The entire letter is comprehensible as such a "secret teaching", communicated to the congregation after the death of the apostle.

Several problems, both grammatical and exegetical, arise from verse 2:6, including the most notorious puzzle of the letter. The introductory conjunction, καὶ νῦν, is consecutive rather than temporal, assuming some sort of logical connection between the previous (fictitious) instruction of the congregation and their knowledge of what τὸ κατέχον represents. This connection appears to require that there was in fact some previous instruction. Scholars since Tertullian have offered various explanations of τὸ κατέχον without reaching any generally satisfying conclusion. How then could the original readers be expected to know what τὸ κατέχον was without some specific previous instruction?

Before we seek to answer this question, we must understand the grammar of the verse. The second half of the verse is a dependent phrase introduced by εἰς τό, indicating that this is a result of the action of the independent clause which begins the sentence. But is the εἰς τό dependent on the articular participle τὸ κατέχον or the verb, οἴδατε? Properly, it should depend on the verb, οἴδατε, since this is the nearest verb. However, the sense of this reading, that the time of the revelation of the Antagonist (the only "he" in the scenario so far) was somehow to be determined by the congregation's knowledge of the identity of the impersonal force, τὸ κατέχον, is inadmissible. The events of the divinely preordained eschatological process are not dependent on human knowledge of their mechanics. Therefore we must construe εἰς τό with τὸ κατέχον, as awkward as this may be, and therefore understand the base verb in the sense of "to restrain". The participial phrase is thus to be rendered "that which restrains".

We may now return to our earlier question and ask how the readers could be expected to know the identity of "that which restrains" if they had not received previous instruction? The answer must be that they understood very well what power regulated the development of the eschatological drama: the will of God, and that alone (cf. Rom. 1:18, 24, 26: παραδοῦναι αὐτοὺς ὁ θεός). There can be no doubt that, ultimately, the power that prevents the Antagonist from appearing before the appointed time is the will of God. God

---

[36] Cf. Dan. 12:9-13; 2 Esdras 12:37-38; Mark 13:23b and parallels.

is in control of the fate of both the good (1:11-12, 2:13b-14) and the evil (2:11-12), and of the events which mete out those fates. This is another major motif of apocalyptic thought, that the course of the end-times is determined, even predetermined, by the will of God, and that it is "God's plan" that is revealed to the apocalyptic seer; this idea stands behind, for example, the vision of the heavenly council in Revelation 4:1-6, 5:1-7 (cf. Jer. 23:18, 22; Zech. 3:1-10). If the will of God is conceded to be the ultimate power that "restrains" the Antagonist until his time, why should it not also be the power identified as τὸ κατέχον in the scenario[37]?

The primary objection to this identification of τὸ κατέχον is the later reference to ὁ κατέχων, a personification of the restraining force; according to the scenario, at the point of crisis, this figure is "out of the way", ἐκ μέσου γένηται. We may ask, however, what "person" would be capable of restraining the power of Satan, which is at work in the present and will be at work in the future through the Antagonist? Various suggestions have been offered, and these are enumerated and critiqued in the commentaries[38]. Of these, the only one that requires comment is the classic solution first suggested by Tertullian, that is, that the restraining force is the Roman empire and its personification is the emperor. Paul was certainly capable of praising the empire whose protection he had most probably enjoyed (cf. Rom. 13:1-7) and even spoke of earthly authority as established by God (Rom. 13:2). However, our own author is thinking not in terms of the present world, but in terms of the final division of humanity between the good and the wicked; in that division, there can be no doubt as to where the empire and its emperors belonged. The empire produced Caligula, who had threatened the sanctity of the Temple; Nero, who had Christians in Rome tortured to death; and Vespasian and Titus, who were responsible for the siege and destruction of Jerusalem. The portrait of the Antagonist himself in 2:3-4 is based, as we have seen, on the model of the blasphemous pagan king. Moreover, since the time of Augustus, the emperors had received divine honors, saying in effect ὅτι ἔστιν θεός (2:4b)[39]. The author could hardly then have seen this self-same empire as a restraint upon the operation of evil.

Giblin, however, has suggested that τὸ κατέχον itself is an evil force that somehow "holds back" the full manifestation of evil[40]. Such a view presumes that various forces of evil may be at odds with one another, while in apoca-

---

[37] Cf. Bassler, "Enigmatic Sign", p. 506–7.
[38] Cf. the excursus in Trilling, *Der zweite Brief*, pp. 94–101, and in Frame, *Thessalonians*, pp. 259–62.
[39] Nilsson, "Der Kaiserkult", pp. 384–95.
[40] Giblin, *Threat to Faith*, pp. 201–4.

lyptic thought in general, evil, like good, is controlled by a single agency, i.e., Satan. While it is comprehensible on God's side that one aspect of good might "restrain" another (for example, God's mercy restraining his justice), a similar scruple on the part of Satan would vitiate the dualism inherent in apocalyptic thought.

However, it remains to explain how God's will may properly lie behind both τὸ κατέχον and its personification as ὁ κατέχων. First, we must recognize that the personification of τὸ κατέχον is a function not of its meaning, but of the nature of the apocalyptic crisis as understood by the author. The description of the career of τὸ κατέχον/ὁ κατέχων is one of three such descriptions. In the first, ἡ ἀποστασία is at work in the present, but in the future, at the point of apocalyptic crisis, it will be manifested in ὁ ἄνθρωπος τῆς ἀνομίας, who is described in terms of political and religious rebellion (2:3-4). In other words, ὁ ἄνθρωπος τῆς ἀνομίας is a personification of ἡ ἀποστασία which is at work in the present. In the same way, τὸ μυστήριον τῆς ἀνομίας is at work in the present, but at the time of the apocalyptic crisis, it will be manifested in the figure of ὁ ἄνομος (2:7-8). By the same token, then, we may see a parallel development in the third description of the scenario; τὸ κατέχον is at work in the present, but at the point of crisis, it will be manifested in the personal figure of ὁ κατέχων (2:6-7). This triple process of a present phenomenon being personified at the future moment of crisis represents the nature of the apocalyptic schema: what has been and continues to be active in the present, will in the future be unveiled as a personal force, part of the battle between the personalized forces of good and evil (cf. Dan. 10:18-11:1; Rev. 12:7-9)[41]. When we understand this pattern, we will also understand that the use of the neuter and masculine participles in verses 2:6-7 was not dictated by the nature of that to which τὸ κατέχον / ὁ κατέχων refers, but to the pattern itself.

Still, it remains to be discovered what figure is designated by ὁ κατέχων; who is the agent of God's will? This role is traditionally filled by "the angel of YHWH", whether a personal manifestation of God himself, as in Genesis 18, or independent spiritual beings, as in later Judaism and in most apocalyptic writings[42]. At the time of crisis, then, when earthly phenomena give way to

---

[41] This dual personal/impersonal nature is typical of demonology and polytheism generally. Eros, for instance, is both a force (love) and a god, as is Hypnos. Demons are often personifications of evil forces, Mark 5:1-20 and parallels, Mark 1:23-28 (Luke 4:33-37), Matt. 9:32-34, 12:22-24 (Luke 11:14-15); see also the character of Tryphon in Plutarch, *De Iside et Osiride* 2. 351E–352A.

[42] Cf. Gen. 16:9-11, 22:11-12; Ex. 14:19-20; Num. 22:34; Judg. 6:19-20; Matt. 1:20-21, 2:19-20; Luke 1:11-13, 19-20, 26-37; Jub. 2:1-2; Vitae Adae et Evae 51; Apoc. Moses 27:1-29:2; 1 Enoch 10:1-16, 20:1-8, 40:1-10, 66:1-3; Tobit 12:11-22; Sus. 55; Bel. 33-39.

supernatural figures, the angel who has restrained the advent of the Antagonist (as an agent of God's will) will be removed. This will not be done by force, but will be the result of the fulfillment of his role, just as the players disappear from *Hamlet* once they have done their part to advance the plot, since they have done what Shakespeare intended them to do. It is God's will that restrains the Antagonist, and at "his time" it is God's will that removes the angel who has done the work of restraint so that the Antagonist may be revealed (cf. Rev. 20:1-3, 7-10). So God's will directs every action of the apocalyptic drama[43].

The next verse, 2:7, falls into two parts: the first explains the present situation, which involves the secret operation of τὸ μυστήριον τῆς ἀνομίας, and the second resumes the chronological sequence of events begun in 2:6. This is actually the second description of what is essentially the same series of events. In 2:3-4, the author has begun to sketch out the progress of events, beginning with the present operation of ἡ ἀποστασία. This will culminate in the arrival of ὁ ἄνθρωπος τῆς ἀνομίας, whose blasphemous career reaches its apogee in his claim of divinity in the Temple (2:4). In 2:6, we have learned that a restraining force is at work to hold back the revelation of this Antagonist until the proper time. The explanatory γάρ of 2:7a appears to explain the need for the restraining force; if it did not exist, the "mystery of lawlessness" would quickly reach fruition in the person of the Antagonist, ὁ ἄνομος.

Τὸ μυστήριον in 2:7a appears in an emphatic position, and its modifying genitive is postponed until the conclusion of the phrase, which position is also emphatic. We may translate, "For the mystery is already in operation, that of lawlessness". It would seem then that this expression does not merely mean "lawlessness"[44], but that τὸ μυστήριον has some definite meaning. We would further argue that it would be no surprise to the congregation to hear that "lawlessness" per se was presently at work, especially in view of the persecution suffered by its members, 1:4, 6-7a. Rather, what is important is that this lawlessness has some eschatological goal, that it is somehow a dynam-

---

Note especially Jub. 15:31-32, in which the spirits are given authority by God over the nations specifically "to lead them astray from Him", and Test. Levi 3:1-3, which refers to the first heaven, the dwelling of "all the spirits of the retributions for vengeance on men" on "the day of judgment, in the righteous judgment of God" (ἐν τῇ δικαιοκρισίᾳ τοῦ θεοῦ; α, β$A^β S^1$).

[43] It is of course possible that an angel, as the agent of God's will, could also be the patron of a political entity (Dan. 10:20-21, 1 Cor. 2:6-8). However, since we would maintain that there was in fact no previous instruction on this point, it seems best not to assume too detailed an understanding of the cryptic term κατέχον.

[44] This is the meaning ascribed in Walter Bauer, *A Greek-English Lexicon of the New Testament and other Early Christian Literature*, trans. William F. Arndt and F. William Gingrich, 2nd. ed., eds. F. William Gingrich and Frederick W. Danker (Chicago: University of Chicago Press, 1979), p. 530.

ic, progressive process that is directed towards culmination in the appearance of the Antagonist.

What is the meaning of τὸ μυστήριον here? It is an active force; it is "already at work", so it is not an abstract concept. This means it is not a "secret" revealed to the author through some sort of revelation (cf. 1 Cor. 15:51) or a "mystery" of God's plan. It is also clear that τὸ μυστήριον does not function adverbally, as though to render "lawlessness is already at work secretly". It should be recalled that this scenario deals in religious and political terms, or rather, religio-political terms. It is a description of an Antagonist who challenges God and is finally destroyed at the advent of the Lord Jesus Christ. The Antagonist makes specifically religious claims by religious means (cf. 2:9), and his followers make up an "anti-church" of the deceived (cf. 2:10-12). The operations of τὸ μυστήριον is parallel to and concurrent with ἡ ἀποστασία, and finds its goal in the revelation of ὁ ἄνομος. We would suggest that the author is using the metaphor of a pagan mystery cult for the apocalyptic antagonism to Christ, a cult that is already "in operation" in the present. Those who rebel against God are "initiated" into τὸ μυστήριον τῆς ἀνομίας, which will have its culmination in the ἀποκάλυψις of the cultic god, ὁ ἄνομος. The apocalyptic dualism is thus made more vivid as all of humanity is envisioned as divided into two groups, those faithful to Christ, and those initiated into τὸ μυστήριον τῆς ἀνομίας, who are opposed to Christ and his people. This idea of course also involves a parody of the mysteries; the "god" who will be revealed is the blasphemous Antagonist, and those who thought themselves "saved" by their initiation are in reality οἱ ἀπολλύμενοι, ἀνθ' ὧν τὴν ἀγάπην τῆς ἀληθείας οὐκ ἐδέξαντο εἰς τὸ σωθῆναι αὐτούς (2:10b).

Although the mystery cult is already in operation, it has not yet received the vision of its false god which will be the confirmation of the initiation of its adherents[45]. This vision will not yet take place: μόνον ὁ κατέχων ἄρτι ἕως ἐκ μέσου γένηται. What should be the verb in this phrase? The only verb readily comprehensible in the context is the cognate, κατέχει, thus, "only the one who restrains (does so) until he is out of the way". This is the situation that prevents the mystery from finding its fulfillment in the ἀποκάλυψις of its "god".

The restatement of the career of the Antagonist begins in 2:8, and it differs from that of 2:3-4 in several respects. The similarities include the repetition of

---

[45] For a description of the initiatory visions of the Isis cult, see Apuleius, *Metamorphosis* 9. 23. For the religious situation in Thessalonike in regard to the cults, see Karl P. Donfried, "The Cults of Thessalonica and the Thessalonian Correspondence", *New Testament Studies* 31 (1985): 336–56.

the idea of a "revelation" of the Antagonist, and again the immediate reference to his destruction. As we noted above, the swift destruction of the Antagonist at the advent of the Lord Jesus Christ appears to be the most important fact about him for our author. This is not mere repetition, however, as 2:8-9 deals with the scene in a different way than 2:3-4. The title of the Antagonist has changed from "the man of [i.e., characterized by] lawlessness" to "the Lawless One" (i.e. the one who personifies the lawless state). The latter title is better suited to the object of worship of τὸ μυστήριον τῆς ἀνομίας.

It is noteworthy that the Antagonist is conceived in terms of "lawlessness" rather than "unrighteousness" or "wickedness"[46]. This implies that the good which is its opposite should be conceived in terms of "obedience" to some sort of "law", which is the behavior enjoined on the readers elswhere in the letter, specifically obedience to the received tradition (cf. 3:4, 6, 14; cf. 1:8b). This suggests also that the Antagonist is not intended to be a supernatural "antiChrist", but rather to embody the rebellion inherent in all of human sinfulness in isolation from faithful obedience to Christ and the tradition. This is why the author is able to see in the false proclamation and disobedience of the ἄτακτοι the working of ἡ ἀποστασία and τὸ μυστήριον τῆς ἀνομίας. In the dualistic state of mind common to apocalyptic eschatology, each moral choice places a person on one side or the other of the eschatological confrontation between good and evil. One is either "faithful" or "deceived". This is the sort of dualistic thought behind 1 John 2:21-23, 4:2-3, 5:10-12; 2 John 7.

The Antagonist continues to be described in Christological terms in 2:8, insofar as he is "revealed" (ἀποκαλυφθήσεσθαι). In this case, the term serves to parody the divine pretensions of the Antagonist, since he is immediately destroyed by the mere appearance of the parousia of Christ, and slain by the breath of his mouth. As Giblin points out[47], the destruction of the Antagonist τῷ πνεύματι τοῦ στόματος αὐτοῦ is intended to show that the Lord's victory is effortless, rather than to be taken in some sort of "pictorial" sense. The career of the Antagonist is the last stage in the eschatological process before the return of Christ, which puts an end to it.

The next verse, 2:9, is marked by an obscurity of relative pronouns, so that the reader is not immediately aware of the intended reference of the description. Everything would seem to indicate that the author intentionally created this confusion of references to emphasize his portrayal of the Antagonist as a demonic mimic of Christ. The last clear reference is to Jesus, who destroys the

---

[46] Cf. 2 Cor. 6:14-15 and the comments of this passage by Hans Dieter Betz, "2 Cor. 6:14-7:1: An Anti-Pauline Fragment?", *Journal of Biblical Literature* 92 (1973): 88–108.

[47] Giblin, *Threat to Faith*, pp. 91–92.

Antagonist at his parousia. The genitive relative pronoun οὗ appears to follow from the phrase, τῆς παρουσίας αὐτοῦ, the more so since the reference forward is also to ἡ παρουσία. It is only when the reader reaches the last word of the phrase, Σατανᾶ, that he realizes that the reference was in reality to the Antagonist, and that the genitive relative pronoun continues a series begun in 2:8b, ὃν ὁ κύριος....

There appear to be two ideas at work here. On the one hand, the two relative clauses recounting the destruction of the Antagonist in 2:8 and his career of deception in 2:9, recall the aretalogies of the pagan gods, notably the gods of the mysteries[48]. In such an aretalogy, the various attributes and accomplishments of the god are recounted in a series of phrases, with each phrase beginning with the same or similar wording. Such aretalogies may be written either in the first or third person, and there are many examples for the goddess Isis[49]. In the case of 2 Thessalonians, 2:8-9 may form an "anti-aretalogy" of the false god of "the mystery of lawlessness"[50]. On the other hand, we have the apparent intention of the author to mislead his readers as to the reference of the phrase in 2:9a by the ambiguity of the relative pronoun. The intention may be to enforce on the reader the error that will characterize the last days, that is, to think that one is dealing with Jesus Christ and to learn instead that one is dealing with the Antagonist, the false god. The reader is momentarily "deceived", just as the lost will be. The "shock of recognition" for the reader, however slight, gives him a premonition of the shock in store for those who are misled by the Antagonist at his appearing.

There is an interesting literary device at work in 2:9, insofar as the Christological ideas of ἡ παρουσία and "miracles and signs and wonders" are each rendered deceptions by a single word at the end of the phrase; the idea of the parousia effected by an ἐνέργεια is corrupted by the single word Σατανᾶ, and the "miracles and signs and wonders" are corrupted by the single word ψεύδους. The various elements of the triad δύναμις καὶ σημεῖον καὶ τέρας appear in various contexts, but the triad itself appears only in Acts 2:22, where the reference is to Christ; in 2 Corinthians 12:12, where these are the signs of the true apostle; and in Hebrews 2:4, where these are God's means of bearing

---

[48] Cf. Plutarch, *De Iside et Osiride*, 2. 351E–352A on the contrast between Isis and Typhon; Hans Dieter Betz, "Ein seltsames mysterien-theologisches System bei Plutarch", *Ex orbe religionum*, studia Geo Widengren, vol. 2 (Leiden: E.J. Brill, 1972), pp. 347–54.

[49] Cf. Oxyrhynchus papyri xi. 1380 (third person) and the "praises of Isis", both translated in *Hellenistic Religions*, ed. Frederick C. Grant, Library of Liberal Arts (Indianapolis, Ind.: Bobbs-Merrill Educational Publishing, 1953), pp. 131–33.

[50] Plutarch derives Typhon from τυφοῦν: δι' ἄγνοιαν καὶ ἀπάτην τετυφωμένος. "He tears to pieces and scatters to the winds the sacred writings" (Plutarch 2. 351F), which are identified with Osiris (ibid., 54. 373A). On this point, see Betz, "Ein seltsames", p. 350.

witness (cf. also Rom. 15:19). The Antagonist "proves" his superior religious status in the appropriate way, by means of wonders, signs, and miracles, except that in his case, these phenomena are false, the product of Satan's deceptive power.

The account of the career of ὁ ἄνομος in 2:9 need not be reconciled with that of ὁ ἄνθρωπος τῆς ἀνομίας in 2:3-4, because the two accounts present the antagonism towards God at the base of every evil, and the deceptive effect of that evil on those who do not remain faithful to the saving truth, codified in the Pauline tradition. More specifically, the description of 2:3-4 is presented from a "God-ward" perspective; it depicts the Antagonist in terms of his rebellion against God. As a result, he is depicted according to the model of the blasphemous pagan king, who typifies all human rebellion against God's sovereignty. In contrast to this, the description of 2:8-9 is presented from a "man-ward" perspective. It depicts the Antagonist in terms of his misrepresentation of himself as divine in his effort to deceive humanity. For this reason, the emphasis in these verses is on the Antagonist's demonic mimicry of Christ, a mimicry which serves the end of deception. This same dichotomy is apparent in the names given in each section to the present activity of evil: in 2:3-4, in relation to God, it is ἡ ἀποστασία, religious rebellion; in 2:8-9, in relation to humanity, it is τὸ μυστήριον τῆς ἀνομίας, a false mystery cult into which the lost are "initiated". Indeed, the dichotomy may even be apparent in the titles of the Antagonist. In relation to God, he is a human being who is characterized by lawlessness, that is, he stands apart from others by his flagrant disobedience which is the extreme expression of all humanity's disobedience and rebellion. In relation to humanity, he is the embodiment of all that opposes God, and thus wrongly perceived as divine himself; he is the one without law, who blasphemously imitates Christ in order to deceive.

The "man-ward" perspective of the scenario in these latter verses is further developed by 2:10. There the attention turns from the figure of the Antagonist as deceiver to those whom he deceives, and contrasts them with the righteous. The mimicry of Jesus by the Antagonist is no longer in view; the emphasis in this verse is on the contrast between the Antagonist and Christ, between "the lost" and the saved. The ploys of the Antagonist are now described in the most general terms; he works ἐν πάσῃ ἀπάτῃ ἀδικίας, recalling the warning of 2:3, μή τις ὑμᾶς ἐξαπατήσῃ κατὰ μηδένα τρόπον. There is the implicit contrast to Jesus, whose attributes are those of ἀλήθεια and δικαιοσύνη.

The primary focus of attention, however, has passed from the figure of the Antagonist to his victims, and the apocalyptic scenario as such is completed. These victims are characterized as οἱ ἀπολλύμενοι. This title stands in contrast to the possibility of salvation through the acceptance of the love of the truth and, by implication, in contrast to the "saved" who do accept it. The initiation of the deceived into τὸ μυστήριον τῆς ἀνομίας has led to their downfall in the company of their false god, the apocalyptic Antagonist[51].

Is this "love of the truth" whose acceptance results in salvation the love of a "saving truth" in the general sense, or does it mean that the love of the truth would have saved "the lost" specifically from the deceptions of the Antichrist? Both are of course possible and arguably intended, but the contrasts πᾶσα ἀπάτη ἀδικίας / ἡ ἀλήθεια and οἱ ἀπολλύμενοι / σωθῆναι αὐτούς suggest the primary idea is that of truth that protects from eschatological deception. The purpose of the letter is to instill faithfulness (expressed as "love" here) to a truth that will save the readers from deception (2:3a). The "truth" contained in the scenario itself is intended to protect the readers against the wiles of the Antagonist. We find a parallel situation in Mark 13:22 (parallel Matt. 24:24), where Jesus warns his disciples about the future presence of false Christs and false prophets, so that they will be wary against their deceptions (cf. Mark 13:5, Matt. 24:4).

Since it is the acceptance of the love of the truth which protects the faithful against the eschatological deception, the rejection of that same love may have taken place at any time before the coming of the Antagonist, but more specifically it is the present time which is in the author's mind. Just as those who persecute *now* will suffer *then* (i.e., in the eschatological future, 1:6) and those who do not know God or obey the gospel *now* will be rejected by the Lord *then* (1:8-9), so the apocalyptic scenario of 2:1-12 extrapolates the current state of affairs into the future as a means of consoling and strengthening the faithful. Those who do not accept the love of the truth *now* will be "the lost" *then* (2:10). On the other hand, those who know the "truth" about the eschatological process will not be shaken from their convictions or upset, as the lost will be (2:2).

The author's attention shifts once more in the following verses, 2:11-12. From the career of the Antagonist and the fall of the lost, he turns to the author of the apocalyptic scenario, God himself. God is the one in control of the eschatological events, and it is only by his permission that Satan and his agent, the Antagonist, are allowed to deceive the unbelievers. However, God has not initiated the action against "the lost"; rather, it is a reaction to their

---

[51] One might suggest contrasting the fate of "the lost" with the purported outcome of their initiation into τὸ μυστήριον τῆς ἀνομίας, i.e., some sort of triumph over death. There appears to be some evidence that initiation into a cult assured a blessed state after death; so George E. Mylonas, *Eleusis and the Eleusinian Mysteries* (Princeton: Princeton University Press, 1961), pp. 283–85; Martin Persson Nilsson, "The Bacchic Mysteries of the Roman Age", *Harvard Theological Review* 46 (1953): 175–202, especially 184–87. However, the evidence on this point is contradictory and liable to misinterpretation, cf. Ramsey MacMullen, *Paganism in the Roman Empire* (New Haven: Yale University Press, 1981), pp. 53–57.

prior rejection of the love of the truth: καὶ διὰ τοῦτο (2:11a). Because of this deliberate choice made by the lost, God takes direct action against them; we may compare Romans 1:24-25, which is also an example of God's "wrath" against the wicked (Rom. 1:18a). In the present case, God sends a "power of deception" upon those who have rejected the love of the truth so that they will believe the false signs of the Antagonist. One believes what is false, therefore, because of the ἐνέργεια πλάνης, but it is not clear by what contrasting power one believes what is true. The ultimate source of both powers is God, but the author does not refer to "the Spirit" as a power of belief[52], nor to any other such power other than God himself (cf. 1:11, 2:13b, 14, 16-17) or "the Lord" (3:5).

This "power of deception" leads to belief in τῷ ψεύδει, either "the Lie" or "what is false". The former would presumably refer to the single greatest lie of the Antagonist, his claim to divinity in 2:4, while the latter would refer to those false miracles, signs, and wonders which supposedly substantiate the claim in 2:9. Since it is these phenomena which are the concern in the second half of the scenario, we would accept the meaning "what is false"; the result of rejection of the love of the truth is belief in what is false.

The division and distinction between the faithful and the wicked is underlined by the chiasmus of 2:10-12:

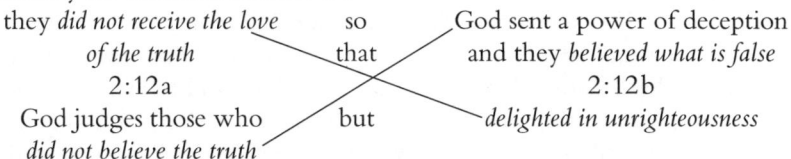

they *did not receive the love* so God sent a power of deception
  of the truth that and they *believed what is false*
   2:12a   2:12b
God judges those who but *delighted in unrighteousness*
did not believe the truth

The wicked are thus defined both by the negation of right actions and by the perpetration of evil actions. Both arise from their belief in what is false, which in turn is a result of God's sending a "power of deception" upon them for their previous refusal to receive the love of the truth. All of their wickedness and their evil end is the ultimate result of unbelief, forsaking faithfulness to the truth.

The idea that God allows the Antagonist to operate and so bring about the downfall of the wicked indicates that he is an agent of God's wrath. God saves those who are faithful despite the free reign of wickedness; this suggests that the appearance of the Antagonist is the central event of "the Day of the Lord", the day of wrath which the faithful will survive. "The Day of the Lord" would then be the middle factor between the present ἀποστασία, which is marked by the operation of τὸ μυστήριον τῆς ἀνομίας, and the parousia of Jesus Christ. His parousia brings the career of the Antagonist to an end and initiates the process of judgment.

---

[52] Cf. our exegesis of 2:13 in chap. 1.

We have already established above that the Day of the Lord is not identical with the parousia of Jesus Christ, but must precede it. In 1 Thessalonians, we learn several more details about the Day of the Lord. It is a day of wrath, but its wrath is intended for the wicked, not the faithful (1 Thess. 5:4-7). The faithful can best prepare for the Day of the Lord by being wakeful and sober (ibid.) and by donning spiritual armor (1 Thess. 5:8). Our author appears to believe that it is the very virtue of steadfastness and obedience to the tradition that will protect the faithful from the deceptions of the Antagonist and so save them. This is why they must not be "shaken from your conviction" (2:2). More specifically, it is important that one realize that the troubles of the present, however severe they may appear to be, are not the "wrath" of the Day of the Lord. If they are believed to be such by someone not fortified by the tradition, the advent of the Antagonist, which marks the true coming of the Day of the Lord, will come as a surprise. The false signs and wonders which comprise his mimicry of Christ will deceive the unwary, and the person who has not been faithful to the tradition will accept the Antagonist as the returned Christ. This deception will be God's wrath at work on such a person, and he will be condemned at judgment. The Antagonist is able to deceive only those who are not equipped with the sure eschatological timetable the author offers as part of the inherited tradition. Therefore, those who falsely proclaim that "the Day of the Lord is here" disarm those who are not protected by faithful adherence to the inherited tradition. False prophets and those they mislead, both will be deceived by the Antagonist when he comes. The false prophets are thus preparing the gullible for the Antagonist's deception, and are part of ἡ ἀποστασία, which is initially rebellion against the author's authority, but is ultimately rebellion against God himself.

We may see, then, that in the author's opinion, the world is already being divided into two lots that will stand before the judgment seat of Christ. On the one hand are those who are faithful to the traditions passed on to them by the apostle, the tradition of Paul as interpreted by the author. On the other hand are those who are not faithful to this tradition, including not only the persecutors of the congregation and other outsiders, but also those insiders who attempt to deceive the congregation with the false proclamations about the Day of the Lord. The author thus displays the dualistic turn of mind typical of apocalyptic thinkers: those who are not obedient to his authority are ultimately no different than those who never believed or even those who persecute the faithful. Both will be punished on the Day of the Lord, when the wrath of God will be revealed through the work of the Antagonist, as it was revealed on an earlier "day" when the Babylonians conquered and destroyed Jerusalem (cf. Lam. 2).

The problem addressed by the author in the *probatio* is then not that of the time of the parousia of Jesus Christ, but the time and nature of the "wrath" that will distinguish the Day of the Lord. The "disorderly" in the congregation believed the Day of the Lord was present; since they, too, shared the instruction given by Paul in 1 Thessalonians and the perception of the Day of the Lord in the Old Testament, they must have believed that the wrath of the Lord was in some way being manifested against the "wicked" in their own day. We already know that the congregation was persecuted (1:4, 6), and this, too, was understood by the ἄτακτοι as a sign of the Day of the Lord, although this persecution would purify the community and strengthen it (cf. Joel 2:15-29, Zeph. 2:1-3; 1 Thess. 5:4-7). The author of 2 Thessalonians, however, argues that the Day of the Lord still lies in the future, and that its "wrath" will be manifested by the deception of the wicked by the Antagonist. This will come about by God's will and by God's abandonment of the wicked to their fate. The author does not specify what aspect the "wrath" of that day will display towards the faithful, apparently because he believes, with Paul, that the tradition will save them from that wrath (1 Thess. 1:10b, 5:4-6).

Thus it appears that, for our author, judgment at the parousia of Jesus Christ will be based on one's "faithfulness", either faithfulness to Christ as manifested in obedience to the Pauline tradition, or loyalty to the "false Christ" proclaimed by the false prophets, the blasphemous Antagonist of God. In the thanksgiving which concludes the *probatio*, the "conditions" of salvation are "holiness in regard to the spirit" and "faithfulness in regard to the truth" (2:13)[53]. Ἁγιασμὸς πνεύματος is also the primary qualification for salvation in 1 Thessalonians 4:3, 4, 7-8, although there the concern is paraenetic rather than eschatological; that is, it is part of a rule for everyday living, not specifically a preparation for the end. Πίστις ἀληθείας, of course, is the primary concern of the author of 2 Thessalonians, insofar as the tradition he espouses embodies the necessary saving truth. However, he does not advocate a doctrine of what might be styled "justification by faithfulness alone", for this loyalty must produce practical results. Among these are holiness (2:13), "good works and words" (1:11, 2:17), steadfastness in persecution (1:4, 3:5), and "worthiness", either of the kingdom or of the call to salvation (1:5, 11; 2:14). The contrast to the saved who know God and obey the tradition handed on by Paul is thus properly found in the present in οἱ μὴ εἰδότες θεὸν καὶ οἱ μὴ ὑπακούοντες τῷ εὐαγγελίῳ τοῦ κυρίου ἡμῶν Ἰησοῦ (1:8). In the future, however, because these same people have rejected ἡ ἀγάπη τῆς ἀληθείας, they are simply οἱ ἀπολλύμενοι.

Now that we have completed the exegesis of 2 Thessalonians 1:5-10 and 2:1-12, there are several points of interest that we need to examine at greater

---

[53] See our exegesis of this verse in chap. 1.

length. The first concerns the Antagonist, whom we have earlier referred to as "supernatural". Although this characterization is appropriate in view of his role in the apocalyptic drama, just what sort of figure did our author intend the Antagonist to be? It is clear that he is not an "anti-Christ" in the dualistic sense of a figure equal in power and status to Christ, but antagonistic to him. We find this sort of dualism in the struggle between Michael and the "princes" of Persia and Greece (Dan. 10:13, 20-21) or between Michael and his angels and the dragon and his angels (Rev. 12:7). The Antagonist, on the other hand, appears κατ' ἐνέργειαν τοῦ Σατανᾶ, himself an angel and subordinate to Christ, especially in consideration of the author's high Christology, which identifies "the Lord" with God. The Antagonist is certainly opposed to Christ, but so are many men and a host of spiritual beings; the author's presentation of the Antagonist's career in terms of a mimicry of Jesus is intended in part, as we have seen, to demonstrate how far short he falls of the equality he claims with Christ. The inevitability of his defeat as indicated by his title ὁ υἱὸς τῆς ἀπωλείας and the ease with which he will be destroyed by the mere appearance of Jesus Christ at his parousia again underlines the futility not only of his rebellion, but of all rebellion against the power of God and Christ. It is clear that the Antagonist is only a tool of God's wrath (2:11-12) and he appears only at the time predetermined by God (2:6-7). He is not an "anti-Christ"; rather, he is an embodiment of human evil, which by its very nature is antagonistic to Christ, because it exalts man to the point of assuming God's place at the center of creation. As we have seen, this evil pride is manifested towards God as opposition to all ideas of the sacred (2:4a), and the usurpation of God's throne (2:4b). This same pride is manifested towards man as a desire to deceive others into accepting the Antagonist's false claim of divinity and thereby bringing them under his control, i.e., religio-political control. The reminiscence of both Antiochus IV and Caligula in 2:3-4 and of both the earthly Jesus and Paul in 2:9b (cf. Acts 2:22, 2 Cor. 12:12) indicates that some sort of human, rather than demonic, figure is in mind. Indeed, the Antagonist is the embodiment not of evil as such, but the embodiment of all of man's rebellion against God (i.e., all human evil), and of man's encouragement of others to rebel against God as well (cf. Rom. 1:32). Thus his distinguishing title is ὁ ἄνθρωπος τῆς ἀνομίας, and, because of his "pagan" (i.e., "godless") nature, he is ὁ ἄνομος.

The unspoken assumption in the scenario of 2 Thessalonians 2:1-12 is that the rise of the Antagonist will result in suffering for the Christian faithful. This suffering, however, is not a direct manifestation of the "wrath", but the natural result of the increase of lawlessness. The rationale of the antagonistic figure in some strands of apocalyptic eschatology is that such a figure precipitates a crisis by his attacks on God through his people. The continual process of the persecution of God's people will at some point reach such an extreme state that God will be "forced" to act on his people's behalf in order to vindicate the sanctity of his name (cf. Dan. 11:36-12:1; Rev. 19:19-21; cf. Gen. 6:5-7). For this reason, we must assume that the advent of the Antagonist will not be without consequences for the congregation. This must have also been the belief of the author, even if he does not spell out these consequences in his scenario; the Day of the Lord would include tribulation for the faithful. However, his concern in the apocalyptic scenario of 2:1-12 is with the fate of the wicked, as it was in 1:8-9. The assurance that divine retribution on the Day of the Lord will lead to the deception and subsequent destruction of the wicked, and that their Deceiver will in turn be easily defeated by the returning Christ, is the consolation this scenario offers to the readers.

The apparently unique apocalyptic scenario forms only a part of the author's eschatology, and it is necessary to discover the relationship between it and the ἔνδειγμα of 1:5-10. The primary difference between the two, we would argue, is between the description of the parousia and what follows it (i.e., judgment) in 1:5-10 and the outline of the events preceding the parousia (i.e., the revelation of the Antagonist and the Day of the Lord) in 2:1-12. The secondary difference is between the adherence to standard apocalyptic motifs in the first scene and a creative reinterpretation of many of these motifs in the second. On the other hand, they are united insofar as the ἔνδειγμα serves to offer support to the argument made by the apocalyptic scenario by depicting the future advantage that will be gained by its acceptance. That is, vindication at the judgment in the company of the author will be the outcome of an acceptance of the proof as a basis for taking the action the author desires, i.e., adherence to the tradition as he interprets it. Therefore, the "scene from the Last Judgment" serves to "introduce" the proof of 2:1-12 by reminding the readers of what is at stake; it thus presents the "facts of the case". If they believe in the coming judgment, they must also know that their future status depends not only on their present suffering (1:7a), but also their solidarity with the author-as-Paul (1:7a, 10b) as well as their holiness and faithfulness (1:10a; cf. 2:13b). It is the traditional nature of the material used in the ἔνδειγμα that puts it above argument. It is the common ground of both author and reader, the base from which any and all "orthodox" eschatologies proceed. The author is thus free to develop his own scenario for the events that precede the parousia, drawing upon such traditional elements as the blasphemous king from Daniel, and reinterpreting them to suit his own ideas. By presenting his own scenario in concert with the traditional picture of the Last Judgment, the author lends the former a similar credibility. His task is to fill in the "empty spaces" in the eschatological tradition he has inherited, empty spaces created by the continuation of the church and of history past the crises of the years 60–70. He must reinterpret the tradition to create a place for his own time, and locate it in some sort of chronological position to the traditional events of tribulation, the reign of evil, and the vindication of the faithful. 2 Thessalonians 1:5-10 provides the context for the reimagining of the tradition in 2:1-12.

What then is the meaning of the apocalyptic scenario? We may first isolate those elements that justify using the expression "apocalyptic scenario" in the first place. 2 Thessalonians 2:1-12 depicts events which must necessarily precede the climactic eschatological event of the parousia of the Lord Jesus Christ. These are depicted as concrete, "historical" events which will occur at an appointed time and continue for an appointed time, so that all things may happen in accord with God's plan. These events are initially manifested in "forces" which are already at work in the world (e.g., ἡ ἀποστασία, τὸ μυστήριον τῆς ἀνομίας, τὸ κατέχον) and then, at some future point of apocalyptic crisis, as persons (ὁ ἄνθρωπος τῆς ἀνομίας, ὁ ἄνομος, ὁ κατέχων). These "persons" are supernatural figures, insofar as they represent extra-human forces (e.g., rebellion, lawlessness) and are under the direct control of supernatural figures (e.g., God, Satan). The Antagonist, for example, is an embodiment of human rebellion against God (2:3-4) and is an agent of Satan's deception of humanity (2:8-9), although he ultimately functions as an instrument of God's wrath (2:10-12). The purpose of the deception is to make final the division of all humanity into two lots for judgment, a division which is already in the process of appearing in the present time (1:6-7a, 8; 2:10-12). So this scenario not only presents a dualistic anthropology, but shows how that dualistic division into the saved and the lost has come into being. God is clearly the power behind the whole eschatological process (1:5, 2:11-12), and his treatment of the wicked is defended in the short theodicy of 2:11-12. The eschatological material is bounded by references to the justice of God's judgment, on the basis of the punishment of the wicked and the vindication of the good.

We may say, then, that the eschatology of the letter is certainly an apocalyptic eschatology, and the two "scenes" of 1:5-10 (the episode in the Last Judgment) and 2:1-12 (the apocalyptic scenario) are both "apocalyptic" in their orientation. This orientation therefore also tells us something about the intention of each scene in and of itself, i.e., apart from its context within the letter: the primary purpose of each scene is to provide consolation to the congregation[54]. This general characteristic of apocalyptic literature is demonstrated clearly in the scenario of 2:1-12. As we have remarked above, the outstanding fact about the apocalyptic Antagonist who deceives the wicked and threatens the faithful is his swift and sure destruction (2:3b, 8). Thus it is

---

[54] Consolation is a major function of Jewish apocalyptic literature; cf. Russell, *Method and Message*, pp. 17–18; Hanson, *The Dawn of the Apocalyptic*, p. 186; but see also the qualifications of John J. Collins, *The Apocalyptic Imagination* (New York: Crossroad, 1984), pp. 31–32.

sure both that the wicked will be destroyed as a result of misplacing their loyalty in the Antagonist, and that the threat to the faithful will come to an early end. Throughout, God is portrayed as being in sure control of all events. It is his will which determines the "appointed time" of the Antagonist and restrains him so that he will not appear too soon (2:6). It is by his will that the wicked are allowed to be deceived (2:11-12). This is the basis of consolation for those who are faithful to God's will as revealed through the tradition: that this same God will be present, as at the beginning, so at the end (cf. Rev. 22:12-13).

However, the intention of the author in presenting the scenario should be differentiated from the intention of such a scenario in itself. Indeed, the apocalyptic material in 2 Thessalonians appears within two concentric contexts: first, within the context of the *narratio* and *probatio*, where it serves a particular rhetorical function, and second, within the context of the letter as a whole, where it serves another but related rhetorical function.

Within the context of the *narratio*, the traditional apocalyptic material of 1:5-10 serves as an ἔνδειγμα intended to show the congregation the final outcome of the eschatological process. This outcome is judgment and God's righteous reversal of the fortunes of good and evil (1:6-7a). This scene from the Last Judgment prepares the reader for the apocalyptic scenario of 2:1-12 by placing it within the context of the ultimate outcome of the eschatological events. The scenario of 2:1-12, in contrast, shows the preliminary process through which God divides humanity into the two opposing groups who will stand before the judgment seat of Christ; as explained above, the eschatological process transforms the present division of humanity into those who are faithful to Christ and those who are not into the final dualism between the saved and the lost.

The function of the apocalyptic scenario of 2:1-12 within the specific context of the *probatio*, however, is formally distinct from its inherent meaning as an eschatological vision. Rather, it is a means of disproving a false doctrinal proclamation. The scenario is included not for its information about the eschatological progression per se, but because this information serves to make the author's argument, which is only incidentally concerned with the time of various eschatological events. In other words, the scenario has a function in itself as a description of apocalyptic events, but within the context of the *probatio* it has another function, i.e., to prove a disputed point of doctrine. The particular point of doctrine is the time of the Day of the Lord, and the author uses this scenario because a proper understanding of the eschatological progression will not only refute the false proclamation, but also guard the believer against other forms of "deception", and promote steadfastness in faithfulness to the tradition. Failure to understand the scenario and the eschatological progression will render one prey to deception in these matters, and ultimately cause one to be condemned at judgment. A proper understanding is thus not only expedient in the present crisis, it is necessary for eschatological salvation. The "consoling" truth of the apocalyptic scenario has become a "saving" truth of a point of doctrine.

Both apocalyptic scenes have another, larger context as well, that of the letter as a whole. Here they serve another function relative to the intention of the entire letter, and serve to prepare the readers to follow the course of action enjoined by the author in 3:1-13, i.e., adherence to the inherited tradition. In simple terms, both apocalyptic scenes promote the purpose of the deliberative rhetoric which carries the message of the letter[55]. In this larger context, the judgment scene of 1:5-10, with its dualistic division of humanity into two groups, the saved and the lost, reminds the congregation of the ultimate consequences of the moral decisions made in the present. Those who do not know God and do not obey the gospel of our Lord Jesus Christ *now* will be outcast from his presence *then*; those who suffer *now* will find rest *then*. We may say that the scene functions as the apocalyptic equivalent of a *momento mori*, a *momento iudicari*. The remembrance of the final outcome of one's actions will ensure that one does what is right; in this case, one will adhere to the tradition as presented by the author.

In the larger context of the whole letter, the apocalyptic scenario of 2:1-12 serves to vindicate this very tradition as opposed to that version of Paul advocated by the ἄτακτοι. If the author's faithfulness to the Pauline tradition is vindicated, however, so is his authority over the congregation, since it is only the leader who is perceived as faithful to the model of the apostle who will be accepted and followed by the congregation the apostle has left behind at his death. As we have seen in the first chapter, those who proclaimed the false message in the congregation thereby gained spiritual status, and claimed the prerogatives allowed spiritual leaders. These "false prophets" were both ἄτακτοι and περιεργαζόμενοι, claiming authority where they in fact had none and meddling in spiritual matters for which they were unsuited. In order for the author to restore the desired "peace" within the congregation, it was necessary for him to refute the ἄτακτοι on the basis of their apocalyptic claims. This would, in turn, eliminate their claim to spiritual leadership and its privileges, rendering them once again ordinary working members of the congregation. The "peace" thereby gained would not only result from the elimination of meddlers and those who are "disorderly", but also from the unification of the congregation in obedience to one tradition, and no less important, one spiritual authority. Acceptance of his apocalyptic scenario and the doctrine it promoted meant for our author the reinforcement of his own spiritual authority and the validation of his instruction to the congregation.

---

[55] See our discussion of the letter as deliberative rhetoric in chap. 1.

The unification of the congregation in acceptance of his authority would guarantee its loyalty to the tradition he espoused and thus its eschatological salvation. This letter, then, represents a battle over spiritual authority, a battle based in the interpretation of the tradition inherited from Paul.

As we have seen, the reason that a conflict over leadership could arise in regard to the whole problem of eschatology was Paul's failure to integrate "the Day of the Lord" (i.e., "the Day of YHWH") as a day of God's wrath into his conception of the parousia of Christ. The reaction of the congregation and our author, on the basis of the Old Testament and some remarks of Paul himself, was to expect the Day of the Lord as a day of wrath that was a necessary preliminary to the return of Jesus Christ as Son of Man (cf. Zeph. 2:1-3, 3:8-10; Joel 2:15-29, 3:17-21; Zech 14:6-21). The reaction of the church at a later stage to this ambiguity in Paul's letters was to equate the Day of the Lord (with "Lord" understood as Jesus, cf. 1 Cor. 1:8, 2 Cor. 1:14) with the parousia (cf. 2 Peter 3:10). This equation, as we have seen, is not justified by Paul's use of the relevant terms.

The author of 2 Thessalonians wrote, then, to offer the proper "Pauline" understanding of "the Day of the Lord" and its place in the eschatological progression. By so doing, he hoped to vindicate his own understanding of the apostle's doctrinal tradition, and so authenticate his own authority in enforcing his understanding of the apostle's ethical tradition upon the congregation. The first task was essential to the second.

At this point, we may well ask whether our author's reinterpretation of Pauline eschatology into a more systematic and overtly apocalyptic form was an isolated phenomenon. Obviously, the letter was written in response to another, "illegitimate" reinterpretation of this sort, but the "problem" of Paul's eschatology may only have been perceived within some Pauline congregations. However, all of Paul's congregations were "apocalyptic" to some extent, and 1 Thessalonians is only one of many letters with some eschatological content. It seems far more likely that 2 Thessalonians is a reflection of a contemporary trend occasioned by the historical events which confronted the second Christian generation. It is now necessary to define this trend or identify some other manifestations of it, and to isolate the particular *Sitz im Leben* which led to the composition of 2 Thessalonians. This shall be the task of our next, concluding chapter.

Chapter IV

2 Thessalonians in the Pauline Tradition

It may be appropriate at this point to review our investigation before attempting to resolve the problem of the place of 2 Thessalonians within the Pauline tradition. In the first chapter, we undertook a rhetorical analysis of 2 Thessalonians and established that it is a work of deliberative rhetoric. This means that the letter was written to convince its readers to follow a particular course of action in the future in order to gain the advantages set out by the author. In this particular case, the intention of the author was to refute the false preaching of the ἄτακτοι in the Pauline congregations, to reinterpret Paul's eschatological teaching, and to bring "peace" to the congregations through the enforcement of obedience to the Pauline tradition as the author understood it. This analysis was then amplified and demonstrated through a verse-by-verse exegesis of the letter. In the second chapter, we compared similar phrases and themes in 1 and 2 Thessalonians in order to determine the nature of the verbal and thematic parallels between the two letters. We discovered that, in spite of structural and verbal similarities between the two, there was little overlap in content except in the most general sense. Indeed, 2 Thessalonians differs from 1 Thessalonians in five major tendencies that indicate its author was someone other than Paul. The author was instead a follower of Paul interpreting Paul's teaching for a later generation. In the third chapter, we investigated the eschatological material of 2 Thessalonians 1:5-10 and 2:1-12, material usually regarded as the "main matter" of the letter. By considering this material within the context of the *probatio* of the letter, we determined that it served both to clarify Paul's own ambiguous eschatological chronology and to provide the readers with an eschatological perspective on the consequences of their present behavior. The apocalyptic scenario of 2:1-12 envisioned three phases of apocalyptic activity: the present, when various forces of evil are already at work in the world; "the Day of the Lord," a day of God's wrath, when those evil forces will be personified at the apocalyptic crisis; and the parousia of Jesus Christ, which will bring history to a close and usher in the Last Judgment.

We are now prepared to find the place of 2 Thessalonians in the Pauline tradition, that is, within the theological movement begun by the apostle and carried on in his name during the subsequent history of the early church. In order to do this, we must examine the historical situation which gave rise to the theological problems the letter addresses, similar reactions in other examples of New Testament literature, and the situation in the Pauline congregations that forms a background to the letter's composition. We shall also examine the author's attitude towards 1 Thessalonians, and reach some conclusions about the various theological trends which are generally labelled "Pauline" by students of the early church.

Before addressing the problem of the historical situation of the churches at the time of the composition of 2 Thessalonians, we must first try to determine an approximate date for the letter. The external evidence is not altogether helpful in this regard. The often-cited passage in Polycarp (Ep. 11:3, 4)[1] appears to refer to 2 Thessalonians 1:4 and 3:15. However, the pertinent text is extant only in Latin, and it is thus unclear that these verses are indeed references to 2 Thessalonians. The first, 11:3, "de vobis etinim gloriatur in omnibus ecclesiis...", recalls ἐν ὑμῖν ἐγκαυχᾶσθαι ἐν ταῖς ἐκκλησίαις..., and the second, 11:4, "non sicut inimicos tales existimetis", recalls μὴ ὡς ἐχθρὸν ἡγεῖσθε, but neither phrase is explicitly linked to the Thessalonian correspondence, and indeed, Polycarp associates the first phrase with the Philippians. Both phrases in Polycarp might well be instances of common Christian phraseology, and it seems unwise to place too much weight upon this evidence. Both of the Thessalonian epistles were included in Marcion's canon around the middle of the second century, and that is the earliest assured attestation for their acceptance as Paul's letters. Even if we were to accept Polycarp's reference as determinative, this would place the acceptance of the letters sometime before 135. Those who have argued for the deutero-Pauline authorship of 2 Thessalonians have tended to place the letter in the last third of the first century[2], and we would agree with this judgment. This period may properly be referred to as the second Christian generation, since it was marked by both a chronological and a situational distance from the days of the earliest disciples, and is also the period that appears to have produced the largest number of those writings that were later incorporated into the New Testament.

The literary output of this generation of Christians was to some extent determined by its historical situation. A series of historical and theological

---

[1] Cited as evidence by, e.g., Milligan, *Thessalonians*, lxxvii; and Frame, *Thessalonians*, p. 39.

[2] Wrede, for example, places the letter around A.D. 100 (Wrede, *Die Echtheit*, p. 114); Masson, around A.D. 100 (Masson, *Les Deux Épitres*, p. 12); Trilling, A.D. 80–100 (Trilling, *Der Zweite Brief*, p. 28); and Lindemann, around A.D. 100 (Andreas Lindemann, "Zum Abfassungszweck des Zweiten Thessalonicherbriefes", *Zeitschrift für die neutestamentliche Wissenschaft* 68 (1977): 35–47, especially 39.

crises faced the believing community after A.D. 70. There was, for example, the Jewish War, which had its climax in the fall of Jerusalem and the destruction of its temple. There is little direct comment on the fall of Jerusalem in the New Testament writings, but it must have been a significant event in the life of the young church[3]. It was, after all, the end of the possibility of traditional Jewish worship, the loss of the central city of both Judaism and Christianity, and the effective end of the priestly aristocracy from which many of the church's most vehement opponents had come. It could also be interpreted as God's judgment on the Chosen People for their rejection of Jesus and his followers, a new beginning of exile at the hands of a new pagan empire.

Before the fall of Jerusalem, however, the Christians had become subject to imperial persecution. They were already the object of popular scorn in Rome when they became Nero's scapegoats for the fire that devastated that city in July of A.D. 64[4]. This was almost certainly a local persecution of the Roman Christians, but it was bloody and violent, to the extent that it even created sympathy for its victims[5]. This was the beginning not only of periodic persecution from Roman officials, but also of the almost continual fear of such persecution. This fear would not have been eased by the accession of Vespasian or his son Titus, both of whom had directed the action against the Jews in Judea[6].

There were also problems within the church, caused by the passing of the first generation of believers, the "eye-witnesses" to the ministry of Jesus. By A.D. 70, the majority of the apostles and the rest of that generation were dead. Papias (c. 60–130), bishop of Hierapolis in Asia Minor, himself learned not from the original disciples or the apostles, but from "those who were their pupils"[7]. Since Papias was a young man during the period of which we speak, it is reasonable to assume that the original disciples were gone, and that "those who were their pupils" were the ones who produced the literature of that period. But this in itself created problems. In the first place, the apostles and other eye-witnesses were the guarantors of the traditions about the Lord, and their loss required the development of a different source of authority and administration within the church. But the loss of the living witness to Jesus' career was itself a blow; Papias zealously sought out those who were followers of the original disciples, "for I supposed that things out of books did not profit

---

[3] This supposition is the basis for John A.T. Robinson's *Redating the New Testament* (London: SCM Press, 1976); cf. the remarks of James Moffatt and Charles F.D. Moule, ibid., pp. 13–14.
[4] Tacitus, *Annals*, 15. 44. 3–4; Seutonius, *Vit. Nero*, 16. 2.
[5] Tacitus, *Annals*, 15. 44. 2–8.
[6] Josephus, *Bell. Jud.* 3. 3–8, 4. 486–90, 657f.
[7] Eusebius, *Hist. Eccles.* 3. 39. 3–4.

me so much as the utterances of a living and abiding voice"[8]. In the second place, the death of the first generation of Christians was further evidence of the delay of the parousia beyond the expectation of the believing community.

The nature of Jesus' own apocalyptic expectation has been a subject of scholarly debate for many years[9], but it seems likely that he envisioned some role for himself and his followers in the apocalyptic drama that was soon to take place, and that his disciples shared this expectation[10]. But the exact nature of that role and of the events surrounding Jesus' return found various expression in the material known collectively as "Q", which underwent redaction even before its inclusion in part in Matthew and Luke[11]. The reinterpretation of Christian eschatology is thus a practice as old as Christian eschatology itself. Paul, for example, modified his original expectation. It appears that he originally led his congregations to believe that Jesus would return before any of the faithful would die of natural causes. Paul later had to modify this view and introduce new instruction about the fate of the dead at the parousia (1 Thess. 4:13-18) and the nature of the resurrection body (1 Cor. 15:35-57)[12]. The longer the church existed in history, the greater the chronological distance between the resurrection of Christ and his parousia. It was necessary to reinterpret the eschatological expectation to account for this delay. This process of reinterpretation continued after Paul's death, into the second century, and on throughout the history of the church.

In spite of this reinterpretation, however, there remain traces of a tradition that the parousia would occur before the last of Jesus' original followers died[13]. The delay of the parousia therefore created a major theological problem for the believers of the second Christian generation. This problem would have been compounded by the occurrence of such "eschatological" events as the "punishment" of the Jews, the destruction of the Temple, and the "tribulation" of persecution at the hands of the imperial authorities.

As we have seen, 2 Thessalonians represents two different interpretations of the eschatological process, but they both reflect a common response to the problem of the delay of the parousia. Their shared solution to the problem is

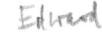

---

[8] Ibid.

[9] For a review of the debate, cf. Ernest P. Sanders, *Jesus and Judaism* (Philadelphia: Fortress Press, 1985), pp. 23–58.

[10] So the analysis of Sanders, ibid., pp. 319–40.

[11] Dieter Lührmann, *Die Redaktion der Logienquelle*, Wissenschaftliche Monographien zum Alten und Neuen Testament 33 (Neukirchen: Neukirchener Verlag, 1969), pp. 69–83; Paul Hoffmann, *Studien zur Theologie der Logienquelle*, Neutestamentliche Abhandlungen 8 (N.F.) (Münster: Verlag Aschendorff, 1972); Athanasius Polag, *Die Christologie der Logienquelle*, Wissenschaftliche Monographien zum Alten und Neuen Testament 45 (Neukirchen: Neukirchener Verlag, 1977).

[12] See our exegesis of 2:5 in chap. 3.

[13] Cf. Mark 9:1, 13:30; Matt. 16:28, 24:34; John 21:20-23; compare Luke 9:27, 21:32.

to reaffirm the imminence of the parousia, but now as part of an eschatological process of several phases, including the present. The present is thus infused with eschatological significance. In the case of the opponents, the present is the time to stand fast in the face of the "wrath" of the Day of the Lord, and presumably to protect oneself with the spiritual "armor" of which Paul speaks in 1 Thessalonians 5:8. In the case of the author, the doctrinal and ethical position of his readers in the present, when the eschatological forces of evil are at work invisibly, will determine their susceptibility to the deceptions of the apocalyptic Antagonist in the future and, as a result, their ultimate fate at the Last Judgment.

As we have noted, this process of reinterpretation was common in Christian apocalyptic literature, as each author attempted to render the apocalyptic tradition coherent to his readers in terms of their own historical experience. Indeed, reinterpretation of earlier texts appears to be as constant as any element in apocalyptic literature. Daniel 9:1-3, 20-27, for example, explains the "seventy years" of exile foretold in Jeremiah 25:11-12, 29:10. Daniel itself was reinterpreted in turn, for example, in 2 Esdras 12:10-36, which offers a novel interpretation of Daniel's vision of the four beasts (Dan. 7:1-9). This reinterpretation is given divine sanction, as the voice addressing Ezra tells him, "The eagle you saw rising from the sea represents the fourth kingdom in the vision seen by your brother Daniel. But he was not given the interpretation which I am now giving you or have already given you" (2 Esdras 12:11-12).

This continual process of reinterpretation was not restricted to Jewish-Christian apocalypticism. The process of development and apocalyptic reinterpretation may also be found in Hellenistic apocalyptic; we find an example in connection with the Oracle of Trophonius. Hans Dieter Betz has traced the development of the tradition concerning the oracle in the various accounts offered by Plutarch, Lucian, Pausanius, and Philostratus[14]. The oracle was located at Lebadeia in Boeotia, in an underground crypt which the consultant entered in order to encounter the God[15]. The oracle apparently became more and more closely identified with a "descent" into the underworld to learn the mysteries of the life to come. Such a descent is familiar not only from the Greek sources going back to Homer (*Odyssey*, book 11), but also from late apocalyptic writings in the Christian tradition[16]. The Trophonius oracle was gradually transformed in the popular mind from a seat of oracular utterance

---

[14] Hans Dieter Betz, "The Problem of Apocalyptic Genre in Greek and Hellenistic Literature: The Case of the Oracle of Trophonius", in *Apocalypticism in the Mediterranean World and the Near East*, ed. David Hellholm (Tübingen: J.C.B. Mohr [Paul Siebeck], 1983), pp. 577–97.

[15] Ibid., pp. 577–78.

[16] Cf. Martha Himmelfarb, *Tours of Hell: An Apocalyptic Form in Jewish and Christian Literature* (Philadelphia: Fortress Press, 1985).

to an entryway to the underworld; its tradition underwent a series of reinterpretations. The process of reinterpretation was thus a common one.

What is perhaps most interesting in this process of reinterpretation as we find it in 2 Thessalonians 2, however, is the accommodation of the present in the apocalyptic drama. This inclusion of the present would appear to arise from the recognition of the death and resurrection of Jesus as the initiatory event of the "last days", which will culminate in his parousia[17]. Since the resurrection of Jesus lay in the church's past and his parousia in the future, the era in which the church existed was itself part of the "last days", a part of the eschatological process. We find the attempt to "fill in the gaps" between the first and the last apocalyptic events not only in 2 Thessalonians 2 but also in the "synoptic apocalypse" of Mark 13 and Matthew 24. That apocalypse, like 2 Thessalonians 2, sets out a series of "stages" through which the church must pass before the return of its Lord.

Several scholars have examined the various similarities between 2 Thessalonians and the synoptic apocalypse[18], but these similarities are of several different sorts. Some points of affinity are more obvious as a result of our rhetorical analysis and exegesis, and these will be dealt with according to their various kinds.

Both 2 Thessalonians and the synoptic apocalypse represent a three-part apocalyptic scenario. In 2 Thessalonians 2, as we have seen, this scenario is composed of the present, the Day of the Lord, and the parousia. The author presents the drama as being in its earliest stage, when the apocalyptic forces are present in impersonal forms. We shall not venture at this point to determine where either Mark or Matthew felt their own time lay within the eschatological process, but both make use of a three-part scenario. In Mark 13, the first stage is called ἀρχὴ ὠδίνων (Mark 13:6-13). This stage is distinguished by the usual tragedies of history, wars, rumors of wars, famines, and earthquakes (Mark 13:7-8). Messianic pretenders will appear during this time (Mark 13:6). The believers will be persecuted by both Jews and Gentiles (Mark 13:9) and families will be divided (Mark 13:12-13). Καὶ εἰς πάντα τὰ ἔθνη πρῶτον δεῖ κηρυχθῆναι τὸ εὐαγγέλιον (Mark 13:10).

The second stage of the schema is ἡ θλῖψις, Mark 13:14-23. The initiatory

---

[17] Cf. Rom. 3:21-28, 5:1-11, 6:1-11, 8:1-11; 1 Cor. 15:12-28; Gal. 3:13-14, 26-29; 1 Thess. 1:9-10; compare Heb. 9:11-28.

[18] Rigaux, *Saint Paul*, pp. 98–101; John Bernard Orchard, "Thessalonians and the Synoptic Gospels", *Biblica* 19 (1938): 19–42; John Pairman Brown, "Synoptic Parallels in the Epistles and Form-History", *New Testament Studies* 10 (1963): 27-48, especially pp. 45–46; Lars Hartmann, *Prophecy Interpreted: The Formation of Some Jewish Apocalyptic Texts and of the Eschatological Discourse Mark 13 par.*, trans. N. Tomkinson and J. Grey (Uppsala: Almquist and Wiksells, 1966), pp. 195–205; Morna D. Hooker, "Trial and Tribulation in Mark XIII", *Bulletin of the John Rylands University Library of Manchester* 65 (1982): 78–99.

event is τὸ βδέλυγμα τῆς ἐρημώσεως ἑστηκότα ὅπου οὐ δεῖ (Mark 13:14a). This event signals the arrival of the apocalyptic crisis, and is followed by a series of consequent actions. These include the flight of those living in Judaea (Mark 13:14b-18) in the face of unparalleled tribulation (Mark 13:19). However, the tribulation will be cut short for the sake of God's elect (Mark 13:20). As a result of the tribulation, false Christs and false prophets will appear and will deceive many people, possibly including some of the faithful (Mark 13:21-22). It is a time that will require extra vigilance from believers (Mark 13:23).

Finally, the parousia comes at the end, Mark 13:24-26. Its coming does not follow immediately upon the end of the tribulation, but occurs at some indefinite time ἐν ἐκείναις ταῖς ἡμέραις μετὰ τὴν θλῖψιν ἐκείνην (Mark 13:24a). The arrival of the parousia is heralded by astrological phenomena familiar from the Old Testament and later Jewish literature[19]. The parousia itself is described in terms taken from Daniel 7:13-14: ὁ υἱὸς τοῦ ἀνθρώπου ἐρχόμενος ἐν νεφέλαις (Mark 13:26). Mark 13:27 refers to the ingathering of the faithful, found also in 1 Thessalonians 4:17. The three phases of the apocalyptic schema in Mark 13, then, are ἀρχὴ ὠδίνων, ἡ θλῖψις, and ὁ υἱὸς τοῦ ἀνθρώπου ἐρχόμενος.

We find a very similar division in Matthew 24. The first stage is ἀρχὴ ὠδίνων, described in terms very similar to those in Mark 13:6-8, 9, 10, 13 (Matt. 24:5-9; compare Matt. 10:17-22a). The second stage is again initiated by the appearance of τὸ βδέλυγμα τῆς ἐρημώσεως (Matt. 24:15a; compare Mark 13:14-23). Matthew refers to this stage as ἡ θλῖψις τῶν ἡμερῶν ἐκείνων (Matt. 24:29a) and θλῖψις μεγάλη (Matt. 24:21). The final stage follows immediately upon "the tribulation of those days", and again is described in terms very like those of Mark 13:24-27 (Matt. 24:29-31). Matthew thus retains the three-part division of the apocalyptic scenario found in Mark, designating the three parts ἀρχὴ ὠδίνων, θλῖψις μεγάλη, and ὁ υἱὸς τοῦ ἀνθρώπου ἐρχόμενος (Matt. 24:30).

Apart from sharing a three-part apocalyptic schema, 2 Thessalonians 2 and the synoptic apocalypses share common features within their respective schema. For example, both include warnings against deceit (2 Thess. 2:3; Mark 13:5, 21-23; Matt. 24:4, 11, 23-26) and warnings against being troubled (θροεῖσθαι, 2 Thess. 2:2, Mark 13:7, Matt. 24:6). There are warnings against false Christs and false prophets (2 Thess. 2:9-10; Mark 13:6b, 21-22; Matt 24:5, 11, 23-24, 26), as well as the explicit statement that the readers have been prepared for these events from an authority in the author's past who is the supposed source of the apocalyptic discourse (2 Thess. 2:5, Mark 13:23,

---

[19] Cf. Isa. 13:10, 34:4; Ezek. 32:7-8; Joel 2:10, 31, 3:15; Sibylline Oracles 3:796-808; Test. Moses 10:3-10; Test. Levi 4:1; 2 Esdras 5:4-5.

Matt. 24:25). Deception is a punishment for the wicked in both scenarios (2 Thess. 2:10-12; Mark 13:6b, 22b; Matt. 24:5b, 10-12, 24), although the persistance of the faithful will result in their ultimate salvation (2 Thess. implies this by contrast with "the lost"; compare Mark 13:13b, 20b, 27; Matt. 24:13, 22, 31). Both scenarios speak of certain "signs" of the end (2 Thess. 2:3b, 8a; Mark 13:6-8, 24-26, 28-31; Matt. 24:5-8, 9-12, 14, 27, 29-30, 32-34), among which is the blasphemy in the Temple (2 Thess. 2:4, Mark 13:14a, Matt. 24:15). The parousia will be followed by the ingathering of the faithful (2 Thess. 2:1b, Mark 13:27, Matt. 24:31).

These common features of the synoptic apocalypse and 2 Thessalonians 2 may reasonably lead us to conclude that their respective authors were drawing on common traditions, traditions found in the Jewish literature and the first generation of Christianity, i.e., the teachings of the apostle Paul and his contemporaries. The prophetic and apocalyptic tradition of Judaism, for example, is the likely source of the idea of the blasphemy in the Temple, based in turn on a historical incident involving Antiochus IV Epiphanes (Dan. 11:30-31). The "ingathering" (ἐπισυναγωγή) of the faithful at the parousia, on the other hand, although possibly derived from Daniel[20], finds its clearest exposition in 1 Thessalonians 4:13-18, where it is presented as a matter previously unknown to the readers[21]. It seems likely that this concept, if not derived directly from Paul, was at least a fairly new one when used in the synoptic apocalypses.

Both 2 Thessalonians and the synoptic apocalypses were also presented in a manner consistent with that of Jewish apocalyptic, i.e., as "prophecies" of a venerated figure out of the past[22]. These two Christian apocalyptic discourses are put into the mouth of an authoritative figure (Paul in the case of 2 Thessalonians, Jesus in the synoptic apocalypse) who provides a "forewarning" of various things that will happen in the figure's "future", which may be past, present, or future from the perspective of the author and his readers. Therefore, when such a figure of the past warns against some "future" danger — in this case, the deceptions of false prophets and false Christs — the warning itself, having been delivered before the advent of such deceivers, that is, sometime in the "past", serves to protect the readers against their deceit. The problem has been anticipated and dealt with in the "past", lending prophetic authority to the warning to be on guard in the present. Indeed, the existence of such false Christs and false prophets, specifically as the false heralds of the approaching "Day of the Lord", finds parallels in polemic directed against false prophets in

---

[20] Cf. Hartmann, *Prophecy Interpreted*, pp. 158, 197.
[21] That this is new information is indicated by the introductory formula, οὐ θέλομεν δὲ ὑμᾶς ἀγνοεῖν, ἀδελφοί....
[22] Russell, *Method and Message*, pp. 127–39.

the Old Testament (cf. Jer. 23:11, 13-17, 21-22, 25-32). It is interesting to note that, while Paul pictures those who are unprepared for the Day of the Lord by echoing the cry of the false prophet, "Peace and security!" (1 Thess. 5:3a; compare Jer. 6:14, 8:11; Ezek 13:10)[23], the false prophets in both 2 Thessalonians 2 and the synoptic apocalypses are those who predict the apocalyptic events before they have truly come (2 Thess. 2:2; Mark 13:6b, 21-22; Matt. 24:5, 11, 23-24, 26).

The particular shape of the apocalyptic tradition as it is reworked in 2 Thessalonians 2 and the synoptic apocalypse seems to derive in large part from a common response to a common historical situation. Both the scenarios are results of an attempt to account for the delay of the parousia after the crises of the decade A.D. 60–70, which could readily have been interpreted as "signs" of the impending end. Another problem, at least in the Pauline churches, was the related problem of finding a place for "the Day of the Lord" as a day of wrath in the eschatological schema. It is difficult to determine to what extent the conflict between "the day of wrath" and "the day of judgement" was perceived as a problem in the congregations not under Paul's influence. On the one hand, the term "the Day of the Lord" and the various forms of "the Day of the Lord Jesus" appear almost exclusively in Paul's writings (but cf. Acts 2:20; parallels in Joel 3:4; 2 Peter 3:10, 13; Rev. 16:14). On the other hand, the idea formed a part of the eschatological tradition with which the authors of the New Testament had to deal. Suffice it to say that the synoptic apocalypse includes a "day" of tribulation in addition to the parousia (Mark 13:14-23, Matt. 24:15-24), and this day is a time of trial for the faithful as well as punishment for the wicked. Indeed, it is for the sake of the elect that the time of tribulation is shortened (Mark 13:20, Matt. 24:22). This "day" of tribulation is prior to and separate from the "day" of judgment, which is initiated by the parousia of Christ (Mark 13: 24-27, Matt 24:29-31). This idea of what Hartmann calls "the preliminary time of evil" is found in apocalyptic works of the Old Testament and the pseudepigrapha[24], and survives in these three-phase apocalyptic scenarios.

We may now turn to the question of where within the eschatological process described in the synoptic apocalypse Mark and Matthew believed their own time to lie. The entire scenario of the synoptic apocalypse is described as a series of events in the future, foretold by Jesus. Since the scenario deals with the whole range of history from the resurrection (since the existence of Jesus' disciples as an organized group in his absence is assumed, cf. Mark. 13:9-13, Matt. 24:9-10) to the parousia, the time of Mark and Matthew must necessarily be included at some point within the eschatological

---

[23] Compare the comments on this slogan by Betz, "De tranquilitate animi".
[24] Hartmann, *Prophecy Interpreted*, pp. 28–34.

process. If we identify an earlier apocalypse or fragments of such as the foundation of Mark 13 and Matthew 24, we must not assume that the "present" of that tradition or traditions was the same as the "present" Mark or Matthew found within it. In other words, each as an author would want his readers to be aware of where they stood in relation to the parousia, in order to prepare them for whatever events might befall them. This is a recurring idea in Mark 13 (cf. Mark 13:5, 9, 13b, 23, 35-37) and it appears in Matthew 24 as well, even apart from the parallels to Mark 13 (Matt. 24:26-28). Therefore, we may expect both authors' versions of the synoptic apocalypse to give some indication of how far they believed the apocalyptic process had progressed by the time they wrote.

Mark 13 includes two chronological notes (Mark 13:10, 14). The first appears to consign Mark's own era to the ἀρχὴ ὠδίνων, since it says that in that stage, εἰς πάντα τὰ ἔθνη πρῶτον δεῖ κηρυχθῆναι τὸ εὐαγγέλιον. However, it is entirely possible that Mark believed that this process of evangelization had been completed in the first Christian generation. We may compare Paul's attitude towards his ministry in Romans 15:17-29, and the remarks of Clement of Rome: "He [Paul] taught righteousness to all the world (ὅλον τὸν κόσμον), and when he had reached the limits of the West, he gave his testimony before the rulers..." (1 Clem. 5:7). Paul intended to preach in Spain, and thus to fulfill his mission to spread the gospel to the Gentiles in "all the world". Mark 13:10 thus does not necessarily indicate at what point Mark wrote; as Vincent Taylor notes, "...Mark is not thinking of centuries of evangelization, but of the world in his day"[25].

The second chronological note (Mark 13:14) involves the prediction of the desecration of the Temple, derived from Daniel 11:31b, 12:11 (cf. Dan. 9:27). Such a "desolating sacrilege" did in fact stand in the Temple when Titus' soldiers erected their battle standards in the courtyard of the Temple in A.D. 70[26]. We may reasonably say, then, that Mark wrote either during the Jewish War, when the fall of Jerusalem seemed certain or, more probably, after the fall of the city and the various unhappy events which followed. The command to flee from Jerusalem may then be seen as a justification after the fact for the flight of the Christians to Pella before the fall of the capital[27], but the historicity of this event is seriously in doubt[28].

It is significant that there is no event between the end of the tribulation

---

[25] Vincent Taylor, *The Gospel According to St. Mark*, 2nd ed. (New York: St. Martin's Press, 1966), p. 637.

[26] Josephus, *Bell. Jud.* 6. 316; cf. *Bell. Jud.* 2. 169–74, *Ant.* 18. 55–59.

[27] Eusebius, *Hist. Eccles.* 3. 5. 3; cf. J. Weiss, *Earliest Christianity*, trans. Frederick C. Grant, 2 vols. (New York: Harper and Row Torchbooks, 1959), 2:714.

[28] Thus the analysis of the Pella tradition by Gerd Lüdemann, *Paulus der Heidenapostel* 2 (Göttingen: Vandenhoeck und Ruprecht, 1983), pp. 265–86.

(Mark 13:14-23) and the astronomical signs which will appear ἐν ἐκείναις ταῖς ἡμέραις μετὰ τὴν θλῖψιν ἐκείνην (Mark 13:24a). This means there is a "breathing space" of indeterminate length between the end of the tribulation and the advent of Jesus Christ. This is a time when the faithful are most in danger of being misled (Mark 13:21-22). It is at this point that we find the dominical admonition, ὑμεῖς δὲ βλέπετε · προείρηκα ὑμῖν πάντα (Mark 13:23). We would argue that Mark wrote his gospel within this "breathing space" after the tribulation following the fall of Jerusalem and before the arrival of the parousia. Mark describes this as the time of greatest spiritual danger, and depicts Jesus confirming that this, as well as the whole eschatological scenario, has been "foretold". The danger of deception apparently arises because the majority of the apocalyptic events have taken place, and the only remaining "sign" is the change in the sun, moon, and stars (Mark 13:24b). The end is indeed imminent, and this is why the elect might be misled, since having survived the great tribulation, they expect the return of Christ at any time. It is only the evangelist's insistence on the preliminary appearance of the astronomical signs of the parousia that could prevent the elect from being misled; the scenario therefore serves as a means of protection for the faithful, as was also the case with 2 Thessalonians. This interpretation is consistent with the disclaimer of Mark 13:32-37, to the effect that no one knows the day or the hour of the parousia except God. The apocalyptic scenario itself does not contradict this statement, since from the perspective of Mark and his readers, all of the premonitionary events and "signs" except the last are in the past. All that remains is the parousia itself. Such disclaimer would also be an effective tool against those within the congregation for which Mark wrote who might proclaim the parousia before the time; again, we might compare 2 Thessalonians 2. This hypothesis of the place of Mark's own time in the apocalyptic scenario also makes sense of the evangelist's retention of the apparently traditional saying of Mark 13:29-31 (cf. John 21:20-23). Addressed to Mark's readers, who have seen all these things take place, it is a reassurance that they shall see the parousia as well. Finally in support of our hypothesis, it need hardly be pointed out that it is between Mark 13:23 and 13:24, between the end of the tribulation and the advent of the parousia, that the predicted events pass from the fulfilled to the unfulfilled.

Matthew, although he shares the tripartite apocalyptic scenario with Mark, perceives his own time as falling elsewhere within the eschatological process than the "breathing space" Mark places between the great tribulation and the parousia. Matthew vitiates the three-phase format of the scenario somewhat by the close association he creates between the second and third phases. The parousia follows "immediately" after the tribulation (εὐθέως δὲ μετὰ τὴν θλῖψιν τῶν ἡμερῶν ἐκείνων, Matt. 24:29a), and "the end" is to come after the world-wide evangelization, which is part of the first stage of the scenario

(Matt. 24:14b: καὶ τότε ἥξει τὸ τέλος). This first stage is also a time when there is a great spiritual danger of deception. Matthew mentions false Christs (Matt. 24:5) and false prophets (Matt. 24:11), noting that both will lead many astray (πλανήσουσιν πολλούς). This is the time when many will fall away, betray and hate their fellows (Matt. 24:10); this verse has no parallel in Mark. However, false Christs and false prophets will also appear in the days of the great tribulation (Matt. 24:23-24). At that point, however, the emphasis seems to be on the unmistakability of the return of Christ. The dominical admonition ὑμεῖς δὲ βλέπετε (Mark 13:23a) has been deleted, and another pair of false proclamations concerning the messiah's whereabouts has been added (Matt. 24:26). The point is made in the following verses: "For as the lightning comes from the east and shines as far as the west, so will be the coming of the Son of Man. Wherever the body is, there the eagles will be gathered together" (Matt. 24:27-28; cf. Luke 17:24, 37b). Matthew uses this second reference to false Christs and false prophets to make it clear that there can be no "secret" return of Christ, no "hidden" parousia, but that when the parousia takes place, Christ's return will be as unmistakable as a flash of lightning. We may note that Matthew here is making the point we should have expected the author of 2 Thessalonians to make if his opponents had indeed been proclaiming the parousia rather than the preliminary "Day of the Lord". We may deduce from this point made in Matthew that there were those who did proclaim such a "secret" return of Christ; Matthew's inclusion of the synoptic apocalypse may have been intended in part to refute such a proclamation. What Matthew says about the false Christs and false prophets in Matthew 24:23-24 may of course also be applied to those who appear during the ἀρχὴ ὠδίνων (Matt. 24:5, 11).

The close association between the great tribulation and the parousia in Matthew 24 leads us to believe he placed his own time in the ἀρχὴ ὠδίνων, the first phase of the apocalyptic drama. In the first place, he has added several verses to Mark's description of this time, specifically referring to apostasy, the appearance of false prophets, and the multiplication of wickedness while the love of many people becomes cold (Matt. 24:10-12). The reference to many falling away (σκανδαλισθήσονται πολλοί; Matt. 24:10) places the events described in verses 10-12 within the church; their insertion just before the reassurance that "he who endures to the end will be saved" (Matt. 24:13; cf. Mark 13:13b) places that verse too within that context, rendering it a call for faithfulness within the church, rather than steadfastness in persecution. This suggests that the evangelist is addressing a situation in his own time, and that his own time is thus that of the ἀρχὴ ὠδίνων. Also suggestive of this theory is the close association between the preaching of the gospel and the end (Matt. 24:14). "This gospel of the kingdom will be preached throughout the whole world, as a testimony to all nations" (εἰς μαρτύριον πᾶσιν τοῖς ἔθνεσιν;

Matt. 24:14a) recalls Matthew 10:18b (εἰς μαρτύριον αὐτοῖς καὶ τοῖς ἔθνεσιν). This latter verse is of course a part of the mission discourse of Matthew 10, specifically the section parallel to Mark 13:9-13 (Matt. 10:17-22a). What Mark relegated to the first phase of the apocalyptic scenario, Matthew regards as the continuing mission of the church, just as he considers its mission the preaching of the gospel to all nations (Matt. 28:19), a mission being carried out in the present time of the ἀρχὴ ὠδίνων.

It appears that Matthew, like the author of 2 Thessalonians, expected a future apocalyptic crisis involving a blasphemy in the Temple (2 Thess. 2:4, Matt 24:15)[29], which would be followed shortly by the parousia (2 Thess. 2:4, Matt. 24:29a). All three authors, Mark, Matthew, and the author of 2 Thessalonians, agreed that their own era, whatever its place in the apocalyptic scenario, was a time of great spiritual danger, when the threat of deception was ever present (Mark 13:21-23; Matt. 24:4-6, 10-13; 2 Thess. 2:2-3a).

Indeed, deception is the major threat to the community in each of these apocalyptic scenarios, specifically deception as to the progress of the eschatological process. The author of 2 Thessalonians writes to discredit the ἄτακτοι who are prematurely announcing the presence of the Day of the Lord (2 Thess. 2:2-3). By so doing, they render their hearers susceptible to the deceptions of the apocalyptic Antagonist who, appearing after what the ἄτακτοι believe is the Day of the Lord, will mislead them through his false signs and wonders into believing that he is the returned Lord (2 Thess. 2:9-12).

The faithful, however, will know when the Day of the Lord arrives (2 Thess. 2:3-4, 6-8), and will thus be prepared for the deceptions of the Antagonist. In the same way, the synoptic apocalypse warns its readers of various false signs of the parousia, most significantly the advent of false prophets (Mark 13:21-22; Matt. 24:5, 26-28; cf. 2 Thess. 2:2-3) and false Christs (Mark 13:5-6, 22; Matt. 24:5, 24; cf. 2 Thess. 2:9). The faithful are not to mistake the various tribulations of history for those unparalleled woes of the "great tribulation" (Mark 13:7-8, 19; Matt. 24:6-8, 21). The parousia itself will be unmistakable (Mark 13:24-27, Matt. 24:29-31), and the faithful must remain steadfast to the end (Mark 13:13b, Matt. 24:13). The idea of avoiding deception and remaining steadfast recurs in each of these apocalyptic scenarios. They reaffirm the imminence of the parousia while accounting for its delay and yet also depict those who announce the approach of the end before the time as perpetrators of deception. The only sure guide for the faithful for

---

[29] This may be a conscious anachronism in both 2 Thessalonians 2 and Matthew 24 (Lindemann, "Zum Abfassungszweck", p. 44), but it seems more likely that the strength of this particular apocalyptic motif had survived in spite of the destruction of the Temple in A.D. 70; ultimate vindication of God's power follows the ultimate abuse of his sanctity.

the development of the eschatological process is the prophetic scenario offered by a venerated teacher of the first Christian generation, either Jesus (as in Mark 13 and Matthew 24) or Paul (as in 2 Thessalonians 2). This is of course consistent with the pseudepigraphic nature of Jewish apocalyptic literature and with the description of the content of the book of Revelation as ἀποκάλυψις Ἰησοῦ Χριστοῦ, ἣν ἔδωκεν αὐτῷ ὁ θεός (Rev. 1:1a). In this way the various authors emphasized the continuity of their eschatological instruction with the inherited traditions upon which it was based and which it reinterpreted.

We find a striking instance of the problem of the delay of the parousia, reinterpretation, and warning of deception in the last chapter of the gospel according to John[30]. It is generally agreed among scholars that this chapter (John 21) is the work of the redactor of John 1–20[31]. Our concern is with John 21:20-23, the conversation of Jesus and Peter about the beloved disciple. In John 21:23, the redactor reports the existence of a λόγος in the Johannine congregations: ἐξῆλθεν οὖν οὗτος ὁ λόγος εἰς τοὺς ἀδελφοὺς ὅτι ὁ μαθητὴς ἐκεῖνος οὐκ ἀποθνῄσκει (John 21:23a). This appears to be a tradition similar to that of Mark 9:1, 13:30; Matthew 16:28, 24:34, to the effect that some of those who heard Jesus would live to see the parousia. In this case, the report is tied to a specific individual, the beloved disciple. This λόγος must have been used as a justification for the delay of the parousia which maintained the idea of imminence; as long as the beloved disciple was alive, the parousia was not "delayed", but could still be expected before he did die. The redactor of John considers this opinion to be wrong; presumably the beloved disciple had died by the time the redactor wrote John 21 (cf. John 19:35, 21:24). The redactor combats this false interpretation of Jesus' oracle by first writing it down within its "historical" context, i.e., as part of the conversation with Peter, and then by giving a "literal" interpretation of the Lord's words (John 21:23b)[32].

This means that the redactor of John, like the author of 2 Thessalonians, is

---

[30] I am indebted to Professor Hans Dieter Betz for this exposition of John 21:20-23.

[31] Cf. Rudolph Bultmann, *The Gospel of John: A Commentary*, trans. G.R. Beasley-Murray (Oxford: Basil Blackwell, 1971), pp. 700–6; Raymond E. Brown, *The Gospel According to John XIII–XXI*, Anchor Bible (Garden City, N.Y.: Doubleday and Co., 1966), pp. 1077–82.

[32] Cf. the theory of Bultmann, *The Gospel of John*, pp. 715–16. Bultmann assumes the work of two redactors in this brief section, the second correcting the impression that the beloved disciple would not die. However, this theory is based on the assumption that the one discrediting that impression would rework Jesus' saying to make its meaning clear. But if indeed ἐξῆλθεν οὖν οὗτος ὁ λόγος εἰς τοὺς ἀδελφούς, the redactor would have to correct the saying as it was known, by offering the correct, "literal" meaning. We may compare the task of the author of 2 Thessalonians in correcting "misinterpretations" that could be made of 1 Thessalonians.

combatting an incorrect interpretation of an inherited eschatological tradition within a community. Just as the author of 2 Thessalonians offers a "correct" interpretation of the disputed meaning of Paul's teaching in 1 Thessalonians, so the redactor of John presents the "correct" meaning of a dominical oracle which was misunderstood in the Johannine congregations. The redactor claims authority for his interpretation of Jesus' λόγος by including it within the scope of the writing which is verified by the witness of the beloved disciple (John 21:24); "these things" includes not only the "original" gospel of John 1-20, but also the redactor's addition, John 21, and, by position, pre-eminently the reinterpretation of the Lord's saying in John 21:22-23. We find a similar verification in 2 Thessalonians 3:17, which validates the entire letter as a Pauline product.

The presence of "error" in the Johannine congregation is refuted by the redactor of John only by the appeal to the reliability of the true witness, the beloved disciple (cf. John 19:35, 21:24), in spite of the fact that the interpretation of the dominical saying in 21:23b is the redactor's own. However, in 1 John we discover a situation that is more serious and requires a stronger refutation. There doctrinal error is explicitly associated with moral error (1 John 1:6, 10; 2:3-6, 9-11; 3:6-10, 17; 4:8; 5:2-3); one's immoral behavior is a sure sign of one's doctrinal error. We may compare 2 Thessalonians 2:15, 3:6, 14. Moreover, the "opposition" perceived by the author of 1 John is not to be corrected by an appeal to a reliable witness, as in John 19:35, 21:24; rather, it is evidence not only of a corrupt doctrine and impure morals, but of the presence of eschatological evil. The author admits that those who are in error are (or were) members of the Johannine congregations (1 John 2:19), but their doctrinal and moral error has revealed that they are the forces of antichrist, and the end is therefore near (1 John 2:18). The one who denies the correct doctrine is antichrist (1 John 2:22), the one who sins is of the devil (1 John 3:8-10). The apocalyptic powers of evil are already at work in the congregation; we may compare 2 Thessalonians 2:3, 7; 3:6-13. Because of this apocalyptic presence in the congregations, the author of 1 John warns his readers against deception (1 John 1:8, 2:26, 3:7, cf. 4:6). This deception is specifically in regard to what is good and what is evil, but is eschatological insofar as the author makes such a close connection between belief and behavior. He believes the world is already divided into the two lots of judgment: the saved and the lost (1 John 1:5-7; 2:9-11, 15-17, 18-25; 3:4-10, etc.). This is because the end is near, and the lost already comprise the hordes of antichrist (1 John 2:18). As in 2 Thessalonians and the synoptic apocalypses, those who disagree with the interpretation of the tradition offered by the author are not simply wrong, but are the representatives of eschatological evil, aiders and abettors of the deceptions of the apocalyptic Antagonist, allies of the devil. The congregations already face the great Adversary, and only by adherence to the instruction of the venerated teachers, as interpreted by the various authors, can the faithful hope to escape the scourge of apocalyptic deception.

The threat of deception appears also in the last, eschatological chapter of the Didache. There we find another apocalyptic scenario of several "stages", just as we have in 2 Thessalonians 2 and the synoptic apocalypse. First, there is a future time designated as "the last days" (ταῖς ἐσχάταις ἡμέραις). This is characterized both by the appearance of false prophets and by the corruption of the faithful through the activities of these false prophets: "For in the last days the false prophets and the corrupters will be multiplied, and the sheep will change into wolves, and love shall turn into hate" (Did. 16:3). That a change is made specifically among the faithful is indicated by their characterization as "sheep" (changed into the chief enemy of sheep, wolves), and by their primary attribute of love (ἀγάπη; changed into its opposite, hate). This change among some of the faithful is a sign of increasing lawlessness (ἀνομία), and has as its consequence mutual hatred, persecution, and betrayal. The author is clearly concerned exclusively with those inside the Christian community, some of whom will remain faithful, but others of whom will be corrupted and prove enemies to their former brothers. That such a change is possible is the reason for the exhortation of the first verse of this chapter, and for the grim reminder presented by the second verse: "... the whole time of your faith shall not profit you unless you have become perfect in the last time."

The increase in lawlessness and its consequences are a prelude to the appearance of the apocalyptic Antagonist, "the deceiver of the world" (ὁ κοσμοπλανής). His deception is specifically that he shall appear "as a son of God, and he will perform signs and wonders, and the earth will be given over into his hands" (Did. 16:4b). He deceives by appearing to be "a son of God", perhaps indicating that he will be mistaken for the returning Christ. The Antagonist's career is one of deception and moral outrage: "he shall commit forbidden acts which have never been since the beginning of the age" (Did. 16:4c). Then follows the "fiery trial" (ἡ πύρωσις τῆς δοκιμασίας) that overtakes all of "the creation of mankind" (ἡ κτίσις τῶν ἀνθρώπων): "many shall be led into sin and be lost, but those who remain steadfast in their faith shall be saved by the accursed one himself" (Did. 16:5b).

This "fiery trial" is followed by a series of three events that usher in the return of the Lord. These are called "signs" (σημεῖα) of the truth (Did. 16:6a), and the first two of the three are designated "the sign of..." (Did. 16:6b). The first is "the sign of an opening in heaven" (σημεῖον ἐκπετάσεως ἐν οὐρανῷ), the second "the sign of the sound of a trumpet" (σημεῖον φωνῆς σάλπιγγος), and the third is the resurrection of the faithful dead. These three signs are followed by the parousia: "Then shall the world see the Lord coming on the clouds of heaven" (Did. 16:8).

Although it is clear that Didache 16 describes the apocalyptic drama as a series of events occuring in a certain order, it is not clear how many "stages" or "acts" are in the author's mind. There are several chronological notes, the first being ἐν... ταῖς ἐσχάταις ἡμέραις (Did. 16:3a), followed in 16:4b by the consecutive καὶ τότε: "and then the deceiver of the world will appear...". The consecutive τότε occurs again at the beginning of verse 5, "then shall the creation of mankind come to the fiery trial...", followed by the series of events preliminary to the parousia: "And then shall appear the signs of the truth. First... then (εἶτα)... and the third..." (Did. 16:6). Finally comes the parousia: τότε ὄψεται ὁ κόσμος τὸν κύριον (Did. 16:8a).

This would seem to indicate a series of five successive events, with the fourth of these, "the signs of the truth", further broken down into three more successive events (Did. 16:6-7). However, the fourth and fifth of the primary successive events are linked in such a way as to form a single "act" of the apocalyptic drama, for the resurrection of the dead is tied explicitly to the parousia of the Lord. In verse 7, the prediction of the resurrection is modified with an allusion to Zechariah 14:5: "... but not all [the dead shall rise], but as it was said, 'The Lord shall come and all his holy ones with him'". In other words, the reason why the resurrection of the faithful dead takes place last in the series of preliminary "signs" is because they must join the Lord at his coming, which is described in the next verse (Did. 16:8). The three "signs of the truth", then, are preliminary to but explicitly associated with the immediate coming of the Lord; they are all part of the single "act" of the parousia.

The emphasis upon these final signs as "signs of the truth" puts them into opposition with the "deception" which has characterized what has gone before. This deception is the work of "the deceiver of the world", the apocalyptic Antagonist, whose entire purpose is to lead astray those who are not protected by their steadfast faithfulness. Those who are lost during the "fiery trial" are precisely those who "shall be led into sin" (σκανδαλισθήσονται), i.e., those who have followed the Antagonist because they were deceived by his appearance as "a son of God" and by his signs and wonders. Thus the appearance of the Antagonist as "the deceiver of the world" and the "fiery trial" are linked together, both by the reference to the many who "shall be led into sin" on the one hand and "those who remain steadfast in their faith" on the other, and by the contrast between "the signs of the truth" and the preceding description of the work of deception (Did. 16:4b-5), which is also manifested by "signs", i.e., the false signs and wonders of the Antagonist (Did. 16:4b).

If this argument is correct, we have in Didache 16 another example of an apocalyptic scenario divided into three main "acts". The first would be that described in 16:3-4a, which takes place "in the last days". This is the time when "the false prophets and the corrupters will be multiplied", that is, when human agents of deception already present in the world shall be greater in number. As a result, the present phenomenon of apostasy from the faith will also increase, as "the sheep will change into wolves" and lawlessness shall increase. But this stage of the apocalyptic scenario does not involve a change in the believers' situation, but merely an increase in the forces that oppose them. The very fact that this situation is described in terms of "increase" indicates that it is linked to the present, and implies that the difference between the present and "the last days" is not very great, a matter of "quantity" rather than "quality". The faithful will know that "the last days" have arrived only when they discover that their continuing situation has taken a turn for the worse. But it is still a time characterized by the activity of human lawlessness, of human corruption, of human deception.

The situation changes at 16:4b, with the introduction of "the deceiver of the world". It is no longer human, natural evil at work but evil which is in some sense supernatural, and which claims to be divine. The Antagonist appears after the increase of lawlessness, but is himself characterized in terms of deception (Did. 16:4b) and the unparalleled nature of his iniquitous acts (Did. 16:4c). He is something new, which sets him apart from the old situation of the present and "the last days". It is his work, as we have seen, which leads to the time of the "fiery trial" (Did. 16:5). It is in opposition to his work of deception that "the signs of truth" which herald the parousia appear.

Briefly stated, then, the three "acts" of the apocalyptic scenario presented in Didache 16 are first, "the last days", characterized by an increase of the evils which already threaten the faithful; second, the appearance of "the deceiver of the world", which culminates in the "fiery trial"; and third, the parousia, which is heralded by the appearance of "the signs of truth".

Whether or not one accepts this analysis of Didache 16 as a three-part apocalyptic scenario, several points remain. The scenario is clearly presented as a series of events moving towards a culmination in the parousia, and consisting of several distinct stages or "acts". The apocalyptic Antagonist is conceived of primarily in terms of deception, a deception aimed at convincing those who do not remain steadfast in their faith that he is some sort of divine figure, attested to by signs and wonders. This coming follows the rise of lawlessness (ἀνομία), and he himself commits forbidden acts (ποιήσει ἀθέμιτα) which have never been since the beginning of the age. The "fiery trial" is a consequence of the work of the Antagonist. Those who are lost are the many who "shall be led into sin", i.e., by the deception of the deceiver of the world, and those who are saved are those who remain steadfast in spite of him. It should especially be noted that the "fiery trial" which brings God's wrath upon the lost takes place as a part of the second "act" of the scenario, and clearly before the signs which indicate the coming of the parousia.

Any literary connection between Didache 16 and 2 Thessalonians 2 is only conjectural. There is a possible allusion to 2 Thessalonians 2:9 in Didache 16:4bc (but cf. Matthew 24:24). It is likely that this last chapter of the Didache was inspired by a wide range of apocalyptic texts[33], and its final form is a product of the author or the community which produced it. But what is of primary interest for our purposes is that this chapter provides another example of an apocalyptic scenario of three "acts" occurring in chronological sequence. Once again we find a preliminary time of lawlessness, a crisis initiated by the appearance of an apocalyptic antagonist and leading to a "fiery trial" which executes God's wrath, and the culminating return of the Lord Christ.

As we have seen, the function of the apocalyptic material in 2 Thessalonians, apart from its specific function within the *probatio* to disprove the false proclamation, was to strengthen the readers in their resolve to do what was right by reminding them of the ultimate outcome of their present behavior. We have ventured to call this use of apocalyptic material a *memento iudicari*. The argument of the author against the deception practiced by the ἄτακτοι was strengthened by a depiction of the consequences of the decision the readers make as to what to believe: blessedness with the Lord after judgment, or destruction in separation from him (2 Thess. 1:9-10). This function of the apocalyptic material is demonstrated by the invocation in the exhortatory section of the letter of Jesus Christ as the authority by whom a command is given. Thus in 3:6a we find: παραγγέλλομεν δὲ ὑμῖν, ἀδελφοί, ἐν ὀνόματι τοῦ κυρίου [ἡμῶν] Ἰησοῦ Χριστοῦ, and in 3:12a: τοῖς δὲ τοιούτοις παραγγέλλομεν καὶ παρακαλοῦμεν ἐν κυρίῳ Ἰησοῦ Χριστῷ.... The author invokes Jesus Christ, who is both eschatological judge (2 Thess. 1:7b-8) and victor (2 Thess. 2:8), and who will destroy all those who are not obedient.

We find an analogous situation in the messages to the seven churches in Revelation 2–3. There, too, certain commands are given explicitly in the name of Jesus; indeed, Jesus dictates the messages to John, the apocalyptic visionary. Jesus is characterized as both eschatological judge (Rev. 2:12; 3:1, 7, 14) and victor (Rev. 2:1, 8, 18), although the military metaphor is clearly predominant here. The seven letters also offer commands and exhortations with an eschatological threat (Rev. 2:5, 16, 22; 3:3) or promise (Rev. 2:7, 10b, 26-27; 3:4, 10-11). Most of the letters deal with a single issue, with the exception of that to Pergamum (Rev. 2:12-17), just as the exhortatory section of 2 Thessalonians deals almost exclusively with the problems of the ἄτακτοι (2 Thess. 3:6-13). The seven letters are linked with an elaborate apocalyptic scenario which depicts past, present, and future events within the terms of

---

[33] Cf. John S. Kloppenborg, "Didache 16:6-8 and Special Matthean Tradition", *Zeitschrift für die neutestamentliche Wissenschaft* 70 (1979): 54–67.

apocalyptic imagery, making clear the connections between present behavior and future eschatological fate (cf. Rev. 6:9-11; 7:13-17).

The letters to the seven churches in Revelation 2-3, then, are exhortations written in the name of the Lord Jesus to correct particular problems in the congregations addressed so that they may be among the blessed when the end comes; they are accompanied by eschatological threat or promise, and are associated with an apocalyptic scenario which depicts the future fate of both good and evil. The affinities with 2 Thessalonians should be obvious. 2 Thessalonians, as we have remarked previously, fulfills an eschatological function by forestalling the power of ἡ ἀποστασία and τὸ μυστήριον τῆς ἀνομίας through exposure of the apocalyptic evil at work in them. It, like the letters of Revelation 2-3, seeks to "put things right" before the dawn of the apocalyptic crises it describes. It, like Revelation 2-3, offers its exhortatory commands in the name of Jesus Christ, who is both eschatological judge and victor. Both works offer examples of letters of exhortation bolstered by explicit apocalyptic expectations. It may well be, then, that the literary genre represented by 2 Thessalonians, that is the apocalyptic letter which itself fulfills an apocalyptic function by influencing the outcome of the events it describes or at least the manner in which those events unfold, was recognized and appropriated by the author of Revelation for the letters to the seven churches with which he introduces his work.

We have found ample evidence of the idea that God's wrath may be manifested as deception of the wicked. We may find the idea also in the Old Testament. The most familiar example is perhaps that of God "hardening" the heart of Pharaoh so that he would not allow the sons of Israel to leave Egypt (Ex. 4:21; 10:20, 27; 11:10; 14:8, 17; cf. 11:9). Mark used the idea in explaining Jesus' use of parables, quoting Isaiah 6:9-10 (Mark 4:10-12). The idea derives in part from consistent monotheism, which sees God as the source both of good and of "evil", and in apocalyptic literature it is used to confirm that God is in ultimate control of all the apocalyptic events, so that there may be no doubt about the outcome. In the book of Revelation, for example, Satan, the Beast and their allies are all deceivers (cf. Rev. 12:9, 13:14), but they are ultimately under God's control, for they are "allowed" to work deception (Rev. 13:14)[34].

As we have seen, the deception of which the false proclamation of the ἄτακτοι was an example was the manifestation of God's wrath which would be fully revealed on "the Day of the Lord". "God sends a powerful delusion upon them so that they will believe what is false, so that all those who are not faithful to the truth but who delighted in unrighteousness may be con-

---

[34] I am indebted to Professor Adela Yarbro Collins for the references from Revelation.

demned" (2 Thess. 2:11-12). We find a similar train of thought in Romans 1:18-32. Paul describes the working of God's wrath in history as deception, but introduces the idea in what we may call "apocalyptic" terms: Ἀποκαλύπτεται γὰρ ὀργὴ θεοῦ ἀπ' οὐρανοῦ ἐπὶ πᾶσαν ἀσέβειαν καὶ ἀδικίαν ἀνθρώπων (Rom. 1:18a; cf. 2 Thess. 1:7b-8a). God's wrath is revealed because, although he is clearly manifest through his works, men prefer to suppress (κατεχεῖν) the truth; they deceive themselves. This leads to a fundamental religious error, and men turn to idolatry (Rom. 1:21-23). Thus God's wrath arises in reaction to a religious error, that of not acknowledging God as God (Rom. 1:21). His wrath is manifested by his "handing over" (παραδοῦναι) humanity to the consequences of its errors. These consequences are moral: religious deception leads to moral deception (Rom. 1:24-25). God "gave them up" to impurity (Rom. 1:24), to "dishonorable passions", which deceive the mind as to what is the "natural" object of sexual desire (Rom. 1:26-27), and to "a base mind and improper conduct" (Rom. 1:28), giving rise to all the vices with which humanity is plagued (Rom. 1:29-32). Humanity's turning from God could only result in its being deceived: φάσκοντες εἶναι σοφοὶ ἐμωράνθησαν (Rom. 1:22). God's wrath is expressed by his allowing men and women to be foolish, to choose what is wrong despite their knowledge of what is right (Rom. 1:32)[35].

The author of 2 Thessalonians has appropriated this Pauline idea of the working out of God's wrath through deception, but he has restricted its scope to the eschatological process, which includes his own time (2 Thess. 2:6-7a). The deception spread by those who proclaim the presence of the Day of the Lord is eschatological deception, a symptom of the presence of ἡ ἀποστασία and τὸ μυστήριον τῆς ἀνομίας (2 Thess. 2:3b, 7a). But because of the close association of religious and ethical error, those who are deceived about the eschatological events are also likely to be deceived about moral behavior. For the author of 2 Thessalonians, the infallible guide for morality is the word and example of the apostle Paul (2 Thess. 2:15, 3:6-10). It is obedience to this tradition that he is seeking to enforce, and his clarification of ἀτάκτως περιπατοῦντες is μὴ κατὰ τὴν παράδοσιν ἣν παρελάβοσαν παρ' ἡμῶν (2 Thess. 3:6b). Disobedience to this tradition is a sign of the presence of eschatological rebellion: εἰ δέ τις οὐχ ὑπακούει τῷ λόγῳ ἡμῶν διὰ τῆς ἐπιστολῆς, τοῦτον σημειοῦσθε (2 Thess. 3:14a). We should take σημειόω

---

[35] Cf, the interpretation of this passage in Ernst Käsemann, *Commentary on Romans*, trans. Geoffrey W. Bromiley (Grand Rapids, Mich.: William B. Eerdmans Publishing Co., 1978), pp. 37–52.

in the middle as "regard it as an omen for yourselves"[36]. Immoral behavior is not only to be shunned for its own sake, but also because it is a symptom of the eschatological evil which will later be manifested in the apocalyptic Antagonist. It is a symptom of the deception of humanity which is the manifestation of God's eschatological wrath (2 Thess. 2:11-12; cf. Rom. 1:18-32). The one who does not obey the Pauline tradition has already chosen sides in the final division between good and evil, and, deceived as a result of God's wrath, is among the lost.

According to our author, the proclamation of the ἄτακτοι arose on the one hand from their disobedience and their deliberate deception by God so that they might later be judged by him (cf. 2 Thess. 3:10-12). Their attempted work of deception, on the other hand, was a means of spreading the eschatological evil before its manifestation in the Antagonist on the Day of the Lord. Our author wrote to check this spread of evil by refuting the false proclamation of the ἄτακτοι and to present Paul's eschatological teaching in a way that would suit the historical experience of the second Christian generation. He chose to do so through the format of 1 Thessalonians, appropriating its structure and much of its language to present his own letter as a work of Paul.

The tone of 1 Thessalonians is generally laudatory. The congregation had experienced persecution after Paul founded it (1 Thess. 2:14, 3:3-4). There was a "disorderly" element in the congregation, but also those who were faint-hearted and weak (1 Thess. 5:14). This "disorderly" group may have been those who did not give due respect to the congregation's leaders (1 Thess. 5:12-13). This problem seems to be related to conflicts over the gift of prophecy (1 Thess. 5:19-22), and possibly over sexual morality (1 Thess. 4:3-8). There was a "lack" in the congregation's understanding of eschatology, since its members were concerned over the death of some of their fellows (1 Thess. 4:13-18) and their own ability to withstand the "wrath" of the Day of the Lord (1 Thess. 5:1-11); they also appear to have been curious about when "the Day" would arrive (1 Thess. 5:1-2). All of these problems, however, Paul apparently felt could be resolved by the instruction of his letter; the congregation was in generally sound health.

We may compare the situation of the congregation as described in 2 Thessalonians. The congregation was founded by Paul (2 Thess. 2:14) and was experiencing or had experienced persecution (2 Thess. 1:4b, 6-7). The congregation accepted the traditional eschatological conception of the Last Judgment, the parousia, and the "day of wrath", but was unsure of how the last

---

[36] Cf. Henry George Liddell and Robert Scott, *A Greek-English Lexicon*, ed. Henry Stuart Jones and Roderick McKenzie (Oxford: Oxford University Press, 1951), p. 1594: "to interpret anything as a sign or portent". In this case, we have seen that disobedience is symptomatic of the presence of eschatological deception. Any instance of disobedience, then, is a "portent" or "omen" of the presence of that deception at work in the community.

was related to the other two. The congregation had received a tradition taught by Paul both in person and by letter (2 Thess. 2:15), which included the command to imitate Paul's example (2 Thess. 3:7-10). The "disorderly" in the congregation spread unrest through a false proclamation that "the Day of the Lord is here", and claimed the material support of the congregation on the basis of their supposedly superior spiritual status (2 Thess. 3:6, 12).

It is clear that the author of 2 Thessalonians had used selected traits from 1 Thessalonians to describe his readers, but that these traits present a very vague and general picture[37]. The only problem he deals with in his exhortation is that of the "disorderly", who are presented as a major threat to the well-being of the congregation. The eschatological concerns raised by the preaching of the ἄτακτοι are the author's own, and the ethical example of Paul is his interpretation of Paul's evocation of his own example. To put it simply, the "portrait" of the congregation addressed by 2 Thessalonians is composed partly of borrowings from 1 Thessalonians and partly of the author's own concerns in writing the letter. The author of 2 Thessalonians is in fact addressing the whole Pauline church.

The author's use of 1 Thessalonians may be explained in part by its appropriateness to the subject he wished to discuss. It offered eschatological instruction and instruction in regard to a group of ἄτακτοι within the context of a generally laudatory letter. But his use of 1 Thessalonians also expressed a certain attitude towards the earlier letter; what was it?

Essentially, there are only two possibilities. Either the author regarded 1 Thessalonians as fundamentally flawed in its eschatology and wrote his letter to replace it as the only "authentic" letter of Paul to the Thessalonians, or he believed that 1 Thessalonians was open to misinterpretation which could be corrected by a supplementary and explanatory letter of his own.

The first theory outlined above was first proposed by Adolf Hilgenfeld in 1862[38]. It was taken up again by Heinrich Julius Holtzmann in 1901[39], but gained few adherents; it has since been revived by Andreas Lindemann[40]. Lindemann bases his argument primarily upon 2 Thessalonians 2:2b: μήτε διὰ πνεύματος μήτε διὰ λόγου μήτε δι' ἐπιστολῆς ὡς δι' ἡμῶν. If one accepts the deutero-Pauline origin of 2 Thessalonians, he argues, this phrase cannot be a reference to another forgery, but only to a letter generally acknowledged to be Pauline, and that letter must be 1 Thessalonians[41]. The

---

[37] Trilling, *Der zweite Brief*, p. 45.
[38] Adolf Hilgenfeld, "Die beiden Briefe an die Thessalonicher, nach Inhalt und Ursprung", *Zeitschrift für wissenschaftliche Theologie* 5 (1862): 225–64.
[39] Heinrich Julius Holtzmann, "Zum zweiten Thessalonicherbrief", *Zeitschrift für die neutestamentliche Wissenschaft* 2 (1901): 97–108.
[40] Lindemann, "Zum Abfassungszweck", pp. 35–47.
[41] Ibid., pp. 36–38.

author is thus leading his readers to believe that 1 Thessalonians is a forgery written in Paul's name, a letter ὡς δι' ἡμῶν. This ruse is further advanced by 2 Thessalonians 3:17, which includes "Paul's" signature and claims that such a signature is a σημεῖον in all of Paul's letters; 1 Thessalonians, of course, has no such signature. The author makes no explicit reference to an earlier letter to the same group with whom the readers are identified. Therefore he presents his letter as the one and only genuine letter to the Thessalonians, and so replaces the "flawed" eschatology of the first letter with his own. As Lindemann puts it, "2 Thess ist also entgegen der üblichen Deutung kein 'Kommentar' zum 1 Thess, sondern er ist geradezu als dessen Widerlegung bzw. 'Rücknahme' konzipiert worden"[42].

We would argue, however, that we must not confuse the interpretations of 1 Thessalonians current in the Pauline congregations of the first century or the fear of such interpretations with the letter itself. There is in 1 Thessalonians no statement comparable to ἐνέστηκεν ἡ ἡμέρα τοῦ κυρίου or even necessarily supportive of such a proclamation. However, as we have seen, Paul's eschatology was not entirely consistent, and it was subject to reinterpretation to account for the continued existence of the church several decades after the resurrection of Jesus Christ. 1 Thessalonians 4:13-5:11 would be an obvious subject of such reinterpretation among those who were familiar with it or its contents, and we have already speculated that Paul's treatment of "the Day of the Lord" as we know it in that letter may have influenced the ἄτακτοι, as well as our author. In refuting the proclamation of the ἄτακτοι, the author is condemning a particular interpretation of 1 Thessalonians, not the letter itself. 2 Thessalonians 2:2b lists the possible sources in themselves; we may compare verses 2:15 and 3:14. Indeed, 1 Thessalonians serves as the model of a Pauline letter for the author of 2 Thessalonians; as Wrede pointed out, it would be at least inconsistent for the author to base the "authority" of his letter on a letter he subsequently denounced as a forgery[43].

We would therefore support the second theory outlined above, that the author of 2 Thessalonians intended his letter as a supplement to 1 Thessalonians and as a corrective to some of the interpretations (or feared interpretations) of that letter. Wrede suggested that our author used 1 Thessalonians as a model because this letter was cited by those who preached the presence of the Day of the Lord[44]. We would agree with Wrede that the ἄτακτοι would have interpreted 1 Thessalonians in such a way as to support their views, if they indeed knew the letter, but we have no evidence that they did know it as such. Trilling argues that 1 Thessalonians was imitated in 2 Thessalonians because it

---

[42] Ibid., p. 39.
[43] Wrede, *Die Echtheit*, pp. 60–62.
[44] Ibid., pp. 67–69.

was the most appropriate means of presenting the author's apocalyptic views. This was so for several reasons: first, the author was concerned with only one theme, and it was necessary to choose a short letter as a model; second, 1 Thessalonians had already dealt with eschatology; and third, 1 Thessalonians was a good source of the apostolic tradition the author of 2 Thessalonians wished to enforce on his readers as a guideline for their behavior[45]. These suggested reasons, however, are not satisfactory. Our analysis has determined, for example, that our author was not solely concerned with eschatology per se, but that the eschatological instruction in the letter is intended to further his purpose of leading his readers to take the proper action in the future, i.e., to adhere to the tradition and live in peace. Admittedly, this was still a limited intention in comparison to some of Paul's longer letters, but length is not really at issue in the work of imitation. The amount of "apostolic tradition" available in 1 Thessalonians also seems a negligible concern, since only the part of the exhortation in 1 Thessalonians 5:14 in regard to the ἄτακτοι is retained in the later letter. Moreover, the "tradition" in 2 Thessalonians is defined by the apostle's words, letters, and example, not by his letters alone (2 Thess. 2:15; 3:7-9, 10, 12, 14-15).

This repeated testimony in 2 Thessalonians to the diversity of the sources of Paul's teaching which composes the tradition should make us deeply aware that we should by no means assume that our author knew the collection of Pauline letters with which we are familiar, or even that he knew any one of them apart from 1 Thessalonians. The congregations founded by Paul were not formed on the basis of his letters, but on the basis of his preaching of the gospel and his subsequent instruction about the new faith[46]. Occasionally his letters served to provide his congregations with new information[47], but none was a systematic presentation of his understanding of the gospel. It is significant that the letter that comes closest to being such a systematic presentation was sent to a congregation Paul himself did not establish, that of Rome[48]. The letters are important to us as a means of attempting to recover something of Paul's teaching, but it was available to the Pauline congregations from the apostle himself, from his associates, and from the leaders of the community who were granted authority by the apostle. It is important to us that Paul wrote letters, and it was a useful fact for the pseudepigraphers (although other Hellenistic pseudepigraphers did not necessarily depend on genuine letters

---

[45] Trilling, *Der zweite Brief*, pp. 25–26.
[46] For a description of Paul's missionary practice provided by the apostle himself, see 1 Thessalonians 2:1-12.
[47] Cf. 1 Thess. 4:13-18, 1 Cor. 10:1-13; compare Rom. 1:13, 1 Cor. 15:51-53.
[48] Rom. 1:8-15.

as support for their own practice)[49], but it was not significant enough a matter for Luke to mention it in the sixteen chapters he devotes to the apostle in Acts. Members of the Pauline congregations had access to Paul's teaching in other forms, including Paul's oral instruction as preserved by their leaders and the example of Paul's own life as it survived in his legend. Therefore, our author knew the apostle's teaching "by word and by letter", but the content of that teaching was not necessarily equivalent to our understanding of Paul based on his letters which have survived.

We cannot assume, therefore, that our author knew of any other letter of Paul than 1 Thessalonians, of which he had a thorough and intimate knowledge. In other words, he may have used 1 Thessalonians as the model for his letter simply because this was the only letter of Paul he knew. This presents a problem, however, since he included a note in 2 Thessalonians 3:17 to the effect that every letter of Paul included a signature as an authenticating sign. We know this to be false not only of Paul's letters in general but of 1 Thessalonians in particular. If we reject, as we have, the position that the author of 2 Thessalonians intended to label 1 Thessalonians a forgery, we are left with two alternatives. Either the author made the statement as a validation of his own letter without regard for its truth, perhaps on the basis of a tradition that Paul added personal notes to his letters, or 1 Thessalonians as he knew it included such a note. The second theory would lead us to the possibility that the author of 2 Thessalonians was the first editor of 1 Thessalonians, that is, the one who presented the letter for the first time to congregations beyond that of the Thessalonians[50]. As we have seen, the false proclamation that "the Day of the Lord is here" is not directly dependent on 1 Thessalonians, but the letter could be interpreted as supporting that position. Therefore, to circumvent such a misinterpretation, the author/editor of the Thessalonians correspondence composed 2 Thessalonians to supplement and explain the eschatological teaching of 1 Thessalonians. This does not mean that the ἄτακτοι were not a real group of prophets or that the threat they posed to the Pauline congregations was not a real threat. It would only mean that 2 Thessalonians was written not to correct a misinterpretation of 1 Thessalonians, but to prevent such a misinterpretation. The authenticating note of 2 Thessalonians 3:17 could then be based on a note that originally belonged to 1 Thessalonians, but which the author transferred to the postscript of 2 Thessalonians to serve as authentication for both letters, which were presented in tandem. If

---

[49] One may cite, for example, the letters attributed to the Cynic philosopher Crates, to Plato, to Apollonius of Tyana, and to Barnabas; for remarks on the characteristics, see Donelson, *Pseudepigraphy*, pp. 22–54.

[50] I am indebted for this suggestion to Prof. Hans Dieter Betz.

one chooses to reject this possibility and accept that the authenticating note of 3:17 was included without regard for its truth, there is the collaborating fact that the presence or absence of the σημεῖον has never been used as a basis for questioning the authenticity of 1 Thessalonians or any other Pauline letter. This also means that if the intention of the author was indeed to displace 1 Thessalonians, the attempt was a manifest failure.

When we come to consider the place of 2 Thessalonians within the Pauline tradition, we must again be wary of over-simplifying the historical circumstances or of picturing the author as a lone figure who recognized a particular situation in the Pauline congregations and took it upon himself to rectify it. Although this image may be appropriate for Paul, who founded the congregations, was informed about them, and considered them his personal responsibility, no figure in the Pauline churches after the apostle's death had this same sort of authority or catholicity of concern. If such a person had existed, it would not have been necessary for him to assume the guise of the apostle. Rather, we must remember that even during Paul's own lifetime he faced opposition not just from outsiders and from other Christians who did not accept his teachings (cf. the "circumcision party" of Galatians), but also from those in the Pauline congregations who misunderstood or misinterpreted his own teaching (cf. the various "parties" of the Corinthian correspondence). Because the congregations knew Paul's teaching first from his missionary preaching and then from its presentation by their congregational leaders, their understanding of Paul's gospel would vary, and sometimes even run counter to Paul's own. The situation certainly did not improve after the apostle's death, and the various Pauline pseudepigrapha bear testimony to the various ways in which the apostle's teaching could be understood. However, it would be wrong to associate the doctrine of any one pseudepigraph with the beliefs of its author alone. Even if the author formulated and developed the content of his letter, his understanding of Paul's teaching arose in part from the particular way it was presented in his home congregation. In the second Christian generation there was apparently a wide range of possible understandings of the gospel in general and Paul's in particular. To a certain extent, 2 Thessalonians is the reaction of one community or group of communities within the Pauline church to the doctrine of another group or community with an equal claim to be "Pauline" and with its own history of interpretation of the apostle's teaching.

As we have remarked before, 2 Thessalonians is witness to two understandings of Paul's eschatology, that of the author (as shaped by the transmission of Paul's teaching within his community) and that of those he calls the ἄτακτοι (also influenced by the teachings within their own communities). Both claimed to be faithful to Paul and both were attempting to systematize and "explain" Paul's eschatology not only in spite of its inconsistencies but also in the light of the continued delay of the parousia Paul had expected long before. That one view, that of the author of 2 Thessalonians, was subsequently accepted by the church as "orthodox" may be a tribute to the viability of that view, but it does not affect the standing of either party at the time the letter was written. This is important to remember, in view of the author's severe indictment of those who held an opposing view of Paul's eschatology; the same charge could easily be (and probably was) made against him with equal "validity" on the basis of the interpretation of Paul's teaching current among the ἄτακτοι.

In other words, we must be careful not to think of 2 Thessalonians as a defense of Pauline eschatology against the claims of a radical apocalyptic sect. There was no agreed-upon Pauline eschatology to defend, but only various interpretations of what Paul had taught on the subject, some more adequate and useful than others. Rather, 2 Thessalonians is a polemical work aimed at persuading its readers to accept one particular interpretation of Pauline eschatology and to submit to the "tradition" espoused by the author as the proper standard of behavior. If this resembles the language of an established church defending its doctrines and traditions, it is because the church as it came to be grew out of such polemical confrontations. More specifically, the understanding of Paul's teaching in the church gradually came to be defined less by a living tradition in the Pauline congregations, such as that represented by 2 Thessalonians, and more by a collection of letters attributed to Paul. The inclusion of the work of some pseudepigraphers in this "Pauline canon" assured the preservation of their particular interpretations of Paul's teaching until the present day. But each interpretation, in its own time, was merely one among many.

We may also now see that the debate in this century between those who find Paul's major orientation to be some form of gnosticism[51] and those who believe his major orientation to be apocalypticism[52] was already anticipated in the decades immediately following the apostle's death. The New Testament includes deutero-Pauline pseudepigrapha which provide a semi-gnostic inter-

---

[51] Richard Reitzenstein, for example, labelled Paul "the greatest gnostic of them all" in his *Die hellenistischen Mysterienreligionen nach ihren Grundgedanken und Wirkung*, 3d ed. (Leipzig: B.G. Teubner, 1927), p. 86 (English translation: *Hellenistic Mystery Religions: Their Basic Ideas and Significance*, trans. John E. Steely [Pittsburgh: Pickwick Press, 1978]). In this opinion he represents the attempt of the "History of Religions" school to associate Paul as closely as possible with the Hellenistic religions.

[52] Albert Schweitzer advanced this theory in conscious opposition to Reitzenstein in *Paul and His Interpreters: A Critical History*, trans. W. Montgomery (New York: Macmillan, 1931). For a recent "apocalyptic" interpretation of Paul, see Johan Christiaan Beker, *Paul the Apostle: The Triumph of God in Life and Thought* (Philadelphia: Fortress Press, 1980).

pretation of Paul's thought, Colossians and Ephesians, as well as 2 Thessalonians, which interprets Paul's work in the light of a vivid apocalypticism.

What is the particular significance of 2 Thessalonians? As we have seen, it is representative not only of the continuation of Pauline theology in the second Christian generation, but also of several currents in the stream of Christian thought at that time. It offers a "definitive" reinterpretation of an earlier, "misunderstood" eschatological tradition. As we have seen, Paul's eschatology was not consistent, and the author of 2 Thessalonians has attempted to present it consistently, while also accounting for the delay of the parousia he still expected to come. He made use of traditional elements of Jewish apocalyptic literature to create his scenario, a process we find at work also in the synoptic apocalypse (Mark 13, Matthew 24) and in the last chapter of the Didache. His reason for doing so was that 1 Thessalonians was a source of real or potential confusion over eschatology, and he wished to provide a supplement to that letter to prevent such confusion. More specifically, he wrote to refute the erroneous interpretation of Paul's eschatology which had arisen in part from the delay of the parousia (cf. John 21:20-23). This doctrine was proclaimed by the "disorderly" element in the Pauline congregations, who apparently claimed superior spiritual status on the basis of their prophetic office and demanded the support of their congregations. Our author labelled the proclamation of the ἄτακτοι a deception and, following Paul's line of thought in Romans 1:18-32, made a close connection between doctrinal error and "deception" in regard to ethics. The proper source of both doctrine and ethics was the "tradition" (2 Thess. 2:15; 3:6, 14-15), and to disregard the tradition was to fall prey to the deception which was a manifestation of God's wrath (2 Thess. 2:10-12). The author thus attacked his opponents both on the grounds of their false proclamation and on that of their "disorderly" behavior (2 Thess. 3:6-12; cf. 1 John). More specifically, the presence of these opponents in the congregation is identified with the deception which is indicative of the presence of apocalyptic evil. They are representative of ἡ ἀποστασία which is the present manifestation of those forces which will be personified in the apocalyptic Antagonist on the Day of the Lord (2 Thess. 2:3-4). In opposing these forces and their work of deception, the letter serves an eschatological function insofar as it calls upon its readers to choose the correct path in the future, the path of belief in the apocalyptic scenario offered by the author and obedience to Paul's example in word and action, so that they may obtain salvation on the Day of the Lord Jesus Christ (2 Thess. 1:7b-10). The author makes no ethical demands on his readers beyond obedience to the tradition based on Paul's words, letters, and personal example. However, he interprets that example as strictly requiring that every member of the community work, primarily as a means of attacking the ἄτακτοι (2 Thess. 3:6-12). The other focus of this attack is the doctrinal exhortation which introduces the apocalyptic scenario (2 Thess. 2:1-2). The two together make it clear that the author's intention is to render the ἄτακτοι harmless and to establish thereby his own interpretation of Paul's teaching as authoritative for his readers.

We have said that the rhetorical structure of 2 Thessalonians provides information about the function of the apocalyptic material it includes. It is now clear that this material is the specific basis on which a battle between contending interpretations of the Pauline tradition was fought. It is a battle carried on by doctrinal argument, claims of authority, and bitter polemic. 2 Thessalonians stands as an example of the absolutist, "dualistic" state of mind which is often considered typical of apocalypticism, but appears to have been endemic in early Christian literature. For its author, the only alternative to his understanding of Pauline tradition was deception, and deception was God's instrument of wrath against the wicked. Those who rejected his interpretation of doctrine or the tradition were to be shunned and accepted back only if they submitted to the authority of "Paul" as our author understood it. It was the part of the faithful to "stand firm and hold to the traditions which you were taught by us, either by word or by letter" (2 Thess. 2:15). Only if the faithful did so could their salvation be assured.

Select Bibliography

Commentaries on 2 Thessalonians

Best, Ernest, *A Commentary on the First and Second Epistles to the Thessalonians*. Harper's New Testament Commentaries. New York: Harper and Row, 1972.
Bornemann, Wilhelm. *Die Thessalonicherbriefe*. Meyer Kommentar. Göttingen: Vandenhoeck und Ruprecht, 1894.
Bruce, Frederick F. *1 & 2 Thessalonians*. Word Biblical Commentary 45. Waco, Texas: Word Books, 1982.
Dibelius, Martin. *An die Thessalonicher I, II, an die Philipper*. Handbuch zum Neuen Testament 11. 3rd ed. Tübingen: J.C.B. Mohr (Paul Siebeck), 1937.
Dobschütz, Ernst von. *Die Thessalonicher-Briefe*. Meyer Kommentar. Göttingen: Vandenhoeck und Ruprecht, 1909.
Frame, James Everett. *A Critical and Exegetical Commentary on the Epistles of St. Paul to the Thessalonians*. International Critical Commentary. Edinburgh: T. and T. Clark, 1912.
Lünemann, Gottlieb. *Critical and Exegetical Commentary on the New Testament: The Epistles to the Thessalonians*. Meyer Commentary. Translated by Paton J. Gloag. Edinburgh: T. and T. Clark, 1880.
Marshall, I. Howard. *1 and 2 Thessalonians*. New Century Bible Commentary. Grand Rapids, Mich.: William B. Eerdmans, 1983.
Marxsen, Willi. *Der zweite Thessalonicherbrief*. Zürcher Bibelkommentare zum Neuen Testament 11.2. Zürich: Theologischer Verlag, 1982.
Masson, Charles. *Les deux épitres de Saint Paul aux Thessaloniciens*. Commentaire du Nouveau Testament 11a. Neuchâtel/Paris: Delachaux Niestlé, 1957.
Milligan, George. *St. Paul's Epistles to the Thessalonians*. London: Macmillan and Co., 1908.
Neil, William. *The Epistles of Paul to the Thessalonians*. Moffatt New Testament Commentaries. London: Hodder and Stoughton, 1950.
Plummer, Alfred. *A Commentary on St. Paul's Second Epistle to the Thessalonians*. London: Robert Scott, 1918.
Rigaux, Béda. *Saint Paul: les épitres aux Thessaloniciens*. Études Bibliques. Paris/Gembloux: Librairie LeCoffre/Éditions J. Duculot, 1956.
Schmiedel, Paul Wilhelm. *Die Briefe an die Thessalonicher und an die Korinther*. Hand-Kommentar zum Neuen Testament. Freiburg: J.C.B. Mohr (Paul Siebeck), 1891.
Trilling, Wolfgang. *Der zweite Brief an die Thessalonicher*. Evangelisch-Katholischer Kommentar zum Neuen Testament 14. Zürich/Neukirchen: Benziger/Neukirchener Verlag, 1980.
Whiteley, Denys Edward Hugh. *Thessalonians*. New Clarendon Bible. Oxford: Oxford University Press, 1969.

Other Works on 2 Thessalonians

Aus, Roger D. "The Liturgical Background of the Necessity and Propriety of Giving Thanks According to 2 Thess. 1:3." *Journal of Biblical Literature* 92 (1973): 422–38.
– "The Relevance of Isaiah 66:7 to Revelation 12 and 2 Thessalonians 1." *Zeitschrift für die neutestamentliche Wissenschaft* 67 (1976): 252–68.
Bailey, John A. "Who Wrote II Thessalonians?" *New Testament Studies* 25 (1979): 131–45.
Bassler, Jouette M. "The Enigmatic Sign: 2 Thessalonians 1:5." *Catholic Biblical Quarterly* 46 (1984): 496–510.
Braun, Herbert. "Zur nachpaulinischen Herkunft des zweiten Thessalonicherbriefs." *Gesammelte Studien zum Neuen Testament und Seiner Umwelt* 2. Durchgesehene und ergänzte Auflage. Tübingen: J.C.B. Mohr (Paul Siebeck), 1967, pp. 205–9.
Ellingworth, Paul, and Nida, Eugene A. *A Translator's Handbook on Paul's Letters to the Thessalonians.* Helps for Translators. New York: United Bible Societies, 1976.
Giblin, Charles H. *The Threat to Faith: An Exegetical and Theological Re-Examination of 2 Thessalonians 2.* Analecta Biblica 31. Rome: Pontifical Biblical Institute, 1967.
Harnack, Adolf von. "Das Problem des zweiten Thessalonicherbriefs." *Sitzungsbericht der königlich Preussischen Akademie der Wissenschaften.* Philosophische-historische Klasse. Berlin: Georg Reimer, 1910, pp. 560–78.
Hurd, John C.. "Concerning the Authenticity of 2 Thessalonians." Paper delivered to the Seminar on the Thessalonian Correspondence, annual meeting of the Society for Biblical Literature, Dallas, Texas, 19–22 December 1983.
Jewett, Robert. "The Thessalonian Church as a Millenarian Movement." Paper delivered to the Social Sciences and New Testament Interpretation Consultation, annual meeting of the Society for Biblical Literature, Chicago, Illinois, 8–11 December 1984.
Kaye, Bruce N. "Eschatology and Ethics in 1 and 2 Thessalonians." *Novum Testamentum* 17 (1975): 47–57.
Krentz, Edgar. "A Stone That Will Not Fit: The Non-Pauline Authorship of II Thessalonians." Paper delivered to the seminar on the Thessalonian Correspondence, annual meeting of the Society for Biblical Literature, Dallas, Texas, 19–22 December 1983.
Lindemann, Andreas. "Zum Abfassungszweck des Zweiten Thessalonicherbriefes." *Zeitschrift für die neutestamentliche Wissenschaft* 68 (1977): 35–47.
Orchard, John Bernard. "Thessalonians and the Synoptic Gospels." *Biblica* 19 (1938): 19–42.
Schweizer, Eduard. "Der zweite Thessalonicherbrief ein Philipperbrief?" *Theologische Zeitschrift* 1 (1945): 90–105, 286–89.
Spicq, Ceslaus. "Les Thessaloniciens 'inquiets' étaient-ils des paresseux?" *Studia Theologica* 10 (1956): 1–13.
Stephenson, Alan M.G. "On the Meaning of ἐνέστηκεν ἡ ἡμέρα τοῦ κυρίου in 2 Thessalonians 2, 2." *Studia Evangelica*, vol. 4, pt. 1. Edited by Frank Leslie Cross. Texte und Untersuchungen zur Geschichte der altchristlichen Literatur. Berlin: Akademie Verlag, 1968.
Trilling, Wolfgang. *Untersuchungen zum 2. Thessalonicherbrief.* Erfurter Theologische Studien 27. Leipzig: St. Benno, 1972.
Wrede, William. *Die Echtheit des zweiten Thessalonicherbriefs.* Texte und Untersuchungen zur Geschichte der altchristlichen Literatur. Leipzig: J.C. Hinrichssche Buchhandlung, 1903.

Select Bibliography   161

Other Works

Achtemeier, Paul J. "An Apocalyptic Shift in Early Christian Tradition: Reflections on Some Canonical Evidence." *Catholic Biblical Quarterly* 45 (1983): 231–48.

Aune, David. *Prophecy in Early Christianity and the Ancient Mediterranean World*. Grand Rapids, Mich.: William B. Eerdmans, 1983.

Barrett, Charles Kingsley. "Pauline Controversies in the Post-Pauline Period." *New Testament Studies* 20 (1973): 229–45.

Baumgarten, Jörg. *Paulus und die Apokalyptik*. Wissenschaftliche Monographien zum Alten und Neuen Testament 44. Neukirchen: Neukirchener Verlag, 1975.

Beker, Johan Christiaan. *Paul the Apostle: The Triumph of God in Life and Thought*. Philadelphia: Fortress Press, 1980.

Betz, Hans Dieter. "Ein seltsames mysterien-theologisches System bei Plutarch." *Ex orbe religionum*. Studia Geo Widengren. 2 vols. Leiden: E.J. Brill, 1972, 2:347–354.

– "De tranquilitate animi (Moralia 464E–477F)." *Plutarch's Ethical Writings and Early Christian Literature*. Edited by Hans Dieter Betz. Studia ad Corpus Hellenisticum Novi Testamenti 4. Leiden: E.J. Brill, 1978.

– *Galatians: A Commentary on Paul's Letter to the Churches in Galatia*. Hermeneia. Philadelphia: Fortress Press, 1979.

– *Essays on the Sermon on the Mount*. Translated by Laurence L. Welborn. Philadelphia: Fortress Press, 1985.

Brown, John Pairman. "Synoptic Parallels in the Epistles and Form-History." *New Testament Studies* 10 (1963): 27–48.

Collins, John J., ed. *Apocalypse: The Morphology of a Genre*. Semeia 14. Missoula, Mont.: Scholars Press, 1974.

– *The Apocalyptic Imagination*. New York: Crossroad, 1984.

de Boer, Martinus C. "Images of Paul in the Post-Apostolic Period." *Catholic Biblical Quarterly* 42 (1980): 359–80.

Donelson, Lewis R. *Pseudepigraphy and Ethical Argument in the Pastoral Epistles.* Hermeneutische Untersuchungen zur Theologie 22. Tübingen: J.C.B. Mohr (Paul Siebeck), 1986.

Goldstein, Jonathan A. *The Letters of Demosthenes*. New York: Columbia University Press, 1968.

Hanson, Paul D. *The Dawn of Apocalyptic*. Revised ed. Philadelphia: Fortress Press, 1975.

Hartmann, Lars. *Prophecy Interpreted: The Formation of Some Jewish Apocalyptic Texts and of the Eschatological Discourse of Mark 13 par*. Translated by Neil Tomkinson and Jean Grey. Uppsala: Almquist and Wiksells, 1966.

Hellholm, David, ed. *Apocalypticism in the Mediterranean World and the Near East*. Tübingen: J.C.B. Mohr (Paul Siebeck), 1983.

Hooker, Morna D. "Trial and Tribulation in Mark XIII." *Bulletin of the John Rylands University Library of Manchester* 65 (1982): 78–99.

Kennedy, George A. *New Testament Interpretation through Rhetorical Criticism*. Chapel Hill, N.C.: University of North Carolina Press, 1984.

Lindemann, Andreas. *Paulus im ältesten Christentum*. Tübingen: J.C.B. Mohr (Paul Siebeck), 1979.

Lüdemann, Gerd. *Paulus der Heidenapostel 2*. Göttingen: Vandenhoeck und Ruprecht, 1983.

MacMullen, Ramsey. *Paganism in the Roman Empire*. New Haven, Conn.: Yale University Press, 1981.

Malherbe, Abraham J. "Ancient Epistolary Theorists." *Ohio Journal of Religious Studies* 5 (1977) 2:3-77.

Metzger, Bruce M. *A Textual Commentary on the Greek New Testament*. New York: United Bible Societies, 1971.

- "Literary Forgeries and Canonical Pseudepigrapha." *Journal of Biblical Literature* 91 (1972): 3–24.
Nilsson, Martin Persson. *Geschichte der Griechischen Religion.* 2nd ed. 2 vols. Munich: C.H. Beck, 1961.
Rist, Martin. "Pseudepigraphy and the Early Christians." *Studies in New Testament and Early Christian Literature: Essays in Honor of Allen P. Wikgren.* Edited by David Aune. Leiden: E.J. Brill, 1972, pp. 75–91.
Rowley, Harold H. *The Relevance of Apocalyptic.* 3rd ed. London: Lutterworth Press, 1963.
Russell, David Syme. *The Method and Message of Jewish Apocalyptic.* Philadelphia: Westminster, 1964.
Sanders, Ernest P. *Jesus and Judaism.* Philadelphia: Fortress Press, 1985.
Schenke, Hans-Martin. "Das Weiterwirken des Paulus und die Pflege seines Erbes durch die Paulus-Schule." *New Testament Studies* 21 (1974): 505–18.
Schmithals, Walter. *Paul and the Gnostics.* Translated by John E. Steely. Nashville: Abingdon Press, 1972.
Speyer, Wolfgang. *Die Literarische Fälschung im Heidnischen und Christlichen Altertum: Ein Versuch ihrer Deutung.* Handbuch der Altertumswissenschaft begründet. Munich: C.H. Beck, 1971.
Stemplinger, Eduard. *Das Plagiat in der griechischen Literatur.* Leipzig/Berlin: B.G. Teubner, 1912.

Index of Passages

Hebrew Bible

Genesis
6,5-7   123
16,9-11   112n
18,1-33   112
22,11-12   112n

Exodus
4,21   148
10,20   148
10,27   148
11,9   148
11,10   148
14,8   148
14,17   148
14,19   112n
14,20   112n

Numbers
22,34   112n

Judges
6,19   112n
6,20   112n

1 Samuel
20,31   107n

Job
33,19-30   38

Psalms
67,36   38n
79,5-7   38n
88,8   38n

Proverbs
3,11-12   38

Isaiah
2,10   38n, 86, 92
2,11   38n
2,12-17   97
2,19   38n, 86, 92
2,21   38n, 86, 92
6,9-10   148
13,1-22   97
13,10   135
34,1-17   97
34,4   135
40,1-2   38
61,1-3   97
66,4   38n
66,15   38n
66,16   92

Jeremiah
6,14   137
8,11   137
10,25   38n, 92
23,11   137
23,13-17   137
23,18   111
23,21-22   137
23,22   111
23,25-32   137
25,11-12   133
29,10   133

Lamentations
1,12   97, 98
2,1   97, 98
2,1-22   120
2,21-22   97, 98

Ezekiel
7,1-27   97
13,10   137
30,1-9   97
32,7-8   135

Daniel
7,1-9   133

Index of Passages

7,13-14	135	3,15	135
9,1-3	133	3,17-21	127
9,20-27	133		
9,27	138	*Amos*	
10,13	122	5,18-20	96-7
10,18-11,1	112		
10,20-21	113n; 122	*Obadiah*	
11,30	136	15-21	97
11,31	136, 138		
11,36	107	*Zephaniah*	
11,36-12,1	123	1,7-18	97
11,37	107	2,1-3	97, 121, 127
12,1	37n	3,8-10	127
12,9-13	110n		
12,11	138	*Zechariah*	
		3,1-10	111
Joel		14,1-21	97
2,10	135	14,5	92,145
2,12-17	97	14,6-21	127
2,15-29	121, 127		
2,18-32	97	*Malachi*	
2,31	135	3,13-4,6	97
3,4	137		

New Testament

Matthew		24,10	136, 137, 140, 141
1,20-21	112n	24,11	135, 136, 137, 140, 141
2,19-20	112n	24,12	136, 140, 141
5,4	93n	24,13	136, 140, 141
5,10-12	36n, 93n	24,14	136, 140, 141
7,21-23	94n	24,15	135, 136, 141
10,16-22	93n, 135, 141	24,15-24	137
10,18	141	24,21	37n, 39n, 135, 141
10,22	51n, 75	24,22	136, 137
10,34-39	93n	24,23	135, 137, 140
13,21	36n	24,23-26	135
13,36-43	94n	24,24	118, 135, 136, 137, 140, 141, 147
16,28	132n, 142		
19,30	93n	24,25	136
20,16	93n	24,26	135, 137, 138, 140, 141
20,25-28	93n	24,27	98, 136, 138, 140, 141
24,4	118, 135, 141	24,28	98, 138, 140, 141
24,5	135, 136, 137, 140, 141	24,29	135, 136, 137, 139, 141
24,5-9	135, 136	24,30	135, 136, 137, 141
24,6	135, 141	24,31	95, 135, 136, 137, 141
24,7	141	24,32	136
24,8	141	24,33	136
24,9	137	24,34	132n, 136, 142
24,9-12	136	24,39	71

25,1-13	94n	16,25	93n
25,31-46	93n, 94n	17,24	98, 140
28,19	141	17,37	140
		21,32	132n
Mark		21,34-35	71
4,10-12	148	21,36	109
9,1	132n, 142	23,42-43	94n
10,31	93n		
13,4	109	*John*	
13,5	118, 135, 138, 141	1,1	47n
13,6	134, 135, 136, 141	4,1	82
13,6-13	134	6,70	107
13,7	134, 135, 136, 141	15,27	47n
13,8	134, 135, 136, 141	17,12	107
13,9	134, 135, 138	19,35	142, 143
13,9-13	137, 141	21,20-23	132n, 139, 142, 157
13,10	134, 135, 138	21,22	143
13,12	134	21,23	142, 143
13,13	51n, 75, 134, 135, 136, 138, 140, 141	21,24	142, 143
13,14	135, 136, 138	*Acts*	
13,14-18	135	2,20	137
13,14-23	134, 135, 137, 139	2,22	116, 122
13,19	37n, 47n, 135, 141	12,24	73
13,20	135, 136, 137		
13,21	135, 139, 141	*Romans*	
13,22	118, 135, 136, 139, 141	1,7	67
13,23	110n, 135, 138, 139, 140, 141	1,8	36n
		1,8-15	153
13,24	135, 136, 139	1,13	153
13,24-27	98, 137, 141	1,18	110, 119, 149
13,25	135, 136	1,18-32	149, 150, 151
13,26	135, 136	1,21	103n, 149
13,27	95, 135, 136	1,22	149
13,28-31	136	1,23	149
13,29	109, 139	1,24	110, 119, 149
13,30	109, 132n, 139, 142	1,25	119, 149
13,31	139	1,26	110, 149
13,32-37	139	1,27	149
13,35	138	1,28	149
13,36	138	1,29-32	149
13,37	138	1,32	88, 103n, 122, 149
		2,1-2	103n
Luke		2,5	102
1,11-13	112n	2,5-16	104
1,19-20	112n	2,12-16	107
1,26-30	112n	2,16	102
4,21	96	2,17-24	103n
6,21	93n	3,3-4	51
6,25-26	93n	3,21-28	134n
9,27	132n	3,24	49n
12,39-40	103	4,16	49n
13,23-30	94n	5,1-2	94n
13,30	93n	5,1-11	134n

Index of Passages

5,2	49n	8,7	86
5,3	36n	9,24-27	50
5,3-5	93n	10,1-13	153
6,1-11	134n	10,13	85n
8,1-11	134n	10,31-11,1	43
8,2-10	78	11,1	53, 75
8,14-17	103	11,2	86
8,31-39	94n	11,2-16	86
8,35	36n	11,16	34n
10,19-21	103n	11,17	86
12,1-21	43	11,18	34n
12,12	36n	11,22	34n
13,1-7	111	11,23	86
13,2	111	13,1-13	61
13,11-14	104	13,13	88
13,12	104	14,33	85n
14,6	101n	15,3	86
14,8-9	101n	15,10	49n
15,17-29	138	15,12-28	134n
15,19	117	15,12-58	109
15,33	85n	15,20-28	94n, 105n
16,1	34n	15,23	105n
16,3-13	101n	15,24	105n
16,4	34n	15,26	105n
16,5	34n	15,35-57	109, 132
16,16	34n	15,51	109, 114
16,20	85n	15,51-55	109, 153
		16,21	57, 89

1 Corinthians

1,1-3	61	*2 Corinthians*	
1,2	34	1,1	35
1,3	67	1,1-2	61
1,4-9	36n	1,2	67
1,7	101	1,3-7	36n, 93n
1,8	101, 127	1,14	101, 127
1,9	85n	4,16-17	36n
1,26	42	6,2	96
2,1-5	45	6,14-15	115n
2,6-8	105n, 113n	8,1-5	37
2,8	101n	9,2	37
3,16	103n	10,7-8	101n
4,4-5	101n	11,2	41, 103, 104
5,5	102	11,23-33	93n
5,6	103n	12,11-18	53
6,2	103n	12,12	116, 122
6,3	103n	13,11	85n, 86
6,9	103n		
6,13-14	101n	*Galatians*	
6,15	103n	1,6	49n
6,15-17	101n	1,6-9	35n
6,16	103n	1,13	34n, 67
6,19	103n	1,14	86
7,10	86	1,19	101n
7,20	42	1,22	34n

2,2	50	2,2	63
2,14	38	2,5	63
3,13-14	134	2,7	29, 76
3,26-29	134	2,9	29, 63, 76
5,2	89	2,10	63
5,7	50	2,11	62, 63, 65, 66, 76
5,13-25	78	2,12	11, 15, 23, 31, 63, 65, 66, 72, 76, 79, 81, 85
6,9-10	54		
6,11	57, 89	2,13	21, 23, 29, 47, 64, 71, 72, 75, 79, 83, 89

Ephesians

1,18	42	2,13-16	72
4,4	42	2,14	62, 64, 93n, 150
		2,15	27, 64, 74
		2,16	27, 64, 71, 74

Philippians

1,3-11	36n	2,19	11, 19, 41, 65, 71, 74
1,6	101	2,20	41
1,9-11	103	3,1-5	69, 70
1,10	101	3,2	25, 68, 70
1,14	73	3,3	68, 81, 93n, 150
1,19-23	94n	3,4	19, 29, 68, 70, 76, 93n, 150
2,16	50, 101, 102, 104	3,6	64
2,29	101n	3,7	23, 64, 72
3,1	101n	3,8	23, 64, 72
4,4-5	101n	3,11	25, 27, 73, 74, 86
4,9	85n, 86	3,12	11, 19, 62, 70, 73, 74
4,10	101n	3,13	13, 17, 19, 21, 27, 41, 65, 70, 71, 73, 74, 78n, 79, 85, 87
4,15	47n		
		4,1	25, 27, 29, 31, 67, 68, 73, 74, 75, 79, 80

Colossians

1,18	47n	4,1-12	74
4,18	58, 77	4,2	19, 70, 74, 87
		4,3	64, 121
		4,3-8	150

1 Thessalonians

1,1	9, 34, 35, 61, 67, 80, 83	4,4	121
1,2	9, 13, 23, 61, 62, 65, 83, 89	4,5	13, 64, 81
1,2-10	36n, 47, 63, 72	4,7	23, 72, 87, 121
1,3	9, 11, 13, 15, 17, 27, 42, 62, 63, 64, 66, 74, 78n, 79, 81	4,8	121
		4,11	31, 76, 86
1,4	11, 23, 64, 81, 85	4,13	109
1,4-7	93n	4,13-18	1, 44, 64, 65, 68, 69, 70, 71, 80, 81, 85, 92, 94n, 95, 96, 103, 109, 132, 136, 150, 152, 153
1,5	11, 13, 21, 23, 63, 64, 71, 79, 81		
1,5-2,16	63	4,14	15
1,5-3,13	79	4,15	73, 101n, 103, 109
1,6	11, 29, 63, 64, 75, 80, 101n	4,16	13, 15, 17, 70, 80, 85, 101n, 109
1,7	11, 13, 62, 64, 80, 81		
1,8	11, 25, 27, 62, 73	4,17	13, 15, 80, 85, 101n, 109, 135
1,9	11, 23, 62, 64, 134n		
1,10	11, 13, 17, 27, 63, 64, 65, 70, 73, 74, 79, 85, 105, 121, 134n	4,18	85
		5,1	15, 19, 69, 70, 150
		5,1-11	1, 44, 64, 69, 70, 71, 73, 80, 81, 85, 92, 100, 150, 152
2,1	29, 63, 75		
2,1-12	64, 153	5,2	17, 69, 85, 103, 104, 150

5,3	17, 69, 71, 81, 85, 103, 104, 137	1,11	12, 14, 37, 40, 41, 42, 63, 65, 66, 67, 78n, 81, 87, 89, 111, 119, 121
5,4	69, 103, 121		
5,4-7	103, 104, 120, 121	1,12	14, 25, 27, 37, 40, 41, 42, 43, 48, 50, 63, 65, 66, 85, 89, 111
5,5	69, 121		
5,6	121		
5,8	25, 104, 120, 133	2,1	6, 14, 35, 39, 44, 48, 65, 68, 70, 72, 99, 136, 158
5,9	21, 23, 69, 71, 72, 80, 105		
5,11	85	2,1-7	46
5,12	15, 31, 65, 68, 77, 82, 150	2,1-12	1, 5, 37, 52, 54, 56, 63, 69, 70, 94, 105, 106, 118, 121, 122, 123, 124, 125, 126, 129
5,12-28	80		
5,13	31, 77, 82, 150		
5,14	27, 29, 31, 52, 56, 75, 76, 77, 80, 82, 150, 153	2,2	6, 13, 14, 16, 23, 35, 44, 48, 49, 55, 56, 67, 68, 69, 70, 72, 81, 99, 100, 104, 118, 120, 135, 137, 141, 151, 152, 158
5,19	82, 150		
5,20	82, 150		
5,21	82, 150	2,3	16, 44, 45, 52, 56, 67, 69, 100, 106, 107, 108, 109, 111, 112, 113, 114, 115, 117, 118, 122, 124, 135, 136, 141, 143, 149, 157
5,22	150		
5,23	21, 31, 33, 71, 72, 77, 80, 85		
5,24	74, 85		
5,25	25, 73		
5,26	33, 80, 89	2,4	16, 45, 100, 107, 108, 111, 112, 113, 114, 115, 117, 119, 122, 124, 136, 141, 157
5,28	33, 77, 80		
2 Thessalonians		2,5	18, 45, 68-69, 70, 100, 109, 135
1,1	8, 34, 35, 80, 83		
1,2	8, 15, 61, 80, 83	2,6	18, 45, 100, 106, 110, 112, 113, 122, 125, 141, 149
1,3	8, 10, 15, 23, 36, 37, 39, 41, 46, 61, 62, 70, 72, 83, 84, 87, 88, 89	2,7	18, 45, 70, 71, 74, 100, 106, 107, 112, 113, 122, 141, 143, 149
1,4	10, 36, 37, 39, 41, 42, 61, 62, 68, 70, 81, 87, 88, 113, 121, 130, 150	2,8	18, 45, 65, 71, 74, 100, 107, 112, 114, 115, 116, 117, 124, 136, 141, 147
1,5	10, 15, 38, 39, 63, 85, 93, 121, 124	2,9	20, 100, 106, 107, 109, 114, 115, 116, 117, 119, 122, 124, 135, 141, 147
1,5-10	5, 36, 38, 39, 40, 41, 63, 64, 68, 69, 70, 84, 92, 94, 95, 97, 121, 123, 124, 125, 126, 129		
		2,9-12	47, 56, 71, 141
1,6	10, 36, 39, 43, 63, 64, 71, 85, 93, 113, 118, 121, 124, 125, 150	2,10	20, 23, 71, 106, 107, 114, 117, 118, 119, 135, 157
		2,10-12	52, 71, 74, 85, 124, 136
1,7	10, 12, 21, 38, 39, 40, 41, 57, 63, 65, 70, 85, 93, 94, 102, 104, 113, 123, 124, 125, 147, 149, 150, 157	2,11	20, 23, 46, 48, 71, 88, 111, 114, 118, 119, 122, 124, 125, 149, 150, 157
		2,12	20, 23, 46, 47, 56, 71, 88, 111, 114, 118, 119, 122, 124, 125, 149, 150, 157
1,8	12, 21, 39, 41, 43, 64, 65, 70, 74, 81, 85, 93, 94, 98, 115, 118, 121, 123, 124, 147, 149, 157	2,13	9, 22, 46, 47, 72, 81, 83, 85, 87, 88, 89, 111, 119, 121, 123
		2,13-17	72
1,9	12, 39, 41, 42, 48, 64, 65, 85, 93, 94, 98, 118, 123, 147, 157	2,14	22, 46, 72, 81, 111, 119, 121, 150
1,10	12, 15, 37, 39, 40, 41, 44, 50, 57, 64, 65, 66, 68, 85, 93, 94, 96, 98, 102, 104, 123, 147, 157	2,15	6, 22, 31, 37, 39, 52, 53, 55, 66, 68, 72, 86, 87, 143, 149, 151, 152, 153, 157, 158

Index of Passages

2,16	24, 37, 39, 49, 51, 73, 75, 86, 119	*1 John*	
2,17	24, 27, 37, 39, 51, 73, 119, 121	1,1	47n
		1,5-7	143
3,1	24, 26, 73, 80	1,8	143
3,1-5	73, 86, 99n	1,10	143
3,1-13	126	2,3-6	143
3,2	26, 73, 74, 87	2,9-11	143
3,3	26, 37, 74, 78n, 85, 87	2,15-17	143
3,4	26, 37, 54, 74, 87, 115	2,18	143
3,5	26, 37, 51, 74, 119, 121	2,18-25	143
3,6	26, 28, 35, 49, 52, 53, 54, 55, 56, 75, 77, 86, 87, 115, 143, 147, 149, 151, 157	2,19	143
		2,21	115
		2,22	115, 143
		2,23	115
3,6-12	39, 52, 54, 55, 56, 63, 75, 76, 86, 143, 147, 149, 157	2,26	143
		3,4-10	143
3,7	28, 49, 53, 75, 151, 153	3,7	143
3,8	28, 49, 53, 76, 151, 153	3,8-10	143
3,9	28, 49, 53, 76, 151, 153	3,17	143
3,10	28, 53, 76, 87, 150, 151, 153	4,2-3	115
3,11	28, 30, 52, 55, 76, 77, 82, 150	4,6	143
		4,8	143
3,12	30, 53, 54, 55, 75, 76, 77, 87, 99n, 147, 150, 151, 153	5,2-3	143
		5,10-12	115
3,13	30		
3,14	6, 30, 39, 52, 53, 55, 56, 75, 77, 87, 115, 143, 149, 152, 153, 157	*2 John*	
		7	115
3,15	6, 30, 53, 55, 56, 75, 77, 99n, 130, 153, 157	*3 John*	
		9-10	53
3,16	6, 25, 30, 32, 53, 55, 58, 75, 77, 80, 85, 86	*Revelation*	
		1,1	142
3,17	32, 57, 77, 80, 84, 89, 90, 143, 151, 154-55	1,9	51n, 75
		2,1	147
3,18	32, 57, 58, 77, 80	2,5	147
		2,7	147
Philemon		2,8	147
4-7	36n	2,9-11	93n
19	57, 89	2,10	147
20	101n	2,12	147
		2,12-17	147
Hebrews		2,16	147
2,4	116	2,18	147
9,9	99	2,22	147
9,11-28	134n	2,26	147
		2,27	147
James		3,1	147
5,1-6	93n	3,3	103, 147
		3,4	147
2 Peter		3,7	147
1,10	42	3,8-13	93n
3,4	47n	3,10	51n, 75, 147
3,10	127, 137	3,11	147
3,13	137		

3,14	47n, 147	16,15	103
4,1-6	111	19,20-21	123
5,1-7	111	20,1-3	113
6,9-11	93n, 148	20,7-10	113
7,13-17	93n, 148	21,6	47n
7,14	37n	22,8	109
12,7	122	22,12-13	125
12,7-9	112	22,13	47n
12,9	148	22,16	109
13,14	148	22,20	109
16,14	137		

Jewish Writings

Apoc. Moses		Josephus	
2,1	112n	*Ant.*	
27,1-29	112n	12. 5-6	107
		18. 55-59	138n
1 Baruch		18, 261-309	108n
4,5-29	38	19. 4-5	108n
		19. 11	108n
2 Baruch			
13,3-10	38	*Bell. Jud.*	
48,47	97n	2. 169-74	138n
49,2	97n	2. 185-203	108n
55,4-8	97n, 99n	3. 3-8	131n
78,5	38	4. 486-90	131n
		4. 657f.	131n
Bel		6. 316	138n
33-39	112n		
		Jubilees	
Eth. Enoch		2,1-2	112n
10,1-16	112n	15,31-32	113n
20,1-8	112n		
40,1-10	112n	*1 Maccabees*	
66,1-3	112n	1,20-24	107
97,3	97n	1,41-51	87n, 107
98,8	97n	1,54-59	107
98,10	97n	2,15-18	87n
99,15	97n	2,37	41
2 Esdras		*2 Maccabees*	
5,4-5	135	5,11-21	107
7,38	102, 104, 113	6,1-6	107
12,10-36	133	6,1-9	87n
12,11-13	133	6,12-16	37
12,37-38	110n		
16,74	97n	*Ps. Sol.*	
		13,9-10	37

Index of Passages

Sib. Orac.
3,796-808   135

Slav. Enoch
18,6   97n

Susanna
55   112n

Test. Dan
6,4   97n

Test. Levi
1,1   97n
3,1-3   97n, 113n

4,1   135
5,5   97n

Test. Moses
10,3-10   135

Tobit
12,11-12   112n

Vit. Ad. et Ev.
51   112n

Wisdom Sol.
11,9-10   38
14,20   108

Early Christian Literature

1 Clement
5,7   138

Didache
11,12   53
12   53
16,1   144
16,2   144
16,3   144, 145
16,4   144, 145, 146, 147
16,5   144, 145, 146

16,6   144, 145
16,7   145
16,8   144, 145

Eusebius, Hist. Eccl.
3. 39. 3-4   131n
3. 5. 3   138n

Polycarp, Ep.
11,3,4   130

Greek and Latin Authors

Apuleius, Met.
9. 23   114n

Aristotle, Ars rhet.
1. 1358b   6n
3. 1419b-1420a   55n, 57n

Demosthenes, De cor.
18. 72   52

Lucian, Peregrinus
13   53

Plato, Apol.
19b   52

Pliny, Epist.
10. 97   87n

Plutarch, De Is. et Os.
2. 351E-352A   116n

Quintillian, Inst. or.
6. 1. 1-2   55n, 57n

Seutonius
Vita Calig.
22. 3-4   108n
22. 33   108n

Vita Nero
16. 2   131n

Tacitus
Annals
15. 44. 2-8   131n
15. 44. 3-4   131n

Hist.
5. 9   108n

Index of Authors

Aune, D., 98
Aus, R. D., 36n

Bailey, J. A., 78, 85n
Bassler, J. M., 37, 111n
Baumgarten, J., 102n
Beker, J. C., 156n
Best, E., 2, 52n
Betz, H. D., 4, 5n, 35, 38, 53n, 57n, 92n, 93n, 115n, 116n, 133, 137n, 142n, 154n
Bornemann, W., 2n
Braun, H., 85n
Brown, J. P., 134n
Bultmann, R., 4n, 142n

Collins, A. Y., 103n, 148
Collins, J. J., 94n, 124n
Conzelmann, H., 103n
Cross, F. M., 99n

Dibelius, M., 3n
Dobschütz, E. von, 1, 35n, 36n, 40, 42, 44n, 45n, 47, 49, 62, 106n
Donelson, L. R., 56n, 58n, 90n
Donfried, K. P., 114n

Everson, A. J., 98n

Frame, J. E., 2, 41, 50n, 52n, 109, 111n, 130n

Giblin, C. H., 106n, 111, 115n
Goldstein, J. A., 6n, 38n

Hanson, P. D., 94n, 124n
Harnack, A. von, 3n
Hartmann, L., 134n, 136n, 137
Hauck, F., 54n
Hilgenfeld, A., 151
Himmelfarb, M., 133n
Hoffmann, P., 132n
Holtzman, H. J., 151
Hooker, M. D., 134n
Hurd, J. C., 54n, 78, 90

Jewett, R., 4n, 5n

Käsemann, E., 149n
Kennedy, G. A., 4n, 5n

Kern, F. H., 1
Kloppenborg, J. S., 147n

Lindemann, A., 130n, 141n, 151-52
Lüdemann, G., 138n
Lührmann, D., 132n
Lünemann, G., 2n

MacMullen, R., 118n
Masson, C., 2, 3n, 130n
Metzger, B. M., 102n
Milligan, G., 2, 34n, 35n, 41, 44n, 45n, 48, 50, 52, 87, 88n, 107n, 130n
Mowinckel, S., 96n
Mylonas, G. E., 118n

Nilsson, M. P., 108n, 111n, 118n

Orchard, J. B., 134n

Peterson, R. J., 78n
Plummer, A., 103n
Polag, A., 132n

von Rad, G., 96n
Reitzenstein, R., 156n
Rigaux, B., 1, 2, 36, 39n, 43n, 44n, 45n, 50-51, 52, 134n
Robertson, A., 103n
Robinson, J. A. T., 131n
Rowley, H. H., 94n
Russell, D. S., 94n, 108n, 124n, 136n

Sanders, E. P., 132n
Schmidt, J. E. C., 1
Schmithals, W., 100n
Schweitzer, A., 156n
Schweizer, E., 3n
Spicq, C., 52

Taylor, V., 138
Trilling, W., 1, 2, 3n, 34, 36n, 37n, 39, 42, 43, 44n, 47n, 50, 51, 53, 56n, 60, 73n, 75n, 111n, 130n, 151n, 152, 153n

Weiss, J., 138n
Wrede, W., 1, 2, 7n, 130n, 152

Zahn, T., 2n

Index of Subjects

Antagonist (Antichrist), 46-47, 70, 100, 107-21, 122-25, 141, 143-47, 150, 157-58
Antiochus IV Epiphanes, 87, 107, 108-9, 122, 136
Apocalyptic scenario, 1, 43, 45-49, 56, 64, 68-71, 78, 84, 123-26, 134-50, 158
Authorship (of 2 Thess.), 2, 59-60, 78-90, 155-58
   date, 130
   theories, 2-3

Caligula, 108-9, 111, 122
Clement of Rome, 138

Day of the Lord, 44-46, 52, 56, 64, 67-71, 81, 83, 92, 96-105, 106, 119-21, 123, 125, 127, 128, 134, 136-37, 141, 148, 149, 150-51, 152, 157-58
Deception, 44-49, 56, 88, 100, 114-21, 124-25, 135-36, 139-150
Disorderly (ἄτακτοι), 52-54, 55-56, 75-76, 77, 80, 81-82, 83, 92, 96, 98-101, 106, 121, 126, 128, 141, 147, 148, 149-51, 152, 154, 155-58

Judgment, 37-43, 51, 56-57, 63, 65, 66, 68, 70-71, 84-85, 92-94, 95, 97-105, 109, 119-121, 123, 124-26, 133, 137

Nero, 1, 111, 131

Papias, 131-32
Parousia (παρουσία), 39-41, 43, 44-46, 48, 63, 64, 65, 68, 70-71, 79, 80, 81, 83, 94, 95-96, 97-98, 99, 100-5, 107, 114-16, 120, 122, 123, 127, 132-33, 134, 135-36, 137-47, 150
Paul, 1-2, 34, 36, 38, 45, 47, 48, 50-51, 53-54, 55-57, 60-66, 68-72, 74, 75, 76, 78-79, 83-84, 86-87, 89, 90, 91, 96, 97, 100, 101-5, 109-10, 111, 121, 122, 126, 127, 128, 132, 136-38, 142, 149, 150-58

as authority, 45
as example, 53-54, 75-76, 153
Polycarp, 130
Pseudepigraphy
   characteristics, 62-63, 84-90, 153-54
   in 2 Thess., 1, 57, 84-90, 91

Relationship of 1 and 2 Thess., 1-4, 6, 59-90, 92, 128, 151-55
Rhetorical analysis, 5, 6, 8-33, 58, 59-60
   epistolary prescript, 8, 34-35, 60-61
   exordium, 8-10, 35-37, 61-63
   narratio, 10-14, 37-43, 63-67, 92-94, 95, 97, 121, 123-27, 128
   probatio, 14-24, 43-49, 67-73, 84, 94-121, 123-27, 128, 147
   exhortatio, 24-30, 50-54, 73-76, 86
   peroratio, 30-32, 54-57, 77
   epistolary postscript, 32, 57, 77, 89-90

Satan, 46-47, 51, 111, 112, 116-18, 122, 124, 143, 148
Second Christian generation, 91, 130-32, 155-58
Silvanus, 8, 35, 61

Timothy, 8, 35, 61, 68, 70
Titus (emperor), 111, 131, 138
Tradition, apocalyptic, 38-39, 56, 93
Tradition, Pauline, 1, 5, 35, 45, 48-49, 52-54, 55-57, 59-61, 67-69, 74-76, 77, 78, 81, 82, 86-87, 90, 91, 96, 109, 117, 120, 121, 127, 128-137, 149-51, 153, 155-58
Tribulation, apocalyptic, 36-37, 44, 68, 70-71, 123, 134-35, 137, 138-41, 144-47

Vespasian, 111, 131

Wrath of God, 65, 69, 79, 102, 104-5, 119-21, 122, 124, 127, 133, 137, 147, 148-51